What Every Special Educator Must Know

Ethics,
Standards,
and
Guidelines

Council for
Exceptional
Children
The voice and vision of special education

Sixth Edition
2009
Revised

Library of Congress Cataloging-in-Publication Data

Council for Exceptional Children

What every special educator must know: The international standards for the preparation and certification of special education teachers
6th edition revised
p. cm.
Includes bibliographical references (p.)

ISBN 0-86586-450-0(paper)

1. Special education teachers—Preparation of—Standards 2. Special education teachers—Certification Standards I. Title

Copyright 2009 by the Council for Exceptional Children, 1110 N. Glebe Road, Suite 300, Arlington, VA 22201

Reference: Council for Exceptional Children. (2008). What every special educator must know: Ethics, standards, and guidelines (6th ed. revised). Arlington, VA: Author.

Stock No. P5904 Printed in the United States of America

10 9 8 7 6 5 4 3 2

Council for Exceptional Children

Core Values

CEC values

The dignity and worth of all individuals
Social justice, inclusiveness, and diversity
Professional excellence, integrity, and accountability
Rich and meaningful participation in society for all individuals with exceptionalities
Effective individualized education for all individuals with exceptionalities
The importance of families in the lives and education of all individuals with exceptionalities
Collaboration and community building to improve outcomes

Mission

CEC is an international community of educators who are the voice and vision of special and gifted education. Our mission is to improve the quality of life for individuals with exceptionalities and their families worldwide through professional excellence and advocacy.

Vision

CEC is a diverse, vibrant professional community working together and with others to ensure that individuals with exceptionalities are valued and included in all aspects of life. CEC is a trusted voice in shaping education policy and practice and is globally renowned for its expertise and leadership. CEC is one of the world's premiere education organizations.

One of the original aims of CEC: ...to establish professional standards for teachers in the field of special education.

First CEC meeting, 1923

The quality of educational services for individuals with exceptionalities resides in the abilities, qualifications, and competencies of the personnel who provide the services.

CEC, 1988

Table of Contents

Section 3: Preparing to Become a Special Education Professional

Section 6: Paraeducators Serving Individuals With Exceptional Learning Needs

Introduction

It was through significant professional and personal commitment that the members of CEC created this edition. In the process, we learned about the standards needed for safe and effective practice. We also learned about each other and developed a deep mutual respect. May those who use these standards experience that same mutual respect from all who serve individuals with exceptionalities and their families.

Preamble to the Common Core, 2nd edition

Like its predecessors, the sixth edition of *What Every Special Educator Must Know* is a collaborative product of the members of CEC and other professionals in the wider educational community. The standards and principles represent the expertise and ideas of literally thousands of special educators. This edition, like its predecessors, is based on the premise that professional standards must emanate from the profession itself. Special education is an international profession, not limited to a single state, province, or location. The standards provide benchmarks to states, provinces, and nations for developing or revising policy and procedures for program accreditation, entry-level licensure, professional practice, and continuing professional growth. For over 85 years, CEC has developed and implemented standards for special educators. The standards presented in this edition continue in this tradition of professional leadership by providing direction to colleges and universities that prepare teachers as well as to states as they develop new licensure frameworks for special educators. The move to performance-based standards places CEC at the forefront in educational reform with other national associations seeking to improve the quality of all teachers who serve exceptional children. These changes can be used by states and teacher preparation programs moving to performance-based accountability systems. The standards have been praised for their reflection of best practice, emphasis on diversity, and for "capturing the essence of special education today."

The sixth edition has been designed to provide information to a variety of stakeholder audiences:

- **Individuals preparing to become professional special educators**
  The sixth edition will introduce you to the ethics and professional practice standards to which you aspire. It also describes the knowledge and skills that will be the foundation of your professional preparation and which have influenced the licensure you seek.

- **Practicing professionals**
  You will not only find your professional ethics and practice standards and your professional standards, you will also find guidance in creating your professional development plan for your continuing professional growth. In addition, you will find knowledge and skill sets for a variety of advanced special education roles.

- **Deans and faculty developing or revising preparation programs**
  You will find the procedures for seeking national recognition of your programs through National Council for Accreditation of Teacher Education (NCATE) and CEC or through CEC alone.

- **State directors and policymakers**
  You will find guidance to align your state licensing standards to the profession's recommendations.

- **Families and other community stakeholders**
  You will find the ethics, professional practice standards, and the knowledge and skills that we as the special education profession use to define ourselves and judge each other's excellence. The preparation standards provide assurance that special educators are prepared for safe and effective practice.

- **Professional colleagues in general education**
  This publication will help you to understand the knowledge and skills that we as special educators bring to our collaborative educational endeavor.

To provide opportunities for career ladders in special education and to encourage practicing special education professionals to develop advanced areas of expertise, CEC has been validating and revalidating knowledge and skill sets for a number of advanced roles in special education. In addition, CEC has validated the Advanced Common Core knowledge and skill set and developed six Content Standards built on the knowledge and skill sets. A number of other new advanced role validation studies are in planning or underway, and the reader is advised to check the CEC Web site, www.cec.sped.org, for updates.

All the knowledge and skills in the sets are now based upon documented literature classified into research, emerging, and practice. The literature is available in a searchable database at the CEC Web site, www.cec.sped.org.

In this edition for the first time are Initial Special Education Content Standards and Advanced Special Education Content Standards. Both were developed based on validated Knowledge and Skill Sets. However, instead of lists of knowledge and skills, the Content Standards consist of rich narrative content descriptions that describe initial and advanced role practice. There are 10 initial content standards and 6 advanced content standards. They are based on, and written to reflect, the content and contexts of the validated Knowledge and Skills Sets in each of the domain areas.

The Content Standards at both levels are the same for special education preparation programs. Although program reviews will be done at the Content Standard level, it is important for faculty to use the Knowledge and Skill Sets appropriate to the area of specialization to inform their curriculum development and to develop their program assessment system. This will be essential to ensure that the program's evaluation system comprehensively addresses each of the 10 or 6 Content Standards.

In the past, CEC had 15 practicum standards. The new *Field Experiences and Clinical Practice Standards* are briefer, focus on the kinds of experiences provided, and no longer have a requirement for a specific number of hours or weeks. CEC remains committed to the importance of practica as an essential part of preparation. The new *Field Experiences and Clinical Practice Standards* require that programs provide appropriate practicum experiences to ensure that candidates are prepared

for safe and effective practice. The *Assessment System Standards* provide guidance to programs on the key components of their assessment systems. These nine standards require programs to build systems that are comprehensive, standards aligned, multiply measured, and that collect data used for program improvement.

Section 1 includes the CEC Code of Ethics and Professional Practice Standards. Central to any profession is its will to abide by a set of ethical principles and standards. As professionals serving individuals with exceptionalities, special educators possess a special trust endowed by the community. As such, special educators have a responsibility to be guided by their professional principles and practice standards. The Code of Ethics is made up of eight fundamental ethical premises to which special educators are bound. The Standards for Professional Practice describe the principles special educators use in carrying out day-to-day responsibilities. Special educators use the Professional Practice Standards to measure each other's professional excellence. It is incumbent on all special educators to use these standards in all aspects of their professional practice. At the time of the revision of this edition, CEC is in the active process of revising and updating the CEC Ethics and Professional Practice Standards. When completed, the revised Ethics and Practice Standards will be available on the CEC Web site.

Section 2 analyzes the role of professional standards as they affect special educators throughout their careers. from preparation through licensure and induction to professional development and advanced certification. This section provides an overview of the work CEC has done and is doing to ensure that quality standards guide the practice of special educators at each step of their career.

Section 3 describes the various CEC standards and guidelines for special education professional candidates.

Section 4 provides strategies and tools that different audiences can use to make the standards accessible. State personnel will find a chart designed to help compare state standards and CEC standards. Teacher educators will find guidance on developing a performance-based assessment system, as well as a strategy for use with teacher candidates to help them become familiar with the standards. Special education teachers will find guidance and tools for using the CEC standards to create professional development plans and advocate for the resources to implement them. Finally, candidates in teacher preparation programs are given a tool to help them measure their progress in developing their professional competence.

Of note is the indexing of the CEC standards by publishers such as Pearson and Merrill throughout their textbooks and resources to help candidates to understand the relationship of the standards to the resources from which they are learning.

Section 5 includes the Initial and Advanced Professional Content Standards as well as the validated Knowledge and Skill Sets for beginning teachers and for those special educators moving into advanced roles. These standards represent the knowledge and skill base that professionals entering practice or assuming advanced roles should possess to practice safely and effectively. The standards that programs are required to meet for CEC and CEC/NCATE accreditation are provided.

Section 6 provides information about the increasingly critical role of paraeducators in special education service delivery, the CEC standards for paraeducator preparation, and tools paraeducators and paraeducator training programs can use to ensure that they are meeting the standards.

APPENDICES

Appendix 1 contains sets of selected CEC Initial Common Core Knowledge and Skills that address topical areas.

Appendix 2 offers a brief description of the relationship of the knowledge and skill sets to the Content Standards.

Appendix 3 contains a flowchart to help faculty identify the appropriate knowledge and skill set for their program(s).

Appendix 4 contains a brief descriptive history of the development of the CEC Standards and a timeline of significant events in the history of special education and professional standards.

Appendix 5 contains the National Board for Professional Teaching Standards for Exceptional Needs.

Appendix 6 contains a table that indexes the CEC Initial Common Core to the INTASC Principles.

Appendix 7 describes the procedures for CEC national program recognition outside of the partnership with NCATE.

Appendix 8 contains a special education mentoring program implementation checklist based on the CEC guidelines for mentorship.

Appendix 9 provides CEC professional policies and position statements directly related to the CEC Standards.

Appendix 10 describes the basics for developing and implementing the programwide performance assessment process with an eye on NCATE unit review.

PROFESSIONAL STANDARDS & PRACTICE COMMITTEE MEMBERS

Scott Sparks (Chair & DDD)
Professor
Department of Special Education
Ohio University

Joni L. Baldwin (DPHD)
Department of Teacher Education
University of Dayton

Joanne Cashman (DISES)
Project Director
National Association of State Directors of Special
Education

Parthenia D. Cogdell (Pioneers)
Consultant
Willingboro, NJ

Sandra Cooley-Nichols (DDEL)
Department of Special Education
University of Memphis

Susan Easterbrooks (DCDD)
Department of Special Education
Georgia State University

Diane Paul (DCDD Alternate)
*Director, Clinical Issues in Speech-Language
Pathology*
American Speech-Language-Hearing
Association

Pat Frawley (CEDS)
Learning Consultant
Westfield, NJ

Pam Fernstrom (DLD)
Professor of Special Education
University of North Alabama

Cheryll Adams (TAG)
*Director, Center for Gifted Studies & Talent
Development*
Ball State University

Susan K. Johnsen (TAG - Alternate)
Department. of Educational Psychology
School of Education
Baylor University

Carol Kochhar-Bryant (DCDT - Alternate)
Professor
Department of Special Education
George Washington University

Karin Lifter (DEC)
Professor
Department of Counseling and Applied
Educational Psychology
Northeastern University

Deborah Newton (TAM)
Department of Special Education & Reading
Southern Connecticut State University

Judy Niemeyer (DEC)
Professor & Director of Graduate Studies
Department of Specialized Education Services
University of North Carolina at Greensboro

Jane Razeghi (DCDT)
Associate Professor
Department of Special Education
George Mason University

Mary Jean Sanspree (DVI)
University of Alabama at Birmingham
School of Education/Optometry

Judith Winn (TED)
Department of Exceptional Education
University of Wisconsin-Milwaukee

Joyce Mounsteven (CCBD)
Learning Consultant
Toronto, ON

Mary Lynn Boscardin (CASE)
Professor of Special Education
University of Massachusetts Amherst

Richard Mainzer, Staff Liaison
*Associate Executive Director for Professional
Services*
Council for Exceptional Children

2008 CEC National Recognition Program Reviewers

Peggy L. Anderson

Joni Baldwin (Auditor)

Mary Ellen Bargerhuff

Beverly Barkon

Anne M. Bauer

William Bauer

Dee Berlinghoff

Latha Bhushan

Marjorie A. Bock

Deanne Borgeson

Susan Brown

Rachelle Bruno (Auditor)

Sumita Chakraborti-Ghosh

Diane Clark

Francis L. Clark

Gail Coulter

Sharon F. Cramer

Mary E. Cronin

Lee Cross

Mary O. Dasovich

Grace Lane Denison

John Doak

Joyce Anderson Downing

Jane Duckett

V. Shelley Dugle

Betty Epanchin

Doreen Ferko

Colleen Finegan

Leigh Funk

Pamela Garriott

Barbara C. Gartin

Dan Glasgow

Marjorie T. Goldstein

William E. Gustashaw

Nancy Halmhuber

Joan Henley

Christy M. Hooser (Auditor)

Marcia D. Horne

Cheryl L. Irish

Melanie Jephson

Melissa Jones

Jan Jones-Wadsworth

Belinda D. Karge

Georgia Kerns

Larry Kortering

Joy Kutaka-Kennedy

Sally Lewis

Carol A. Long

Barbara Ludlow

Patricia S. Lynch

Virginia M. MacEntee

Michael Madden

Linn Maxwell

Gail McMahan

Tammy McMahan

Martha Michael

Dorothy Millar

April D. Miller

Diane Miller

Sandra Miller

Frank E. Mullins

Nikki Murdick

Dava O'Connor

Jane Partanen

Robert Perkins

Mary Anne Prater

Latisha L. Putney

Eileen B. Raymond

Jane Razeghi

Melisa Reed

Ann Richards

Mary Ring

Shirley Ritter

Pam Robinson

Diana Rogers-Adkinson

Mary Jean Sanspree

Regina H. Sapona

Marilyn L. Scheffler

Randall Scott

Kathlene S. Shank (Auditor)

William Sharpton

Delar K. Singh

Cathleen Spinelli

Georgine Steinmiller

Don M. Stenhoff

Stephen W. Stile

Roberta Strosnider

Mary Ulrich

Ronna J. Vanderslice

Lisa Vernon-Dotson

Shirley T. Wallis

Elizabeth Whitten

Jane Williams

Eleanor B. Wright

Sheri Wynn

Section 1: CEC Code of Ethics and Standards for Professional Practice for Special Educators[1]

One of the central characteristics of a mature profession is its willingness to abide by a set of ethical principles. As professionals serving individuals with exceptionalities, special educators possess a special trust endowed by the community and recognized by professional licensure. As such, special educators have a responsibility to be guided by their professional principles and practice standards. This section delineates the CEC Code of Ethics and Standards for Professional Practice. They are intended to provide the kind of leadership and guidance that makes each of us proud to be special educators and provides us with the principles by which our practice is guided.

The Code of Ethics is made up of eight fundamental principles to which all special educators are bound. The Standards for Professional Practice describe the guidelines special educators use in carrying out day-to-day responsibilities. The Professional Practice Standards are how special educators measure themselves and their colleagues' professional excellence. It is incumbent on all special educators to use these standards.

ETHICS OF SPECIAL EDUCATORS

We declare the following principles to be the Code of Ethics for educators of persons with exceptionalities. Members of the special education profession are responsible for upholding and advancing these principles. Members of the Council for Exceptional Children agree to judge and be judged by them in accordance with the spirit and provisions of this Code.

A. Special education professionals are committed to developing the highest educational and quality of life potential of individuals with exceptionalities.

B. Special education professionals promote and maintain a high level of competence and integrity in practicing their profession.

C. Special education professionals engage in professional activities that benefit individuals with exceptionalities, their families, other colleagues, students, or research subjects.

D. Special education professionals exercise objective professional judgment in the practice of their profession.

E. Special education professionals strive to advance their knowledge and skills regarding the education of individuals with exceptionalities.

F. Special education professionals work within the standards and policies of their profession.

G. Special education professionals seek to uphold and improve where necessary the laws, regulations, and policies governing the delivery of special education and related services and the practice of their profession.

H. Special education professionals do not condone or participate in unethical or illegal acts, nor violate professional standards adopted by the Delegate Assembly of CEC.

---

[1] At the time of the printing of this edition, CEC is in the process of revising and updating the CEC Ethics and Professional Practice Standards. When completed, the revised Ethics and Practice Standards will be available at the CEC Web site.

Professionals in Relation to Persons With Exceptionalities and Their Families

Instructional Responsibilities

Special education personnel are committed to the application of professional expertise to ensure the provision of quality education for all individuals with exceptionalities. Professionals strive to

1. Identify and use instructional methods and curricula that are appropriate to their area of professional practice and effective in meeting the individual needs of persons with exceptionalities.

2. Participate in the selection and use of appropriate instructional materials, equipment, supplies, and other resources needed in the effective practice of their profession.

3. Create safe and effective learning environments, which contribute to fulfillment of needs, stimulation of learning, and self-concept.

4. Maintain class size and caseloads that are conducive to meeting the individual instructional needs of individuals with exceptionalities.

5. Use assessment instruments and procedures that do not discriminate against persons with exceptionalities based on race, color, creed, sex, national origin, age, political practices, family or social background, sexual orientation, or exceptionality.

6. Base grading, promotion, graduation, and/or movement out of the program on the individual goals and objectives for individuals with exceptionalities.

7. Provide accurate program data to administrators, colleagues, and parents, based on efficient and objective recordkeeping practices, for decision-making.

8. Maintain confidentiality of information except when information is released under specific conditions of written consent and statutory confidentiality requirements.

Management of Behavior

Special education professionals participate with other professionals and with parents in an interdisciplinary effort in the management of behavior. Professionals

1. Apply only those disciplinary methods and behavioral procedures that they have been instructed to use, and that do not undermine the dignity of the individual or the basic human rights of persons with exceptionalities, such as corporal punishment.

2. Clearly specify the goals and objectives for behavior management practices in the persons' with exceptionalities individualized education program.

3. Conform to policies, statutes, and rules established by state/provincial and local agencies to judicious application of disciplinary methods and behavioral procedures.

4. Take adequate measures to discourage, prevent, and intervene when a colleague's behavior is perceived as being detrimental to exceptional students.

5. Refrain from aversive techniques unless repeated trials of other methods have failed and only after consultation with parents and appropriate agency officials.

Support Procedures

Professionals

1. Seek adequate instruction and supervision before they are required to perform support services for which they have not been prepared previously.

2. May administer medication, where state/provincial policies do not preclude such action, if qualified to do so or if written instructions are on file that state the purpose of the medication, the conditions under which it may be administered, possible side effects, the physician's name and phone number, and the professional liability if a mistake is made. The professional will not be required to administer medication.

3. Note and report to those concerned whenever changes in behavior occur in conjunction with the administration of medication or at any other time.

Parent Relationships

Professionals seek to develop relationships with parents based on mutual respect for their roles in achieving benefits for the exceptional person. Special education professionals

1. Develop effective communication with parents, avoiding technical terminology, using the primary language of the home, and other modes of communication when appropriate.

2. Seek and use parents' knowledge and expertise in planning, conducting, and evaluating special education and related services for persons with exceptionalities.

3. Maintain communications between parents and professionals with appropriate respect for privacy and confidentiality.

4. Extend opportunities for parent education utilizing accurate information and professional methods.

5. Inform parents of the educational rights of their children and of any proposed or actual practices, which violate those rights.

6. Recognize and respect cultural diversities that exist in some families with persons with exceptionalities.

7. Recognize that the relationship of home and community environmental conditions affects the behavior and outlook of the exceptional person.

Advocacy

Special education professionals serve as advocates for exceptional students by speaking, writing, and acting in a variety of situations on their behalf. They

1. Continually seek to improve government provisions for the education of persons with exceptionalities while ensuring that public statements by professionals as individuals are not construed to represent official policy statements of the agency that employs them.

2. Work cooperatively with and encourage other professionals to improve the provision of special education and related services to persons with exceptionalities.

3. Document and objectively report to one's supervisors or administrators inadequacies in resources and promote appropriate corrective action.

4. Monitor for inappropriate placements in special education and intervene at appropriate levels to correct the condition when such inappropriate placements exist.

5. Follow local, state/provincial, and federal laws and regulations that mandate a free appropriate public education to exceptional students and the protection of the rights of persons with exceptionalities to equal opportunities in our society.

Professionals in Relation to Employment

Certification and Qualification

Professionals ensure that only persons deemed qualified by having met state/provincial minimum standards are employed as teachers, administrators, and related service providers for individuals with exceptionalities.

Employment

1. Professionals do not discriminate in hiring based on race, color, creed, sex, national origin, age, political practices, family or social background, sexual orientation, or exceptionality.

2. Professionals represent themselves in an ethical and legal manner concerning their training and experience when seeking new employment.

3. Professionals give notice consistent with local education agency policies when intending to leave employment.

4. Professionals adhere to the conditions of a contract or terms of an appointment in the setting where they practice.

5. Professionals released from employment are entitled to a written explanation of the reasons for termination and to fair and impartial due process procedures.

6. Special education professionals share equitably the opportunities and benefits (salary, working conditions, facilities, and other resources) of other professionals in the school system.

7. Professionals seek assistance, including the services of other professionals, in instances where personal problems threaten to interfere with their job performance.

8. Professionals respond objectively when requested to evaluate applicants seeking employment.

9. Professionals have the right and responsibility to resolve professional problems by utilizing established procedures, including grievance procedures, when appropriate.

Assignment and Role

1. Professionals should receive clear written communication of all duties and responsibilities, including those that are prescribed as conditions of their employment.

2. Professionals promote educational quality and intra- and interprofessional cooperation through active participation in the planning, policy development, management, and evaluation of the special education program and the education program at large so that programs remain responsive to the changing needs of persons with exceptionalities.

3. Professionals practice only in areas of exceptionality, at age levels, and in program models for which they are prepared by their training and/or experience.

4. Adequate supervision of, and support for, special education professionals is provided by other professionals qualified by their training and experience in the area of concern.

5. The administration and supervision of special education professionals provides for clear lines of accountability.

6. The unavailability of substitute teachers or support personnel, including aides, does not result in the denial of special education services to a greater degree than to that of other educational programs.

Professional Development

1. Special education professionals systematically advance their knowledge and skills in order to maintain a high level of competence and response to the changing needs of persons with exceptionalities by pursuing a program of continuing education including, but not limited to, participation in such activities as inservice training, professional conferences/workshops, professional meetings, continuing education courses, and the reading of professional literature.

2. Professionals participate in the objective and systematic evaluation of themselves, colleagues, services, and programs for the purpose of continuous improvement of professional performance.

3. Professionals in administrative positions support and facilitate professional development.

Professionals in Relation to the Profession and to Other Professionals

The Profession

1. Special education professionals assume responsibility for participating in professional organizations and adherence to the standards and codes of ethics of those organizations.

2. Special education professionals have a responsibility to provide varied and exemplary supervised field experiences for persons in undergraduate and graduate preparation programs.

3. Special education professionals refrain from using professional relationships with students and parents for personal advantage.

4. Special education professionals take an active position in the regulation of the profession through use of appropriate procedures for bringing about changes.

5. Special education professionals initiate, support, and/or participate in research related to the education of persons with exceptionalities with the aim of improving the quality of educational services, increasing the accountability of programs, and generally benefiting persons with exceptionalities. They:

   • Adopt procedures that protect the rights and welfare of subjects participating in the research.
   • Interpret and publish research results with accuracy and a high quality of scholarship.
   • Support a cessation of the use of any research procedure that may result in undesirable consequences for the participant.
   • Exercise all possible precautions to prevent misapplication or misuse of a research effort, by self or others.

Other Professionals

Special education professionals function as members of interdisciplinary teams, and the reputation of the profession resides with them. They

1. Recognize and acknowledge the competencies and expertise of members representing other disciplines as well as those of members in their own disciplines.

2. Strive to develop positive attitudes among other professionals toward persons with exceptionalities, representing them with an objective regard for their possibilities and their limitations as persons in a democratic society.

3. Cooperate with other agencies involved in serving persons with exceptionalities through such activities as the planning and coordination of information exchanges, service delivery, evaluation, and training, so that duplication or loss in quality of services may not occur.

4. Provide consultation and assistance, where appropriate, to both general and special educators as well as other school personnel serving persons with exceptionalities.

5. Provide consultation and assistance, where appropriate, to professionals in nonschool settings serving persons with exceptionalities.

6. Maintain effective interpersonal relations with colleagues and other professionals, helping them to develop and maintain positive and accurate perceptions about the special education profession.

Section 2: Assuring Well-Prepared Special Education Professionals

The education of teachers must be driven by:

- a clear and careful conception of the educating we expect our schools to do,
- the conditions most conducive to this educating (as well as conditions that get in the way), and
- the kinds of expectations that teachers must be prepared to meet.

Goodlad, 1990

From its earliest days, the Council for Exceptional Children (CEC) recognized the significance of professional standards to the quality of educators, and CEC accepted responsibility for developing and disseminating professional standards for the field of special education. At the first meeting of CEC in 1922, the establishment of professional standards for teachers in the field of special education was identified as one of the primary aims of CEC. In 1965, CEC held a national conference on professional standards, but it was not until 1981 that the CEC Delegate Assembly charged CEC to develop promote and implement preparation and certification standards along with a professional code of ethics. In its current strategic plan, CEC reiterates this commitment to professional standards leadership by identifying the promotion of professional standards that support high quality teaching and learning as a way to advance the education of individuals with exceptionalities.

In 1988, the CEC Delegate Assembly recognized the relationship between the skills and knowledge with which special education teachers enter the profession and the quality of educational services for individuals with exceptionalities. More recently, the significance of the well-prepared teacher as the within-school variable having the greatest influence on a student's learning has been widely documented and recognized.

However, for at least 3 decades, the issue of the quality preparation and continuing development of special educators has been overshadowed by a chronic and severe shortage of personnel to deliver special education services (Boe, Cook, & Sunderland, 2008). As any special education administrator knows, the shortage of available well-prepared special educators overshadow the quality issue. They know the dilemma of having to use unqualified personnel. They worry about the negative consequences on the learning of individuals with disabilities. They fear the violation of the trust of parents and families when they call unqualified individuals special educators. And they harm their collegiality with fully licensed and well-prepared teachers. Figure 2.1 shows that the number of individuals practicing special education without appropriate preparation has continued to grow since the about 1993. The most recent data from the U.S. Education Department (ED) to the U.S. Congress puts the number of unqualified individuals practicing special education of over 50,000, a larger number than the total CEC membership. Even a conservative estimate is that the shortage of well-prepared special educators directly influences the learning of over a million children with exceptionalities.

In addition, retaining the well-prepared special educators has been made difficult by negative working conditions (Billingsley, 2006; CEC, 2000, Gersten, Keating, Yovanoff, & Harness, 2003). The percentage of special educators who leave special education each year is almost double the rate of educators in general. In fact, over half of all entering special educators leave special education before their fifth year of practice. Although very little data is available regarding what proportion of these leavers are less than fully prepared special educators, Rosenberg and Sindelar, (2003) have pointed out that it is likely that many of these individuals cycling in and out so quickly are individuals who are not fully prepared and licensed.

The recent emphasis in federal legislation in the United States on accountability and high expectations

Figure 2.1 Practicing Special Education Teachers Who Are Not Licensed

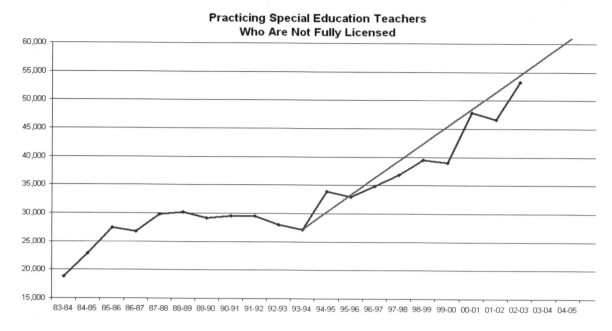

Practicing Special Education Teachers
Who Are Not Fully Licensed

for individuals with disabilities makes it even more imperative that all special educators are well-prepared and have the conditions that allow them to provide individuals with exceptional needs the most effective interventions and encourage entering special educators to become career-oriented special education professionals. It is within this context that CEC has used multiple strategies to enhance the influence of the CEC standards to ensure that entry-level personnel have the skill and knowledge to practice safely, ethically, and effectively and that practicing special educators have effective mentoring.

STANDARDS FOR THE PREPARATION OF SPECIAL EDUCATORS[2]

The preparation of candidates for entry to special education professional practice begins with appropriate preparation. At a minimum CEC expects that every entry-level special education professional (Figure 2.2)

- Possess appropriate pedagogical knowledge and skills
- Hold at least a bachelor's degree from an accredited institution, and
- Master appropriate core academic subject matter content.

In addition, CEC expects that professional special educators in new positions undergo a systematic and structured discipline-specific period of induction.

Pedagogy

Historically, pedagogy or teaching skill has been at the heart of special education. Special educators have always recognized that the individualized learning needs of children are at the center of special education instruction. Whether helping individuals with

exceptional learning needs master addition, cooking, independent living, or world history, special educators have focused on how to alter the instructional variables to optimize learning.

Among the characteristics of mature professions is the identification of the specialized knowledge and skill along with the assurance that practicing professionals possess the specialized knowledge and skill to practice safely and effectively. In addressing this responsibility, CEC uses a rigorous consensual validation process to identify, update, and maintain sets of knowledge and skills for entry-level and advanced special educators. As a part of this validation process, CEC documents the literature upon which the knowledge and skill sets are based. This process has involved thousands of practicing special educators (teachers, administrators, and teacher educators) in consonance with a national CEC committee with representation of the 17 national divisions within CEC. The result is the most rigorous and comprehensive sets of knowledge and skills available anywhere for the preparation of high quality special educators.

Figure 2.2 Minimum CEC Expectations for Entry-Level Special Educators

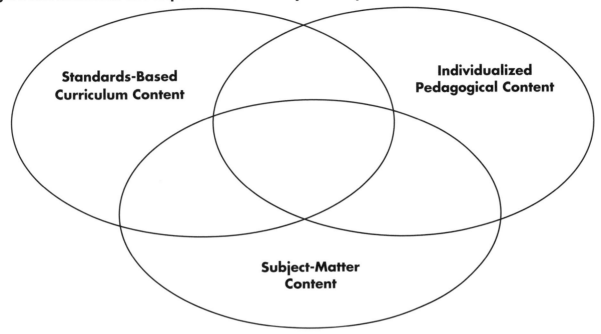

Standards-Based Curriculum Content

Individualized Pedagogical Content

Subject-Matter Content

These knowledge and skills sets are the foundation upon which CEC builds its work at both the state and national levels to ensure that preparation programs incorporate CEC standards into their curricula and that state and provincial jurisdictions incorporate the standards into their licensing requirements. It is through professional standards used by preparation programs and aligned with licensing systems that the public can be assured that special educators are appropriately prepared for safe, ethical, and effective practice (CEC, 2002a).

At the entry level, CEC preparation standards are developed around 10 initial roles and 6 advanced roles content domains that describe the knowledge, skills,

and dispositions shared by all professional special educators. At the advanced level, CEC preparation standards are developed around six content standards that describe the knowledge, skills, and dispositions shared by all professional special educators practicing at advanced levels. Although the content standards cross special education specialty areas, the specific sets of knowledge and skills inform and differentiate the content, context, and issues of the respective specialty areas (e.g., early childhood, mild/moderate, developmental disabilities, and learning disabilities). They provide the knowledge and skills that special educators must master for safe, ethical, and effective practice. The knowledge and skill sets are located in the Appendix. CEC continuously conducts validation

---

[2] CEC standards are not intended to identify and prescribe at a micro level of detail all evidence-based interventions along with all components of each for which preparation programs should be required to account. CEC professional preparation standards do not identify specific methods or strategies, (e.g., the xyz learning strategy or the xyz reading method). CEC does not use such a heavy-handed top down approach in validating its professional preparation standards. This decision was based on the dynamic nature of evidence bases. Additionally, CEC felt that such an approach was inconsistent with the collegiality across professions.

This does not imply that CEC eschews the value of evidence-based practice. In fact, the fifth edition of *What Every Special Educator Must Know* states, "A foundation assumption of the CEC standards is that all special education professionals will use evidence-based research in their decision making." The CEC standards frequently use the term "effective practice" specifically to connote that preparation programs will teach the current state of knowledge for evidence-based practices. There are also Initial and Advanced Common Core Standards that deal specifically with this issue. CEC initial common core standards make clear that candidates for special education licensure should know how to access and use evidence-based practices. The language does not attempt to delineate every evidence-based practice and its components. Rather knowledge and skills, along with the balance of the CEC Content Standards, affirm the significance of evidence-based professional practice broadly.

Although the CEC Standards are not designed to identify specific evidence-based practices along with their components for which preparation programs might be required to account, the CEC Standards make clear the expectation that special education teacher candidates should understand appropriate research methods for special education practice, know validated evidence-based practices, know how to evaluate and modify their practice, and engage in evidence-based practices.

studies, and readers are advised to check the CEC Web site for updates.

Liberal Arts and Core Academic Subject Matter Content

Although pedagogy is central to special education, special educators must have a solid grounding in the liberal arts ensuring proficiency in reading, written and oral communications, calculating, problem-solving, and thinking by holding at least a bachelor's degree from an accredited institution.

In addition, special educators should possess a solid base of understanding of the content areas of the general curricula, (i.e., math, reading, English/language arts, science, social studies, and the arts), sufficient to collaborate with general educators in:

- Teaching or co-teaching academic subject matter content of the general curriculum to individuals with exceptional learning needs across a wide range of performance levels, and
- Designing appropriate learning and performance accommodations and modifications for individuals with exceptional learning needs in academic subject matter content of the general curriculum.

Because of the significant role that content-specific subject matter knowledge plays at the secondary level, special education teachers routinely teach secondary level academic subject matter classes in consultation or collaboration with one or more general education teachers appropriately licensed in the respective content area. However, when a special education teacher assumes sole responsibility for teaching a core academic subject matter class at the secondary level, the special educator must have a solid knowledge base in the subject matter content sufficient to assure individuals with exceptional learning needs can meet state general curriculum standards (CEC, 2002b).

Mentoring and Induction

In addition to these three critical elements, professionals entering initial practice in special education should receive a minimum of a 1-year mentorship during the first year of professional special education practice. The mentor should be an experienced professional in the same or a similar role as the individual being mentored who can provide expertise and support on a continuing basis. Even with quality preparation, the beginning special education professional faces new challenges in applying and generalizing newly

acquired skills and knowledge. Like other professionals, special educators who have the support of more senior colleagues become proficient more quickly, and are more likely to remain in the profession (Billingsley, 2006). The goals of the mentorship program should include

- Facilitating the application of knowledge and skills learned
- Conveying advanced knowledge and skills
- Acculturating into the school's learning community
- Reducing job stress and enhancing job satisfaction
- Supporting professional induction

When special educators begin practice in a new area of licensure, they should have the opportunity to work with mentors who are experienced professionals in similar roles. The purpose of mentors is to provide expertise and support to the teachers on a continuing basis for at least the first year of practice in that area of certification. The mentorship is part of continuing education; thus, it is a requirement for maintaining licensure, not a requirement for initial licensure. The mentorship is a professional relationship between the new teacher and an experienced teacher that aids the new teacher in further developing knowledge and skills in the area of certification and provides the support required to sustain the new teacher in practice.

The mentorship is collegial, not supervisory. It is essential that a mentor have knowledge, skills, and experience relevant to the new teacher's position in order to provide the expertise and support the new teacher requires. Thus, it is essential that new teachers practice in environments where mentors are available. Members of the special education profession are expected to serve as mentors as part of their professional responsibilities, and they should receive the resources and support necessary to carry out this responsibility effectively. The CEC Standards provide that special education teachers should receive mentorships when they begin practice in each area of licensure. Thus, for example, an experienced teacher of individuals with visual impairments who, after the necessary preparation, becomes licensed to teach individuals in early childhood should receive a mentorship during the first year of practice in early childhood in order to maintain the license in early childhood.

Using CEC Standards to Assure Well-Prepared Special Educators

In the landmark report, *What Matters Most: Teaching and America's Future*, the National Commission on

Teaching and America's Future (NCTAF, 1996) used a three-legged stool to describe the three primary levers to influence teacher quality:

- **Accreditation** of teacher preparation programs,
- **Initial licensing** of entry-level teaching professionals, and
- Advanced **certification** of teaching professionals.

CEC National Recognition of Preparation Programs

In 2002, CEC made it policy that preparation programs, whether traditional or alternative, should demonstrate their alignment with CEC standards through submission to CEC performance-based review. The first leg of the metaphorical stool for assuring teacher quality is national recognition of programs preparing educators. In the United States, there are currently two government-recognized agencies to accredit teacher education programs: National Council for Accreditation of Teacher Education (NCATE) and the Teacher Education Accreditation Council (TEAC). Both of these agencies base their accreditation approaches on the importance of establishing teaching as a full and mature profession. However, the two are built on different concepts to achieve professionalism.

National Council for Accreditation of Teacher Education

To NCATE, the foundation of a strong profession is a shared body of specialized knowledge and skill based on research, and public confidence that professionals are fit to practice. Speaking for NCATE, Art Wise states that only a strong degree of consensus among practitioners and practitioner educators can build that confidence (Wise, 2005). NCATE is built on the premise that strong professions depend upon "collective organization" and that accrediting bodies in the "mature professions" have played a catalytic role as the repositories of the consensus about the professions' specialized knowledge and skill.

Since 1977, NCATE has been accrediting teacher education programs using an inclusive model of collaborating with the respective professional associations representing the various professional disciplines (i.e., English, Social Studies, Math, School Psychology) For almost 20 years, CEC has been the partner of NCATE representing the disciplines within the special education profession.

Candidates preparing to work in schools as teachers or other professional school personnel know and demonstrate the content, pedagogical, and professional knowledge, skills, and dispositions necessary to help all students learn. Assessments indicate that candidates meet **professional** (emphasis added), state, and institutional standards.

In addition to requiring preparation programs to demonstrate that their candidates have a positive influence on student learning, NCATE expects preparation programs to demonstrate through performance information that the programs address the professional standards of the respective associations in preparing candidates for both initial and advanced roles. Through this process, NCATE expects programs preparing special educators to demonstrate candidates' mastery CEC standards.

NCATE currently has formal agreements with 50 of the U.S. states and territories. It has reviewed and approved over 600 teacher education units with approximately 100 units in the process (Wise, 2005). Over 70% of entering educators each year currently graduate from NCATE accredited programs. Currently 29 states require all of their special education preparation programs to submit for CEC recognition. The remaining states have signed agreements that they will to move their state program approval standards into alignment with CEC standards. Through 2007, CEC has reviewed and approved over 1,000 special education preparation programs. For every teacher education institution undergoing NCATE accreditation, CEC reviews an average of three programs.

In its partnership with NCATE, CEC operates comprehensive systems to prepare and provide program reviewers, and to provide multiple levels of program preparation technical assistance. Please note that CEC has not included information in this section to help faculty prepare for CEC and NCATE accreditation. To ensure that faculty receives the most accurate and up-to-date guidance, information on the multiple ways CEC offers support in the development of program reports can be found on the CEC Professional Standards Web site.

Teacher Education Accreditation Council

It has been TEAC's position that educators have not achieved the consensus on specialized knowledge and skill of true professionals and that without this consensus the appropriate strategy is to base accreditation on what TEAC refers to as an "academic audit." The TEAC academic audit requires programs to identify whatever claims the program faculty of a given institution make and then provide evidence regarding how well the program does regarding its claims. The TEAC model leaves the identification of program standards to each faculty. In addition to creating a cacophony of expectations, the TEAC model neither expects nor encourages faculty to address the national professional standards of the various professional societies. In fact, in discussing the standards of the various professional societies, Frank Murray (2005), the president of TEAC, writes, "In the public mind, these professionally self-serving standards are the problem, not the solution to the problem" p. 315. Although the TEAC approach is advertised as offering freedom to faculty to create special educators in whatever mold they choose, it plays no responsible role as the repository of consensual knowledge and skills of the profession. At least as important, TEAC does not require special education preparation programs to demonstrate that their graduates possess the profession's entry-level knowledge and skills by seeking CEC national recognition through the evidence-based process of program review. Finally, the TEAC approach does not give the public confidence that a professional special educator has the skills and knowledge to practice safely and effectively.

In an informal survey of several of the teacher education programs in the institutions TEAC has accredited, the program chairs of the special education departments report that CEC standards "play an influential role" in their programs (personal communications, 2007). While such anecdotal reports are positive, they do not meet the CEC expectation that special education preparation programs submit their programs to a performance review by CEC. CEC continues to communicate with and monitor TEAC for opportunities to help TEAC move to a more professional model and provide a viable role for CEC standards[3].

CEC Program Recognition

In the United States and in other regions of the world a third possibility exists for programs to receive CEC recognition. Although CEC is not recognized to accredit programs, special education preparation programs may directly seek a review of their program performance data from CEC and have CEC grant recognition of the program. No state that currently requires national program recognition allows this option, but is has been used twice in the last 2 decades. CEC in fact updated its program review policies in 2003 to make the CEC review process performance-based similar to the NCATE performance review.

CEC expects stand-alone program recognitions will most likely continue to be chosen infrequently. Analysis of the implications of whether CEC should consider application to become recognized by the federal government as an accreditation agency yields the conclusion that CEC has the most opportunity to maximize the influence of its standards collectively through the NCATE consensual process.

Coordinating for Quality Licensure

The second leg of the NCTAF three-legged stool of quality assurance is professional teacher licensing. Professional licensing in our society implies that the individual professional possesses a common set of specialized knowledge and skills to practice safely and effectively. It is a trust between the profession and the public that individuals who hold a license are prepared to use the specialized skills safely and effectively. CEC engages in multiple initiatives and collaborations to enhance the influence of its standards in the licensing process.

Historically, the licensing of individuals to practice in special education has been the responsibility of states in the United States and the provinces in Canada. Although approaches to licensing special educators taken by jurisdictions have been variable and sometimes idiosyncratic, a clear majority of states align their licensing process with CEC standards. Currently, 50 states are committed to aligning their licensing processes with CEC standards. CEC collaborates with the appropriate personnel in the states to help them align their respective licensing requirements with CEC standards. This collaboration provides a more stable expectation to the public that licensed special educators possess the nationally validated and recognized special knowledge and skill to practice safely, ethically, and effectively. Although there is no requirement that states adopt CEC standards for licensure, the overwhelming majority of states report that CEC standards significantly align with their licensing requirements. There are procedures described in the 6th edition of *What Every Special Educator Must Know: Ethics, Standards, and Guidelines for Special Educators* for state personnel to align state and CEC Standards.

---

[3] As of the writing of this edition, representatives of NCATE and TEAC are discussing possible strategies for moving closer together.

Several issues are confronting states and preparation programs related to licensure. These include preparing special educators for multicategorical practice, the use of high stakes assessments in licensing, the interfacing of skills needed by general and special educators to work in integrated collaborative teams.

Multicategorical Licensure

The majority of individuals are now licensed for multi-categorical practice in special education (IPEDS, 2003, U.S. Department of Education, 2005). Many states use variations of titles such as Teachers of Individuals With Mild/Moderate Exceptionalities and Teachers of Individuals With Severe/Profound Exceptionalities to describe these multicategorical licenses. When states and provinces combine the essential knowledge and skill of special educators in the special education specialty areas, this is using a multicategorical licensing approach. Although most states and provinces now use a multicategorical licensing approach in special education, it is important that states balance the need for both breadth and depth of knowledge and skills for special education teachers. On the one hand, overly broad licensing approaches result in teachers who are not adequately prepared for the complex challenges of teaching individuals with exceptional learning needs. On the other hand, overly narrow licensing approaches at an entry-level do not prepare special education candidates for the increasing diversity of individuals with exceptional learning needs that special educators serve today. As the breadth of categories grow within

a multicategorical license, the challenge to prepare candidates for professionals practice becomes more challenging.

To support states/provinces that use a multicategorical approach to licensing, CEC has the Curriculum Referenced Licensing and Program Accreditation Framework. The Individualized General Education Curriculum and the Individualized Independence Curriculum delineate the consensually validated knowledge and skills for multicategorical licenses, and reference the curricula in which the licensed teacher will practice.

Complementary General and Special Educator Roles

Based on the premise that the standards for national program recognition and state licensure should align, CEC organized its professional standards to align explicitly with the INTASC 10 principles for model licensing standards at the entry level and with the NBPTS at the advanced level. It is encouraging that the licensing and certification approaches suggested by both the Council of Chief State School Officer's Interstate New Teacher Assessment and Support Consortium (INTASC) and National Board for Professional Teaching Standards (NBPTS) align with the CEC Curriculum Referenced Licensing and Program Accreditation Framework. This alignment reflects a strong national convergence regarding the balance of depth and spread (Figure 2.3), and it reflects the explicit intentions of CEC, INTASC,

Figure 2.3 Comparison of Professional Standards Frameworks

CEC Curriculum Referenced Licensing and Accreditation Framework	INTASC*	NBPTS Exceptional Needs Certificate
Individualized General Curriculum	Mild/moderate disabilities (ages 5-14,12-21)	Mild and Moderately Impaired
Individualized Independence Curriculum	Severe/multiple disabilities (ages 5-21)	Severe and Multiply Impaired
Deaf/Hard of Hearing	Deaf/hard of hearing (ages birth-21)	Deaf/Hard of Hearing
Blind/Visually Impaired	Visual Impairments (ages birth-21)	Visually Impaired
Early Childhood Special Education	Early childhood (ages birth-21)	Early Childhood
Gifted/Talented Special Education		

*As suggested in INTASC (2001, May), Appendix A, p. 40.

and the NBPTS to collaborate and coordinate with each of other.

In 1990, the Council for Chief State School Officers (CCSSO) created its INTASC with the purpose of helping states improve licensing processes. In collaboration with CEC, INTASC undertook a project to interface the knowledge and skills that general and special educators should each have in common in order to work in integrated collaborative teams. INTASC also delineated special knowledge and skills that special educators in various subdisciplines should possess. For those states that have adopted the INTASC framework, CEC explicitly coordinates its framework with the INTASC framework.

It is important for states and provinces to differentiate complementary general and special educator skills that lead to integrated collaborative practice from attempts to merge general and special educator skills. To be able to integrate, collaborate, and co-teach productively, the skills and knowledge of general and special educators must complement each other. There is scant evidence that it is realistic to build a licensure that assumes entry-level professionals can master special educator and general educator knowledge and skills simultaneously.

High Stakes Assessment of Professional Competence

Developments in national, state, and provincial policy are moving toward more accountability systems for teachers, most notably through the provisions of laws such as the No Child Left Behind Act (NCLB, 2001) in the United States. Although CEC embraces efforts to ensure that individuals with exceptional needs have well-prepared teachers, CEC remains concerned about policies that allow or even advocate the use a single high stakes test to make critical decisions about educators' professional competence. It is not sound policy to permit individuals with a bachelor's degree and no training in special education to be considered a "highly qualified" special educator. Currently, NCLB includes a provision that permits states to define a "highly qualified" special educator as one who passes a single test on the day the individual enrolls in a preparation program. The use of a single test score raises serious validity issues and could have a negative impact on otherwise qualified persons from groups who do not

typically perform well on standardized tests. There is consensus in the teaching and technical test development communities that high stakes decisions should never rest on a single test score. To address these concerns, the CEC Board of Directors approved the following position in 2004:

It is CEC policy that in determining an individual's professional competence multiple measures, rather than a single test score, shall be used in the decision-making process to enhance the validity and reliability of decisions related to content and pedagogical competence. As a minimum assurance of fairness, when a test is used as part of the decision-making process, the individual should be provided multiple opportunities to pass the test. If there is credible evidence that a test score may not accurately reflect the individual's level of performance, the agency shall provide an alternative means by which the individual may demonstrate performance relative to professional standards.

Other Coordination Initiatives

Collaboration With the Educational Testing Service and Textbook Publishers

The Educational Testing Service (ETS) is the major producer of assessments that states use in licensure. CEC has for some years now collaborated with ETS to ensure that the PRAXIS II special education tests have content validity with CEC standards. CEC has also approached the National Evaluation Systems Company (NES), the second largest teacher license assessment company, to establish a relationship. However, the NES business model preempts their collaboration with any of the professional associations. The NES strictly produces individual tests for its state clients and leaves it up to the state to align with professional association standards. This is somewhat similar to the business model TEAC uses in that professional association standards such as CEC are not a formal recognized part of the process.

In its ongoing collaborations with special education textbook publishers (e.g., Pearson), CEC staff advocates for the identification and indexing of the CEC Standards in relevant textbooks to help special education teacher candidates identify and understand the significance of the standards in their preparation.

Both state/provincial licensure and advanced certification of individuals for professional practice in the field of special education should be for limited periods with renewal based on planned, organized, and recognized professional development related to the professional's field of practice. CEC expects practicing special educators to develop and implement a Professional Development Plans (PDP). The PDP should be reviewed and amended at least annually. The professional development activities in the PDP should go beyond the routine job functions of the professional, and no single activity or category should make up the plan. This PDP should include participation in an average of at least 36 contact hours (or an average of 3.6 continuing education units) each year of planned, organized, and recognized professional development related to the professional's field of practice within the following categories

- Career related academic activities
- Conducting or supporting research
- Participating in district and/or school-based professional development programs
- Teaching courses (other than those for regular employment)
- Delivering presentations
- Publishing books and/or journal articles
- Participating in mentoring or supervised collegial support activities
- Providing service to professional association(s)
- Participating in approved educational travel
- Other professional projects approved by state, district, or other agencies

In 2001, the CEC surveyed State Education Agencies (SEAs) regarding special education career ladders. Of the states that responded, less than a third indicated that they offer an advanced special education licensure. The Bright Futures Report (CEC, 2000) found that when special educators have viable career paths, retention is enhanced. Advanced certification options are an important component of special education career ladder programs.

National Board for Professional Teaching Standards

Approximately 20 years ago, NBPTS was created to fill the void of advanced certification of classroom-based educators in the various education disciplines. Since its creation, CEC has collaborated with the NBPTS to assure the NBPTS and the CEC standards are complementary. Currently, the NBPTS has procedures for advanced certification of teachers of individuals with

exceptional needs through five pathways. Through the NBPTS, special educators may earn the advanced certification for teachers of individuals with exceptional needs. The NBPTS recognizes five advanced areas of specialization

- Mild/Moderate Disabilities Exceptional Needs Specialist
- Severe and Multiple Exceptional Needs Specialist
- Early Childhood Exceptional Needs Specialist
- Visual Impairments Exceptional Needs Specialist
- Deaf/Hard of Hearing Exceptional Needs Specialist

CEC is currently collaborating with the NBPTS in the review and revision of the special education standards. With the input of CEC staff, the NBPTS will be examining the possibility of adding a sixth pathway for teachers of individuals with exceptional gifts and talents.

CEC Standards for Advanced Roles in Special Education

As special educators progress in their teaching careers, many seek to develop and deepen their skills and broaden their knowledge base through advanced study in classroom or specialty areas. Others choose to pursue new roles within special education. Within the field of special education, CEC has developed advanced standards for the following roles

- Special Education Administrators
- Educational Diagnosticians
- Technology Specialists
- Transition Specialists

CEC recently validated the Advanced Common Core for advanced roles in special education, and is currently validating advanced specialty area knowledge and skill sets for additional advanced roles including a number of categorical specialty areas. CEC is developing a plan for a process by which preparation programs that have earned CEC national recognition may award CEC Advanced Specialty Area Certificates to their program graduates. Mastery of Advance Role Certificates can be of significant value within a career ladder for special educators who want to identify their special skills on a resume regardless of whether the state or province has a specific license in the certificate area. PSPC is currently in planning with several CEC affiliates to conduct validation studies in a number of advanced role areas.

Still other special educators will pursue doctoral level studies in special education. There are currently over 150 programs preparing special educators at the doctoral level. Like all other preparation programs, CEC expects doctoral programs to demonstrate their quality through CEC performance-based recognition.

Of interest is the fact that independently NCATE has likewise made the accreditation of advanced programs a priority focus.

ASSURING ETHICAL PROFESSIONAL PRACTICE

Central to any profession is its will to abide by a set of ethical principles and standards. As professionals serving individuals with exceptionalities, special educators possess a special trust. As such, special educators have a responsibility to be guided by their professional principles and practice standards. Appendix 4 contains the CEC Code of Ethics and Standards by which professional special educators practice. The Code of Ethics has eight fundamental ethical premises to which special educators are bound. The Standards for Professional Practice describe the principles special educators use in carrying out daily responsibilities. The Professional Practice Standards are how special educa-

tors measure their own and each other's professional excellence. It is incumbent on all special educators to understand and use these standards in all aspects of their professional practice.

CEC first approved the Ethics and Professional Practice Standards in 1983 and charged the PSPC to implement them. They are published in Section 1 of *What Every Special Educator Must Know*, as well as on the CEC Web site. Special education preparation programs routinely use the Ethics and Practice Standards to help prepare special education candidates.

ASSURING QUALITY PROFESSIONAL SERVICES

CEC is currently developing procedures for identifying and disseminating quality service standards that will assure the conditions to permit special educators

to deliver quality professional services. The reader is invited to visit the professional standards page on the CEC Web site for progress in this area.

REFERENCES

Billingsley, B. S. (2005 cited as 2006). *Cultivating and keeping committed special education teachers: What principals and district leaders can do.* Thousand Oaks: Corwin Press.

Boe, E. E., Cook, L. H., & Sunderland, R. J. (2008). Teacher turnover in special and general education: Exit attrition, teaching area transfer, and school migration. *Exceptional Children*, 75, 7-31.

Bonnie, S. B. (2004, cited as 2006). Special education teacher retention and attrition: A critical analysis of the research literature. *Journal of Special Education*, 38, 39-55.

Council for Exceptional Children. (2000). *Bright futures for exceptional learners: An agenda to achieve quality conditions for teaching and learning.* Reston, VA: Author.

Council for Exceptional Children. (2002a). *CEC professional policy section four part 3 special purpose resolutions and government actions: Position on preparation program accountability.* Arlington, VA: Author.

Council for Exceptional Children. (2002b). *CEC professional policy section four part 3 special purpose resolutions and government actions: Position on academic subject matter content of the general curriculum and special educators.* Arlington, VA: Author.

Council for Exceptional Children. (2003). *What Every Special Educator Must Know: Ethics, Standards, and Guidelines for Special Educators.* Reston, VA: Author

Council of Chief State School Officers. (2001). *Model standards for licensing general and special education teachers of students with disabilities: A resource for state dialogue.*

Washington, DC: Author. Retrieved October 15, 2008 from http://serge.ccsso.org/pdf/standards.pdf

Gersten R., Keating, T., Yovanoff, P., & Harniss, M. (2001 cited as 2003). Working in special education: Factors that enhance special educators' intent to stay. *Exceptional Children, 67*, 549-567.

Goodlad, J. I., (1990). *Teachers for Our Nation's Schools*, Jossey-Bass: San Francisco.

Mason, C., & White, M. (2007). *Anatomy of a Mentoring Program for New Special Education Teachers*. Arlington, VA: Council for Exceptional Children.

Murray, F. (2005). *Teacher education accreditation council guide to accreditation*. Washington, DC: Teacher Education Accreditation Council. Retrieved October 15, 2008 from http://www.teac.org/wp-content/uploads/2009/03/teac-guide-to-accreditation.pdf.

National Commission on Teaching and America's Future. (1996). *What matters most: Teaching and America's future*. Woodbridge, VA: Author.

No Child Left Behind Act of 2001. (H.R.1), Title II (2002).

Rosenberg, M. S., & Sindelar, P. T. (2001, cited as 2003). *The proliferation of alternative routes to certification in special education: A critical review of the literature*. Arlington, VA: Council for Exceptional Children. Retrieved October 2008 from: http://www.cec.sped.org/AM/Template.cfm? Section=Search&section= Careers_Center&template=/ CM/ContentDisplay. cfm&ContentFileID =725.

U.S. Department of Education. (2005). Twenty-fifth Annual Report to Congress on the implementation of the Individuals With Disabilities Education Act. Washington, DC: Author.

U.S. Department of Education National Center for Education Statistics. (2003, cited as IPEDS). *Digest of education statistics 2002*. (NCES 2003-060). Washington, DC: Author.

U.S. Department of Education Office of Special Education Programs. (2008). Individuals With Disabilities Education Act Data Accountability Center. Retrieved October 1, 2008 from http://www.ideadata. org/arc_toc9.asp#partbPEN

Wise, A. (2005). *Professional accreditation, NCATE, and TEAC*. Retrieved October 15, 2008 from http://www. ncate.org/public/artAwiseProfAccred.asp?ch=87

Section 3: Preparing to Become a Special Education Professional

CEC professional standards are built on the premise that well-prepared special education professionals are the cornerstone to the delivery of quality evidence-based practices **to individuals with exceptional learning needs**[4]. It has long been common sense that well-prepared and qualified teachers get the best learning results. Research has verified that a well-prepared teacher has more influence on a child's learning than any other factor under school control (Darling-Hammond, 2000).

In most mature professions, a strong national professional organization validates standards that institutions use for preparing candidates and that credentialing agencies use for licensing individuals (Connelly & Rosenberg, 2003). As the professional organization of special educators, CEC has advocated for well-prepared and high-quality special education professionals for over 75 years. To this end, CEC develops and maintains professional standards for entry-level and advanced special education roles, as well as for guiding continuing professional growth. CEC expects preparation programs to incorporate the CEC standards into their curricula and jurisdictions to coordinate the standards with their licensing requirements. It is through professional standards used by preparation programs and aligned with licensing systems that the public can be assured that special educators are prepared to practice safely and effectively.

Today, CEC professional standards for teacher quality are rigorously validated, research informed, and pedagogically grounded, CEC national recognition of preparation programs is performance-based for results-oriented accountability. Over the past 28 years, CEC has validated the knowledge and skills that are essential for well-prepared beginning special educators and for special educators preparing for advanced roles.

Figure 3.1 Special Education Continuum

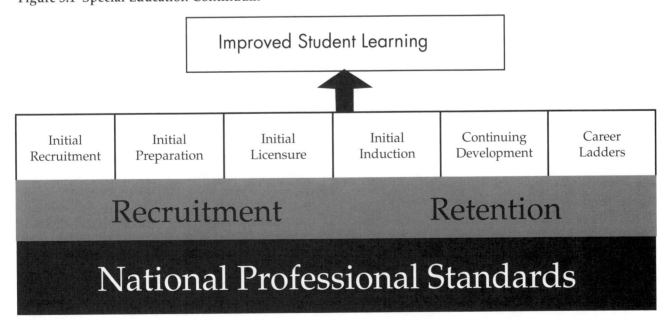

4 This document uses "individual with exceptional learning needs" to include both individuals with disabilities and individuals with exceptional gifts and talents.

This process involved thousands of practicing special educators in consonance with a national committee representing the 17 national CEC divisions. The result is the most rigorous and comprehensive set of national standards available anywhere for the preparation of well-prepared special educators. (See Appendix 2 for a description of the validation process.)

The careers of special educators can be thought of as a continuum, including initial preparation, induction, and continuing professional growth (Figure 3.1). The standards and guidelines relevant to each part of the continuum are described in the following pages.

CEC expects at a minimum that entry-level special educators possess a bachelor's degree from an accredited institution, have mastered appropriate core academic subject matter content, and appropriate curricular standards, along with the specialized pedagogical knowledge and skills for teaching individuals with exceptional learning needs in the respective areas of specialization.

CORE ACADEMIC SUBJECT MATTER CONTENT AND CURRICULAR STANDARDS[5]

CEC expects all special educators to have a solid grounding in the liberal arts curriculum ensuring proficiency in reading, written and oral communications, calculating, problem-solving, and thinking. All special educators should also possess a solid base of understanding of the general content area curricula, that is, math, reading, English/language arts, science, social studies, and the arts, sufficient to collaborate with general educators in

- Teaching or co-teaching academic subject matter content of the general curriculum to individuals with exceptional learning needs across a wide range of performance levels
- Designing appropriate learning and performance accommodations and modifications for individuals with

exceptional learning needs in academic subject matter content of the general curriculum

Because of the significant role that content specific subject matter knowledge plays at the secondary level, special education teachers routinely teach secondary level academic subject matter content classes in consultation or collaboration with one or more general education teachers appropriately licensed in the respective content area. However, when a special education teacher assumes sole responsibility for teaching a core academic subject matter class at the secondary level, the special educator must have a solid knowledge base in the subject matter content sufficient to assure the individuals with exceptional learning needs can meet state curriculum standards.

ASSURING QUALITY PREPARATION PROGRAMS

Today there are different approaches to preparing individuals to become special educators. However, all share the responsibility to assure at a minimum that their entry-level and advanced special education teacher candidates have mastered appropriate knowledge and skill in content and pedagogy to practice safely and effectively. Currently, the most common approach to the preparation of entry-level special educators in the United States (U.S. Department of Education, 2003) is through programs that prepare individuals for practice with individuals across a variety of exceptionalities, (e.g., multicategorical). It is important that prospective special educators prepared for multicategorical practice possess the knowledge and skills to teach individuals with each of the relevant exceptionalities. Although

multicategorical preparation is most common, the challenge for preparation programs lies in preparing individuals with both the depth and breadth of professional knowledge and skills.

CEC expects all preparation programs to acquire national program recognition from CEC. With the adoption of performance-based approach to national recognition, preparation programs now demonstrate that their candidates have mastered appropriate knowledge and skills for the roles for which they are prepared. This includes demonstrating the positive impact of their teacher candidates on increased student learning. In national program recognition, the programs undergo a process in which the evidence is

---

5 In the United States, states have set widely diverse requirements to meet the designation of "highly qualified" as mandated by U.S. Federal legislation. Candidates are advised to consult the regulations for the state in which they plan to practice.

submitted assuring that the graduates of the program possess appropriate knowledge, skill, and dispositions to practice within the respective professional role safely and effectively.

Colleagues review the performance of the program assessment results to determine how well the program has prepared their prospective teachers in alignment with CEC national professional standards. Only when a special education preparation program has CEC national recognition is the public assured that program graduates are prepared to practice safely and effectively.

For individuals looking for a preparation program, it is important for them to assure that the program is nationally recognized by CEC. For over 27 years, CEC alone and in partnership with NCATE has provided recognition to quality special education preparation programs.

Through the CEC partnership with NCATE, CEC has agreements with 50 states or territories in the United States. To date CEC has evaluated and approved approximately one third of all special education preparation programs in the United States.

Additionally, CEC maintains procedures to conduct performance-based program reviews outside the United States and in those instances in which a preparation program does not seek national accreditation through NCATE (Appendix 7).

Alternative Preparation Programs

Currently it is estimated that almost a million individuals with exceptional learning needs receive their special education services from approximately 50,000 individuals who are not even minimally qualified under licensing standards to practice special education. Many other children receive special education services from teachers doing double duty because over 3,000

special education teaching positions remain vacant each year or school districts have assigned them unreasonably large caseloads. This crisis in demand for special education teachers is fueling a good deal of interest in alternative ways to prepare special educators. Many of these alternatives hold promise, and CEC actively embraces innovative approaches preparing well-qualified special educators. However, some poorly conceptualized alternative approaches appear to have sacrificed standards in attempting to place unprepared individuals in poorly supported teaching positions. The result has been an expensive revolving door through which ill-prepared individuals are rushed into classrooms only to become overwhelmed and disillusioned. These individuals leave special education in large numbers. Most significant, a large price is extracted from the learning of individuals with exceptional learning needs.

Alternative preparation programs have historically played and can continue to play a positive role in addressing the demand deficit in special education. However, decision makers must not be seduced by "quick fixes." School districts cannot afford to waste precious dollars on recruitment and induction of unprepared individuals. Most important, too many individuals with exceptional learning needs will never benefit from the promise of the Individuals With Disabilities Education Act (IDEA) unless decision makers embrace solutions that address both quantity and quality in teacher preparation. Regardless of whether a preparation program is traditional or alternative, campus-based or school-based, distance or face-to-face, CEC expects all programs preparing special educators to meet CEC nationally validated standards by undergoing a performance-based review. As stated in the introduction, this approach provides the most reasonable assurance to the parents and the public that beginning special education teachers are prepared for their professional responsibilities.

ASSURING HIGH-QUALITY LICENSURE

Historically, the licensing of individuals to practice has been the responsibility of states and provinces. Although approaches to licensing special educators taken by jurisdictions have been variable and somewhat idiosyncratic, most states today base their licensing process on the standards of the national societies representing the various disciplines within education.

Currently, over 40 states are committed to align their licensing processes with the CEC standards. As mentioned previously, most individuals are now licensed for multicategorical practice. Many states use terms

such as Teaching of Individuals With Mild/Moderate Exceptionalities and Teaching of Individuals With Severe/Profound Exceptionalities to describe these multicategorical licenses. According to the latest figures from the U.S. Department of Education, over 90% of the titles of the special education degrees granted each year are multicategorical (U.S. Department of Education, 2003). For those states that use a multicategorical approach, CEC has developed the Curriculum Referenced Licensing and Program Accreditation Framework. The Individualized General Education Curriculum and Individualized Independence

Figure 3.2 Comparison of Professional Frameworks

	CEC	INTASC	NBPTS
1. Individualized General Curriculum	•	•	•
2. Individualized Independence Curriculum	•	•	•
3. Deaf/Hard of Hearing	•	•	•
4. Blind/Vision Impaired	•	•	•
5. Early Childhood Special Education	•	•	•
6. Gifted/Talented Special Education	•		•

Curriculum describe these multicategorical licenses, and reference the curricula in which the licensed teacher will primarily practice. In using multicategorical licensing approaches, it is important that states balance the need for both breadth and depth of knowledge and skills for special education teachers. Licensing approaches that are overly broad result in teachers who are not adequately prepared for the complex challenges of individuals with exceptional learning needs. Conversely, licensing approaches that are overly narrow do not prepare prospective special educators for the increasing diversity of individuals with exceptional learning needs that special educators serve.

Based on the premise that the standards for national program recognition and state licensure should align,

CEC has organized its professional standards to align with the 10 INTASC principles for model licensing standards at the entry level and with the National Board for Professional Teaching Standards (NBPTS) at the advanced level. It is encouraging, that the initial licensing model of INTASC and advanced certification approaches suggested by the NBPTS align closely with the CEC Curriculum Referenced Licensing and Program Accreditation Framework, reflecting a strong national convergence regarding the balance of depth and spread (see Figure 3.2). This alignment also reflects the explicit intentions of CEC, INTASC, NCATE, and the NBPTS to collaborate and coordinate with each other.

INDUCTION AND MENTORING

Even with well-designed and implemented preparation, the beginning special educator faces a myriad of challenges in applying and generalizing learned skills during their beginning teaching. Like other professionals, special educators who have the focused support of veteran colleagues as mentors become proficient more quickly, and are more likely to remain in the profession. Every new professional in special education must receive an intensive focused induction program under a mentor during the first year or so of special education practice. The mentor must be an accomplished special educator in the same or a similar role to the mentored individual who can provide expertise and support on a continuing basis throughout the induction (Mason & White, 2007). The goals of the mentorship program include

- Facilitating the application of knowledge and skills learned
- Conveying advanced knowledge and skills
- Acculturating into the school's learning communities
- Reducing job stress and enhancing job satisfaction
- Supporting professional induction

In addition, whenever a special educator begins practice in a new area of licensure, they should also have the opportunity to work with mentors who are accomplished professionals in similar roles. The purpose of mentors is to provide expertise and support to the individual on a continuing basis for at least the first year of practice in that area of licensure. The mentorship is a professional relationship between the individual in a new area of practice and an accomplished individual in the area that supports the individual in further developing knowledge and skills in the given area of licensure and provides the support required to sustain the individual in practice. The mentorship must be collegial rather than supervisory. It is essential that the mentor have accomplished knowledge, skills, and experience relevant to the position in order to provide the expertise and support required to practice effectively. Mentorship can be an effective part of career ladders. Veterans of the special education profession are expected to periodically serve as mentors as part of their professional responsibility, and they must receive the resources and support necessary to carry out this responsibility effectively.

CONTINUOUS PROFESSIONAL GROWTH

Like their colleagues in general education, special educators are lifelong learners committed to developing the highest educational and quality-of-life potential of individuals with exceptionalities. The fifth principle in the CEC Code of Ethics states that special educators strive to advance their knowledge and skills regarding the education of individuals with exceptionalities.

CONTINUING LICENSURE/CERTIFICATION

Both state/provincial licensure and advanced certification of individuals for professional practice in the field of special education should be for a limited period, and renewal should be based on planned, organized, and recognized professional development related to the professional's field of practice. CEC expects practicing special educators to develop and implement a Professional Development Plan (PDP). The PDP is reviewed and amended at least annually. The professional development activities in the PDP should go beyond routine job functions of the professional, and no single activity or category should make up the plan. This PDP should include participation in an average of at least 36 contact hours (or an average of 3.6 continuing education units) each year of planned, organized, and recognized professional development related to the professional's field of practice within the following categories:

- Career related academic activities
- Conducting or supporting research
- Participating in district- and/or school-based professional development programs
- Teaching courses
- Delivering presentations
- Publishing
- Participating in mentoring or supervised collegial support activities
- Providing service to professional association(s)
- Participating in approved educational travel
- Other projects

Section 4 contains resources for developing the annual Professional Development Plan.

ADVANCED SPECIAL EDUCATION STUDY

In 2001, the CEC National Clearinghouse for Professions in Special Education queried state education agencies (SEAs) regarding special education career ladders. Of the 16 states that responded, only 5 indicated that they offer an advanced special education licensure. The Bright Futures Report (Council for Exceptional Children, 2000) found that when special educators have viable career paths to pursue, retention is enhanced. Advanced licensure options are an important component of any special education career ladder program. As special educators progress in their teaching careers, many seek to deepen their teaching skills through advanced study in specialty areas. Other special educators will pursue new roles within special education. Within the field of special education, CEC has developed advanced standards for the following roles

- Special Education Administrators
- Special Education Diagnosticians
- Special Education Technology Specialists
- Special Education Transition Specialists
- Early Childhood Special Education Specialists
- Specialists for Deaf and Hard of Hearing

CEC is developing standards in other advanced role areas including a number of categorical specialty areas. CEC is developing a process through which professional development programs that have earned CEC national recognition may apply to award CEC Advanced Certificates to their program graduates. National Board for Professional Teaching Standards (NBPTS) offers another avenue for advanced certification for teachers (see Appendix 5). CEC has had a long and fruitful relationship with the NBPTS. Through the NBPTS, special educators may earn the advanced certification for teachers of exceptional needs individuals. The NBPTS recognizes five areas of specialization

- Mild/Moderate Disabilities Exceptional Needs Specialist

- Severe and Multiple Exceptional Needs Specialist
- Early Childhood Exceptional Needs Specialist
- Visual Impairments Exceptional Needs Specialist
- Deaf/Hard of Hearing Exceptional Needs Specialist

Still other special educators will pursue doctoral level studies in special education. There are currently over 150 programs preparing special educators at the doctoral level. Like other preparation programs, CEC expects doctoral programs to demonstrate their quality through CEC performance-based recognition.

REFERENCES

Connelly, V. J., & Rosenberg, M. S. (2003). *Developing teaching as a profession: Comparison with careers that have achieved full professional standing*. (COPSSE Document No. RS-9). Gainesville: University of Florida, Center on Personnel Studies in Special Education.

Council for Exceptional Children. (2000). *Bright futures for exceptional learners: An agenda to achieve quality conditions for teaching and learning*. Reston, VA: Author.

Darling-Hammond, L. (2000). *Teacher quality and student achievement: A review of state policy evidence*. Education

Policy Analysis Archives, 8(1). Retrieved 10/21/03 from http://epaa. asu.edu/epaa/v8n1.

Mason, C., & White, M. (2007). *Anatomy of a Mentoring Program for New Special Education Teachers*. Arlington, VA: Council for Exceptional Children.

U.S. Department of Education. National Center for Education Statistics. (2003). *Digest of education statistics 2002*. (NCES 2003-060). Washington, DC: Author.

NOTES:

Exceptional Condition is used throughout to include both single and co-existing conditions. These may be two or more disabling conditions or exceptional gifts or talents co-existing with one or more disabling conditions.

Special Curricula is used throughout to denote curricular areas not routinely emphasized or addressed in general curricula; (e.g., social, communication, motor, independence, self-advocacy).

As used, the phrase, "core academic subject matter content of the general curriculum," means only the content of the general curriculum including math, reading, English/language arts, science, social studies, and the arts. It does not per se include the additional specialized knowledge and skill that special educators possess in areas such as reading, writing, math, social/emotional skills, functional independent living skills, and transition skills.

Advanced specialty areas are those areas beyond entry-level special education teacher preparation programs. Advanced specialty area programs are preparation programs that require full special education teacher licensure as a program entrance prerequisite.

Section 4: Tools and Strategies for Using the Standards

Section 4 provides tools that different audiences can use to make the standards more accessible. State personnel will find a chart to help them compare state and CEC standards. Teacher educators will find guidance on developing a performance-based assessment system, as well as a strategy they can use with teacher candidates to help them become familiar with the standards.

Special education teachers will find guidance and tools to help them use the CEC standards to develop professional development plans and advocate for the resources to implement them. Finally, candidates in teacher preparation programs are provided a tool to help them measure their progress in developing their professional competence.

STATE LICENSING: ALIGNING CEC AND STATE STANDARDS

As described earlier, CEC has organized the Knowledge and Skill Sets so that each explicitly aligns with the organization used by the Interstate New Teacher and Assessment and Support Consortium's (INTASC) Model Standards for Teacher licensure. Each set has been reorganized into 10 domain areas that parallel the domain of each of the 10 INTASC Core Principles. This alignment is demonstrated in Figure 4.1 (see Appendix 6 for a complete description of this re-organization). One of the primary purposes of this alignment was to support those states that use the INTASC standards as a key component of their licensure frameworks, to use the CEC Standards as they develop state standards for licensure of special education teachers.

CEC Standards for Preparation and Licensure are written in two tiers. The foundational standards are the Knowledge and Skill Sets. These sets have been developed to meet the variety of state licensure frameworks. There are standards for both categorical and multicategorical licensure frameworks. CEC also developed a set of 10 Content Standards, based on the Knowledge and Skill Standards, one for each of the domain areas listed in Figure 4.1. The Content Standards are written at a rich narrative level and are a single set—that is, they do not delineate the differences between the knowledge and skills needed by early childhood special education teachers, teachers of individuals with mild to moderate disabilities, teachers of individuals who are deaf and hard of hearing, and so forth. This level of specificity is found in the Knowledge and Skill Sets. Figure 4.2 will be helpful to states as they go through the process of determining the alignment of their state standards and the CEC standards. This could be done at the Content Standard level or the Knowledge and Skill Standards level. Figure 4.2 is a model chart that lists the CEC Content Standards in the left column and provides a column for states to enter the state standards that align with the respective CEC Content Standards. Worksheet 4.2 will help states to compare their state standards for in a given area with the respective CEC Knowledge and Skill Sets. Figure 4.3 uses Early Childhood Special Education with the CEC Knowledge and Skill Standards as an example. All of the CEC Standards, along with electronic versions of these worksheets, can be found at www.cec.sped.org/ps

Figure 4.1 Alignment of INTASC Core Principles and CEC Standard Domain Areas

CEC Standard Domain Areas	INTASC Core Principles
Foundations	Content Knowledge
Characteristics of Learners	Learner Development
Instructional Strategies	Instructional Strategies
Individual Differences	Learner Diversity
Learning Environments and Social Interactions	Learning Environment
Instructional Planning	Planning for Instruction
Language	Communication
Ethics and Professional Practice	Reflective Practice and Professional Development
Assessment	Assessment
Collaboration	Community

Figure 4.2 Comparing CEC Content Standards and State Content Standards

CEC Content Standards	Corresponding State Standards
1. Foundations Special educators understand the field as an evolving and changing discipline based on philosophies, evidence-based **principles and theories**, relevant **laws and policies**, diverse and **historical** points of view, and **human issues** that have historically influenced and continue to influence the field of special education and the education and treatment of individuals with exceptional needs in both school and society. Special educators understand how these **influence professional practice**, including assessment, instructional planning, implementation, and program evaluation. Special educators understand how **issues of human diversity** can impact families, cultures, and schools, and how these complex human issues can interact with issues in the delivery of special education services. They understand the **relationships of organizations** of **special education** to the organizations and functions of schools, school systems, and other agencies. Special educators use this knowledge as a ground upon which to construct their own personal understandings and philosophies of special education. Beginning special educators demonstrate their mastery of this standard through the mastery of the CEC Common Core Knowledge and Skills, as well as through the appropriate CEC Specialty Area(s) Knowledge and Skills for which the program is preparing candidates.	

CEC Content Standards	Corresponding State Standards
2. Development and Characteristics of Learners Special educators know and **demonstrate respect** for their students first as unique human beings. Special educators understand the **similarities and differences in human development** and the characteristics between and among individuals with and without exceptional learning needs. Moreover, special educators understand how **exceptional conditions** can **interact** with the domains of human development and they **use this knowledge to respond to the varying abilities and behaviors of individuals** with exceptional learning needs. Special educators understand how the experiences of individuals with exceptional learning needs can impact families, as well as the individual's ability to learn, interact socially, and live as fulfilled contributing members of the community. Beginning special educators demonstrate their mastery of this standard through the mastery of the CEC Common Core Knowledge and Skills, as well as through the appropriate CEC Specialty Area(s) Knowledge and Skills for which the program is preparing candidates.	
3. Individual Learning Differences Special educators understand the **effects that an exceptional condition** can have on **an individual's learning** in school and throughout life. Special educators understand that the beliefs, traditions, and values across and within cultures can affect relationships among and between students, their families, and the school community. Moreover, special educators are **active and resourceful in seeking to understand how primary language, culture, and familial backgrounds interact with the individual's exceptional condition** to impact the individual's academic and social abilities, attitudes, values, interests, and career options. The understanding of these learning differences and their possible interactions **provides the foundation** upon which **special educators individualize instruction** to provide meaningful and challenging learning for individuals with exceptional learning needs. Beginning special educators demonstrate their mastery of this standard through the mastery of the CEC Common Core Knowledge and Skills, as well as through the appropriate CEC Specialty Area(s) Knowledge and Skills for which the program is preparing candidates.	
4. Instructional Strategies Special educators possess a repertoire of evidence-based **instructional strategies to individualize instruction** for individuals with Exceptional learning needs. Special educators select, adapt, and use these instructional strategies to promote **positive learning results in general and special curricula** and to **modify learning environments appropriately** for individuals with exceptional learning needs. They enhance the **learning of critical thinking, problem-solving, and performance skills** of individuals with exceptional learning needs, and increase their self-awareness, self-management, self-control, self-reliance, and self-esteem. Moreover, special educators emphasize the **development, maintenance, and generalization** of knowledge and skills across environments, settings, and the life span. Beginning special educators demonstrate their mastery of this standard through the mastery of the CEC Common Core Knowledge and Skills, as well as through the appropriate CEC Specialty Area(s) Knowledge and Skills for which the program is preparing candidates.	

CEC Content Standards	Corresponding State Standards
5. Learning Environments and Social Interactions Special educators actively **create learning environments** for individuals with exceptional learning needs that foster cultural understanding, safety and emotional well-being, positive social interactions, and **active engagement** of individuals with exceptional learning needs. In addition, special educators **foster environments in which diversity is valued** and individuals are taught to live harmoniously and productively in a culturally diverse world. Special educators shape **environments to encourage the independence**, self-motivation, self-direction, personal empowerment, and self-advocacy of individuals with exceptional learning needs. Special educators **help their general education colleagues integrate individuals** with exceptional learning needs in general education environments and engage them in meaningful learning activities and interactions. Special educators use **direct motivational and instructional interventions** with individuals with exceptional learning needs to teach them to respond effectively to current expectations. When necessary, special educators can safely **intervene with individuals with exceptional learning needs in crisis**. Special educators coordinate all these efforts and **provide guidance and direction to paraeducators and others**, such as classroom volunteers and tutors. Beginning special educators demonstrate their mastery of this standard through the mastery of the CEC Common Core Knowledge and Skills, as well as through the appropriate CEC Specialty Area(s) Knowledge and Skills for which the program is preparing candidates.	
6. Language Special educators understand **typical and atypical language development** and the ways in which exceptional conditions can interact with an individual's experience with and use of language. Special educators use individualized strategies to **enhance language development** and **teach communication skills** to individuals with exceptional learning needs. Special educators are familiar with **augmentative, alternative, and assistive technologies** to support and enhance communication of individuals with exceptional needs. Special educators match their communication methods to an individual's language proficiency and cultural and linguistic differences. Special educators provide **effective language models** and they use communication strategies and resources to **facilitate understanding of subject matter for individuals with exceptional learning needs whose primary language is not English.** Beginning special educators demonstrate their mastery of this standard through the mastery of the CEC Common Core Knowledge and Skills, as well as through the appropriate CEC Specialty Area(s) Knowledge and Skills for which the program is preparing candidates.	

CEC Content Standards	Corresponding State Standards

7. Instructional Planning

Individualized decision-making and instruction is at the center of special education practice. Special educators develop **long-range individualized instructional plans** anchored in both general and special education curricula. In addition, special educators systematically translate these individualized plans into carefully selected **shorter-range goals and objectives** taking into consideration an individual's abilities and needs, the learning environment, and a myriad of cultural and linguistic factors. Individualized instructional plans emphasize **explicit modeling** and **efficient guided practice** to assure acquisition and fluency through maintenance and generalization. Understanding of these factors as well as the implications of an individual's exceptional condition, guides the special educator's selection, adaptation, and creation of materials, and the use of powerful instructional variables. Instructional plans are **modified based on ongoing analysis of the individual's learning progress**. Moreover, special educators facilitate this instructional planning in a **collaborative context** including the individuals with exceptionalities, families, professional colleagues, and personnel from other agencies as appropriate. Special educators also develop a variety of **individualized transition plans**, such as transitions from preschool to elementary school and from secondary settings to a variety of postsecondary work and learning contexts. Special educators are comfortable using **appropriate technologies** to support instructional planning and individualized instruction.

Beginning special educators demonstrate their mastery of this standard through the mastery of the CEC Common Core Knowledge and Skills, as well as through the appropriate CEC Specialty Area(s) Knowledge and Skills for which the program is preparing candidates.

8. Assessment

Assessment is integral to the decision-making and teaching of special educators and special educators use **multiple types of assessment information** for a variety of educational decisions. Special educators use the results of assessments to help identify exceptional learning needs and to develop and implement individualized instructional programs, as well as to adjust instruction in response to ongoing learning progress. Special educators understand the **legal policies and ethical principles of measurement and assessment** related to referral, eligibility, program planning, instruction, and placement for individuals with exceptional learning needs, including those from culturally and linguistically diverse backgrounds. Special educators understand **measurement theory and practices** for addressing issues of validity, reliability, norms, bias, and interpretation of assessment results. In addition, special educators understand the appropriate **use and limitations** of various types of assessments. Special educators collaborate with families and other colleagues to assure **nonbiased, meaningful assessments and decision-making**.

Special educators conduct **formal and informal assessments** of behavior, learning, achievement, and environments to design learning experiences that support the growth and development of individuals with exceptional learning needs. Special educators use assessment information to **identify supports and adaptations** required for individuals with exceptional learning needs to access the general curriculum and to participate in school, system, and statewide assessment programs. Special educators **regularly monitor the progress** of individuals with exceptional learning needs in general and special curricula. Special educators **use appropriate technologies** to support their assessments.

Beginning special educators demonstrate their mastery of this standard through the mastery of the CEC Common Core Knowledge and Skills, as well as through the appropriate CEC Specialty Area(s) Knowledge and Skills for which the program is preparing candidates.

CEC Content Standards	Corresponding State Standards
9. Professional and Ethical Practice Special educators are guided by the profession's ethical and professional practice standards. Special educators practice in multiple roles and complex situations across wide age and developmental ranges. Their practice requires ongoing attention to **legal matters** along with serious professional and **ethical considerations**. Special educators engage in **professional activities** and participate in learning communities that benefit individuals with exceptional learning needs, their families, colleagues, and their own professional growth. Special educators view themselves as **lifelong learners** and regularly reflect on and adjust their practice. Special educators are aware of how their own and others' attitudes, behaviors, and ways of communicating can influence their practice. Special educators understand that culture and language can interact with exceptionalities, and are **sensitive to the many aspects** of diversity of individuals with exceptional learning needs and their families. Special educators actively plan and engage in activities that foster their professional growth and keep them **current with evidence-based best practices**. Special educators know their own limits of practice and practice within them. Beginning special educators demonstrate their mastery of this standard through the mastery of the CEC Common Core Knowledge and Skills, as well as through the appropriate CEC Specialty Area(s) Knowledge and Skills for which the program is preparing candidates.	
10. Collaboration Special educators routinely and effectively **collaborate with families, other educators, related service providers, and personnel from community agencies in culturally responsive ways**. This collaboration assures that the needs of individuals with exceptional learning needs are addressed throughout schooling. Moreover, special educators embrace their special role as advocate for individuals with exceptional learning needs. Special educators promote and advocate the learning and well-being of individuals with exceptional learning needs across a wide range of settings and a range of different learning experiences. Special educators are viewed as specialists by a myriad of people who actively seek their collaboration to effectively include and teach individuals with exceptional learning needs. Special educators are a **resource to their colleagues** in understanding the laws and policies relevant to individuals with **exceptional learning needs**. Special educators use collaboration to **facilitate the successful transitions** of individuals with exceptional learning needs across settings and services. Beginning special educators demonstrate their mastery of this standard through the mastery of the CEC Common Core Knowledge and Skills, as well as through the appropriate CEC Specialty Area(s) Knowledge and Skills for which the program is preparing candidates.	

Figure 4.3 Comparing CEC Initial Common Core Set and State Standards

Special Education Standard 1: Foundations

CEC Knowledge and Skills		State Standard
ICC1K1	Models, theories, philosophies, and research methods that form the basis for special education practice	
ICC1K2	Laws, policies, and ethical principles regarding behavior management planning and implementation	
ICC1K3	Relationship of special education to the organization and function of educational agencies	
ICC1K4	Rights and responsibilities of students, parents, teachers, and other professionals, and schools related to exceptional learning needs	
ICC1K5	Issues in definition and identification of individuals with exceptional learning needs, including those from culturally and linguistically diverse backgrounds	
ICC1K6	Issues, assurances and due process rights related to assessment, eligibility, and placement within a continuum of services	
ICC1K7	Family systems and the role of families in the educational process	
ICC1K8	Historical points of view and contribution of culturally diverse groups	
ICC1K9	Impact of the dominant culture on shaping schools and the individuals who study and work in them	
ICC1K10	Potential impact of differences in values, languages, and customs that can exist between the home and school	
ICC1S1	Articulate personal philosophy of special education	

Special Education Standard 2: Development and Characteristics of Learners

ICC2K1	Typical and atypical human growth and development	
ICC2K2	Educational implications of characteristics of various exceptionalities	
ICC2K3	Characteristics and effects of the cultural and environmental milieu of the individual with exceptional learning needs and the family	
ICC2K4	Family systems and the role of families in supporting development	
ICC2K5	Similarities and differences of individuals with and without exceptional learning needs	
ICC2K6	Similarities and differences among individuals with exceptional learning needs	

| ICC2K7 | Effects of various medications on individuals with exceptional learning needs | |

Special Education Standard 3: Individual Learning Differences

ICC3K1	Effects an exceptional condition(s) can have on an individual's life	
ICC3K2	Impact of learners' academic and social abilities, attitudes, interests, and values on instruction and career development	
ICC3K3	Variations in beliefs, traditions, and values across and within cultures and their effects on relationships among individuals with exceptional learning needs, families, and schooling	
ICC3K4	Cultural perspectives influencing the relationships among families, schools and communities as related to instruction	
ICC3K5	Differing ways of learning of individuals with exceptional learning needs including those from culturally diverse backgrounds and strategies for addressing these differences	

Special Education Standard 4: Instructional Strategies

ICC4K1	Evidence-based practices validated for specific characteristics of learners and settings	
ICC4S1	Use strategies to facilitate integration into various settings	
ICC4S2	Teach individuals to use self-assessment, problem solving, and other cognitive strategies to meet their needs	
ICC4S3	Select, adapt, and use instructional strategies and materials according to characteristics of the individual with exceptional learning needs	
ICC4S4	Use strategies to facilitate maintenance and generalization of skills across learning environments	
ICC4S5	Use procedures to increase the individual's self-awareness, self-management, self-control, self-reliance, and self-esteem	
ICC4S6	Use strategies that promote successful transitions for individuals with exceptional learning needs	

Special Education Standard 5: Learning Environments and Social Interactions

ICC5K1	Demands of learning environments	
ICC5K2	Basic classroom management theories and strategies for individuals with exceptional learning needs	
ICC5K3	Effective management of teaching and learning	
ICC5K4	Teacher attitudes and behaviors that influence behavior of individuals with exceptional learning needs	

ICC5K5	Social skills needed for educational and other environments	
ICC5K6	Strategies for crisis prevention and intervention	
ICC5K7	Strategies for preparing individuals to live harmoniously and productively in a culturally diverse world	
ICC5K8	Ways to create learning environments that allow individuals to retain and appreciate their own and each other's respective language and cultural heritage	
ICC5K9	Ways specific cultures are negatively stereotyped	
ICC5K10	Strategies used by diverse populations to cope with a legacy of former and continuing racism	
ICC5S1	Create a safe, equitable, positive, and supportive learning environment in which diversities are valued	
ICC5S2	Identify realistic expectations for personal and social behavior in various settings	
ICC5S3	Identify supports needed for integration into various program placements	
ICC5S4	Design learning environments that encourage active participation in individual and group activities	
ICC5S5	Modify the learning environment to manage behaviors.	
ICC5S6	Use performance data and information from all stakeholders to make or suggest modifications in learning environments	
ICC5S7	Establish and maintain rapport with individuals with and without exceptional learning needs	
ICC5S8	Teach self-advocacy	
ICC5S9	Create an environment that encourages self-advocacy and increased independence	
ICC5S10	Use effective and varied behavior management strategies	
ICC5S11	Use the least intensive behavior management strategy consistent with the needs of the individual with exceptional learning needs	
ICC5S12	Design and manage daily routines	
ICC5S13	Organize, develop, and sustain learning environments that support positive intracultural and intercultural experiences	
ICC5S14	Mediate controversial intercultural issues among students within the learning environment in ways that enhance any culture, group, or person	

ICC5S15	Structure, direct, and support the activities of paraeducators, volunteers, and tutors.	
ICC5S16	Use universal precautions.	

Special Education Standard 6: Communication

ICC6K1	Effects of cultural and linguistic differences on growth and development	
ICC6K2	Characteristics of one's own culture and use of language and the ways in which these can differ from other cultures and uses of languages	
ICC6K3	Ways of behaving and communicating among cultures that can lead to misinterpretation and misunderstanding	
ICC6K4	Augmentative and assistive communication strategies	
ICC6S1	Use strategies to support and enhance communication skills of individuals with exceptional learning needs	
ICC6S2	Use communication strategies and resources to facilitate understanding of subject matter for students whose primary language is not the dominant language	

Special Education Standard 7: Instructional Planning

ICC7K1	Theories and research that form the basis of curriculum development and instructional practice	
ICC7K2	Scope and sequences of general and special curricula	
ICC7K3	National, state or provincial, and local curricula standards	
ICC7K4	Technology for planning and managing the teaching and learning environment	
ICC7K5	Roles and responsibilities of the paraeducator related to instruction, intervention, and direct service	
ICC7S1	Identify and prioritize areas of the general curriculum and accommodations for individuals with exceptional learning needs	
ICC7S2	Develop and implement comprehensive, longitudinal individualized programs in collaboration with team members	
ICC7S3	Involve the individual and family in setting instructional goals and monitoring progress	
ICC7S4	Use functional assessments to develop intervention plans	
ICC7S5	Use task analysis	

ICC7S6	Sequence, implement, and evaluate individualized learning objectives	
ICC7S7	Integrate affective, social, and life skills with academic curricula	
ICC7S8	Develop and select instructional content, resources, and strategies that respond to cultural, linguistic, and gender differences	
ICC7S9	Incorporate and implement instructional and assistive technology into the educational program	
ICC7S10	Prepare lesson plans	
ICC7S11	Prepare and organize materials to implement daily lesson plans	
ICC7S12	Use instructional time effectively	
ICC7S13	Make responsive adjustments to instruction based on continual observations	
ICC7S14	Prepare individuals to exhibit self-enhancing behavior in response to societal attitudes and actions	
ICC7S15	Evaluate and modify instructional practices in response to ongoing assessment data	

Special Education Standard 8: Assessment

ICC8K1	Basic terminology used in assessment	
ICC8K2	Legal provisions and ethical principles regarding assessment of individuals	
ICC8K3	Screening, pre-referral, referral, and classification procedures	
ICC8K4	Use and limitations of assessment instruments	
ICC8K5	National, state or provincial, and local accommodations and modifications	
ICC8S1	Gather relevant background information	
ICC8S2	Administer nonbiased formal and informal assessments	
ICC8S3	Use technology to conduct assessments	
ICC8S4	Develop or modify individualized assessment strategies	
ICC8S5	Interpret information from formal and informal assessments	
ICC8S6	Use assessment information in making eligibility, program, and placement decisions for individuals with exceptional learning needs, including those from culturally and/or linguistically diverse backgrounds	

ICC8S7	Report assessment results to all stakeholders using effective communication skills	
ICC8S8	Evaluate instruction and monitor progress of individuals with exceptional learning needs	
ICC8S9	Create and maintain records	

Special Education Standard 9: Professional and Ethical Practice

ICC9K1	Personal cultural biases and differences that affect one's teaching	
ICC9K2	Importance of the teacher serving as a model for individuals with exceptional learning needs	
ICC9K3	Continuum of lifelong professional development	
ICC9K4	Methods to remain current regarding research-validated practice	
ICC9S1	Practice within the CEC Code of Ethics and other standards of the profession	
ICC9S2	Uphold high standards of competence and integrity and exercise sound judgment in the practice of the professional	
ICC9S3	Act ethically in advocating for appropriate services	
ICC9S4	Conduct professional activities in compliance with applicable laws and policies	
ICC9S5	Demonstrate commitment to developing the highest education and quality-of-life potential of individuals with exceptional learning needs	
ICC9S6	Demonstrate sensitivity for the culture, language, religion, gender, disability, socio-economic status, and sexual orientation of individuals	
ICC9S7	Practice within one's skill limit and obtain assistance as needed	
ICC9S8	Use verbal, nonverbal, and written language effectively	
ICC9S9	Conduct self-evaluation of instruction	
ICC9S10	Access information on exceptionalities	
ICC9S11	Reflect on one's practice to improve instruction and guide professional growth	
ICC9S12	Engage in professional activities that benefit individuals with exceptional learning needs, their families, and one's colleagues	
ICC9S13	Demonstrate commitment to engage in evidence-based practices	

Special Education Standard 10: Collaboration

ICC10K1	Models and strategies of consultation and collaboration	
ICC10K2	Roles of individuals with exceptional learning needs, families, and school and community personnel in planning of an individualized program	
ICC10K3	Concerns of families of individuals with exceptional learning needs and strategies to help address these concerns	
ICC10K4	Culturally responsive factors that promote effective communication and collaboration with individuals with exceptional learning needs, families, school personnel, and community members	
ICC10S1	Maintain confidential communication about individuals with exceptional learning needs	
ICC10S2	Collaborate with families and others in assessment of individuals with exceptional learning needs	
ICC10S3	Foster respectful and beneficial relationships between families and professionals	
ICC10S4	Assist individuals with exceptional learning needs and their families in becoming active participants in the educational team	
ICC10S5	Plan and conduct collaborative conferences with individuals with exceptional learning needs and their families	
ICC10S6	Collaborate with school personnel and community members in integrating individuals with exceptional learning needs into various settings	
ICC10S7	Use group problem-solving skills to develop, implement and evaluate collaborative activities	
ICC10S8	Model techniques and coach others in the use of instructional methods and accommodations	
ICC10S9	Communicate with school personnel about the characteristics and needs of individuals with exceptional learning needs	
ICC10S10	Communicate effectively with families of individuals with exceptional learning needs from diverse backgrounds	
ICC10S11	Observe, evaluate, and provide feedback to paraeducators	

NOTES:

Individual with exceptional learning needs is used throughout to include individuals with disabilities and individuals with exceptional gifts and talents.

Exceptional condition is used throughout to include both single and co-existing conditions. These may be two or more disabling conditions or exceptional gifts or talents co-existing with one or more disabling conditions.

Special curricula is used throughout to denote curricular areas not routinely emphasized or addressed in general curricula; (e.g., social, communication, motor, independence, self-advocacy).

CEC is the world's leader in the development of standards for special education teachers. These standards are used by hundreds of colleges and universities to develop their curricula and as a measure to assess their graduates' competence. Over half of the states use the CEC standards as models for their state licensure frameworks. But do these standards have any use or relevance for special education teachers working every day in classrooms? The answer is resoundingly yes. There are numerous ways that practicing special educators can and should use the CEC standards to ensure that they have and maintain the knowledge and skills necessary to meet the needs of individuals with exceptional learning needs. The standards are an excellent yardstick that can be used by individuals to assess their own competence as well as to determine the best use of their professional development hours. Practitioners can also use the standards to evaluate their ability and proficiency as they contemplate a job change or a move to working with individuals with different kinds of disabilities.

The CEC standards can be a powerful tool for special educators to request and receive the professional development opportunities they need to update their current skills and learn new skills required for the challenges they face every day. The standards can be and are being used by schools and districts as the basis for helping their teachers develop professional development programs that will ensure that all teachers have the knowledge and skills they need to work successfully with individuals with disabilities.

The CEC standards can be used as a road map to help practicing teachers structure a professional development plan, to ensure that they maintain an appropriate level of expertise, and to evaluate their competence as they move into new areas. Beginning teachers can find them particularly useful as a way of measuring their developing expertise. The following steps outline a process teachers can use:

- Select the most appropriate set of standards from the CEC Web site.
- Rate your level of mastery on each of the individual standards. Two suggested formats for creating an evaluation form are shown in Figures 4.4 and 4.5.
- After you have evaluated your level of mastery, add up the number of items checked in each domain area (e.g., Characteristics of Learners, Assessment, etc.). Pay closest attention to those domains that have the highest scores.

- Choose the domain(s) in which you want to work and develop your professional development plan accordingly.

For example, a beginning teacher who is working with individuals with mild to moderate disabilities could select the Individualized General Curriculum set of standards. This set is designed for teachers working with individuals with disabilities who are expected to be successful in the general curriculum and most closely aligns with a mild/moderate licensure framework. By going through the steps, outlined previously, beginning teachers can identify in which areas they feel the least confident. This information can be used to help select course work required for continuing education licensure, inservice or conference sessions needed for CEUs, extra reading, and so forth.

If a teacher is considering moving into a new special educator role or working with individuals with exceptionalities different from those in his or her preparation, he or she can identify the knowledge and skills they should target. For example, perhaps a teacher has been asked to teach individuals with exceptionalities who are developmentally delayed though their previous preparation and experience has been with individuals with mild to moderate learning disabilities. Following the steps outlined previously and using the CEC Developmental Disabilities set of standards, the teacher can determine which knowledge and skills to target. This documentation can be used in collaboration with a principal or special education administrator as part of a request for additional training.

This process could also be used by a group of special educators. Each could complete a self-evaluation and then identify the domains and skills the group shares together to help plan or request the inservice educational opportunities that would benefit them. This documentation could be provided to the principal, district supervisor, or inservice director as a part of request for coverage of specific topic areas.

Teaching is a life-long learning process. Men and women who leave training programs are novices entering their profession. Using the CEC standards to gauge their professional development is a way for ALL teachers to ensure that their knowledge and skills are up-to-date and sufficient to meet the needs of their individuals with exceptional learning needs.

Figure 4.4 Professional Development Plan Self-Assessment in Collaboration

Knowledge		Focus Area	Action Steps
ICC10K1	Models and strategies of consultation and collaboration		
ICC10K2	Roles of individuals with exceptional learning needs, families, and school and community personnel in planning of an individualized program		
ICC10K3	Concerns of families of individuals with exceptional learning needs and strategies to help address these concerns		
ICC10K4	Culturally responsive factors that promote effective communication and collaboration with individuals with exceptional learning needs, families, school personnel, and community members		
IGC10K1	Parent education programs and behavior management guides that address severe behavior problems and facilitation communication for individuals with exceptional learning needs		
IGC10K2	Collaborative and/or consultative role of the special education teacher in the reintegration of individuals with exceptional learning needs		
IGC10K3	Roles of professional groups and referral agencies in identifying, assessing, and providing services to individuals with exceptional learning needs		
IGC10K4	Co-planning and co-teaching methods to strengthen content acquisition of individuals with learning exceptional learning needs		

Skills		Focus Area	Action Steps
ICC10S1	Maintain confidential communication about individuals with exceptional learning needs		
ICC10S2	Collaborate with families and others in assessment of individuals with exceptional learning needs		
ICC10S3	Foster respectful and beneficial relationships between families and professionals		
ICC10S4	Assist individuals with exceptional learning needs and their families in becoming active participants in the educational team		
ICC10S5	Plan and conduct collaborative conferences with individuals with exceptional learning needs and their families		
ICC10S6	Collaborate with school personnel and community members in integrating individuals with exceptional learning needs into various settings		
ICC10S7	Use group problem-solving skills to develop, implement, and evaluate collaborative activities		
ICC10S8	Model techniques and coach others in the use of instructional methods and accommodations		
ICC10S9	Communicate with school personnel about the characteristics and needs of individuals with exceptional learning needs		
ICC10S10	Communicate effectively with families of individuals with exceptional learning needs from diverse backgrounds		
ICC10S11	Observe, evaluate, and provide feedback to paraeducators		

IGC10S1	Use local community, and state and provincial resources to assist in programming with individuals with exceptional learning needs		
IGC10S2	Select, plan, and coordinate activities of related services personnel to maximize direct instruction for individuals with exceptional learning needs		
IGC10S3	Teach parents to use appropriate behavior management and counseling techniques		
IGC10S4	Collaborate with team members to plan transition to adulthood that encourages full community participation		

NOTE:
Implicit to all of the knowledge and skills standards in this section is the focus on individuals with disabilities whose education focuses on an individualized general curriculum.

CANDIDATES: DO I KNOW WHAT I NEED TO KNOW?

The following chart (see Figure 4.5) is a self-evaluation instrument designed to be used by candidates of special education to evaluate their progress in learning the knowledge and skills they will need upon graduation from the preparation program. Candidates can use it in a variety of ways. Candidates can check each knowledge and skill as they are acquired; they can also include the course number, as well as the specific activity that they completed as they mastered each item.

Several colleges and universities have used a similar instrument for their candidates to use to self-evaluate their mastery of the CEC Standards periodically throughout the preparation program, including dur-

ing their first year of teaching. This has provided rich data for the preparation program that can then be used to improve the program.

The matrix included in this chart is for the Individualized General Curriculum Referenced Standards; page limitations have prevented us from including the other Area of Specialization matrices. Similar matrices for each Area of Specialization could easily be prepared using the same format. All of the CEC standards can be found on the CEC Web site at www.cec.sped.org .

Figure 4.5 Sample Candidate Self-Assessment in Collaboration

Knowledge		Proficiency Level	Comments
ICC10K1	Models and strategies of consultation and collaboration		
ICC10K2	Roles of individuals with exceptional learning needs, families, and school and community personnel in planning of an individualized program		
ICC10K3	Concerns of families of individuals with exceptional learning needs and strategies to help address these concerns		
ICC10K4	Culturally responsive factors that promote effective communication and collaboration with individuals with exceptional learning needs, families, school personnel, and community members		
IGC10K1	Parent education programs and behavior management guides that address severe behavior problems and facilitation communication for individuals with exceptional learning needs		
IGC10K2	Collaborative and/or consultative role of the special education teacher in the reintegration of individuals with exceptional learning needs		
IGC10K3	Roles of professional groups and referral agencies in identifying, assessing, and providing services to individuals with exceptional learning needs		
IGC10K4	Co-planning and co-teaching methods to strengthen content acquisition of individuals with learning exceptional learning needs		

Skills		Proficiency Level	Comments
ICC10S1	Maintain confidential communication about individuals with exceptional learning needs		
ICC10S2	Collaborate with families and others in assessment of individuals with exceptional learning needs		
ICC10S3	Foster respectful and beneficial relationships between families and professionals		
ICC10S4	Assist individuals with exceptional learning needs and their families in becoming active participants in the educational team		
ICC10S5	Plan and conduct collaborative conferences with individuals with exceptional learning needs and their families		
ICC10S6	Collaborate with school personnel and community members in integrating individuals with exceptional learning needs into various settings		
ICC10S7	Use group problem-solving skills to develop, implement, and evaluate collaborative activities		
ICC10S8	Model techniques and coach others in the use of instructional methods and accommodations		
ICC10S9	Communicate with school personnel about the characteristics and needs of individuals with exceptional learning needs		
ICC10S10	Communicate effectively with families of individuals with exceptional learning needs from diverse backgrounds		
ICC10S11	Observe, evaluate, and provide feedback to paraeducators		

Skills		Proficiency Level	Comments
IGC10S1	Use local community, and state and provincial resources to assist in programming with individuals with exceptional learning needs		
IGC10S2	Select, plan, and coordinate activities of related services personnel to maximize direct instruction for individuals with exceptional learning needs		
IGC10S3	Teach parents to use appropriate behavior management and counseling techniques		
IGC10S4	Collaborate with team members to plan transition to adulthood that encourages full community participation		

Proficiency Levels: N=Novice, B=Beginning User, P=Proficient, A=Accomplished

PREPARATION PROGRAM DEVELOPERS: CEC PROGRAM RECOGNITION

In 2002, CEC made it policy that all special education preparation programs, whether traditional or alternative, should demonstrate their alignment with CEC standards through CEC performance-based review.

There are currently two pathways to apply for CEC Program recognition, through NCATE and directly to CEC. In the United States, there are currently two government-recognized agencies to accredit teacher education programs: National Council for Accreditation of Teacher Education (NCATE) and the Teacher Education Accreditation Council (TEAC). Both of these agencies base their accreditation approaches on the importance of establishing teaching as a full and mature profession. However, the two are built on different concepts to achieve professionalism.

From the NCATE perspective, the foundation of a strong profession is a shared body of specialized knowledge and skill based on research, and public confidence that professionals are fit to practice. Speaking for NCATE, Art Wise states that only a strong degree of consensus among practitioners and practitioner educators can build that confidence. NCATE is built on the premise that strong professions depend upon "collective organization," and that accrediting bodies

in the "mature professions" have played a catalytic role as the repositories of the consensus about the professions' specialized knowledge and skill.

Since 1977, NCATE has been accrediting teacher education programs using an inclusive model of collaborating with the respective professional associations representing the various professional disciplines (i.e., English, Social Studies, Math, School Psychology) For almost 20 years, CEC has been the partner of NCATE representing the disciplines within the special education profession.

Candidates preparing to work in schools as teachers or other school professionals know and demonstrate the content knowledge, pedagogical content knowledge and skills, pedagogical and professional knowledge and skills, and professional dispositions necessary to help all students learn. Assessments indicate that candidates meet professional, state, and institutional standards.

NCATE Unit Standard 1

In addition to requiring preparation programs to demonstrate that their candidates have a positive influence on student learning, NCATE expects preparation programs to demonstrate through performance information that the programs address the professional standards of the respective associations in preparing candidates for both initial and advanced roles. Through this process, NCATE expects programs preparing special educators to demonstrate candidates' mastery CEC standards.

NCATE currently has formal agreements with 50 of the U.S. states and territories. It has reviewed and approved over 600 teacher education units with approximately 100 units in the process. Over 70% of entering educators each year currently graduate from NCATE accredited programs. There are several varieties of agreements that NCATE negotiates several varieties of agreements with the states and territories. Currently 29 states require all of their special education preparation programs to submit for CEC recognition. In the other states, the states have signed agreements that they will to move their standards into alignment with CEC standards. Through 2005, CEC has reviewed and approved over 800 special education preparation programs. For every teacher education institution undergoing NCATE accreditation, CEC reviews an average of three programs.

The process of preparing a program for CEC review is complex and technical. In its partnership with NCATE, CEC operates multiple levels of program report developer technical assistance, including:

- Web-based resources
- Electronic seminars and past seminar recordings
- Group workshops twice annually
- State workshops by request
- On-site individualized technical support

NCATE offers a variety of additional technical supports and materials for program developers.

It is not presently possible to acquire CEC program recognition through TEAC. From the TEAC perspective, educators have not achieved the consensus on specialized knowledge and skill of true professionals, and that without this consensus the appropriate strategy is to base accreditation on what TEAC refers to as an "academic audit." In addition to creating a cacophony of expectations, the TEAC model neither expects nor encourages faculty to address the national professional standards of the various professional societies. In fact, in discussing the standards of the various professional societies, Frank Murray, the president of TEAC, writes, "In the public mind, these professionally self-serving standards are the problem, not the solution to the problem." Thus, whereas the TEAC approach is advertised as offering freedom to faculty to create special educators in whatever mold they choose, it plays no responsible role as the repository of consensual knowledge and skills of the profession. At least as important, TEAC does not require special education preparation programs to demonstrate that their graduates possess the profession's entry-level knowledge and skills by seeking CEC national recognition through the evidence-based process of program review. Finally, the TEAC approach does not give the public confidence that a professional special educator has the skills and knowledge to practice safely and effectively. CEC continues to communicate with and monitor TEAC for opportunities to help TEAC move to a more professional model and provide a viable role for CEC standards. Currently, NCATE and TEAC are engaged in exploratory discussion to see if there are possibilities for potential merger.

Direct CEC Program Recognition

There is an alternative pathway for preparation programs to receive CEC recognition. Although CEC does not **accredit** (emphasis added) programs, special education preparation programs may directly seek review of their program performance data from CEC and have CEC grant **recognition** (emphasis added) of the program. CEC expects stand-alone program recognition will continue to be chosen infrequently. However, CEC has been receiving queries from universities in other countries. Analysis of the implications of whether CEC should consider becoming recognized by the federal government as an accreditation agency continues to conclude that CEC can maximize the influence of its standards collectively through the NCATE consensual process. For inquiries regarding program recognition directly from CEC email profstandards@cec.sped.org

Standards for the Preparation of Special Education Personnel

a. Programs preparing individuals for entry level or advanced special education professional roles shall adhere to CEC professional standards, by seeking CEC official recognition through the evidence-based process of program review.

b. Program review includes examination of evidence to document quality practice in:

   (1) Conceptual Framework Programs have a conceptual framework that establishes the program vision and its relationship to the program components and curricula.

   (2) Candidate Content, Pedagogical, and Professional Knowledge, Skills, and Dispositions
       i.   *Content Standards* Programs ensure that prospective special educators have mastered the CEC Special Education Content Standards for their respective roles.
       ii. *Liberal Education* Programs ensure that prospective special educators have a solid grounding in the liberal curricula ensuring proficiency in reading, written and oral communications, calculating, problem- solving, and thinking.
       iii. *General Curriculum*
            (a) Programs ensure that prospective special educators possess a solid base of understanding of the general content area curricula (i.e., math, reading, English/ language arts, science, social studies, and the arts), sufficient to collaborate with general educators in:

            Teaching or collaborative teaching academic subject matter content of the general curriculum to individuals with exceptional learning needs across a wide range of performance levels

            Designing appropriate learning and performance accommodations and modifications for individuals with exceptional learning needs in academic subject matter content of the general curriculum

            (b) Programs preparing special educators for secondary level practice and licensure in which the teachers may assume sole responsibility for teaching academic subject matter classes, ensure that the prospective special educators have a subject matter content knowledge base sufficient to assure that individuals with exceptional learning needs can meet state curriculum standards.

   (3) **Assessment System and Program Evaluation** Programs have an assessment system to collect and analyze data on the applicant qualifications, candidates and graduate performance, and program operations sufficient to evaluate and improve the program.

   (4) **Field Experiences and Clinical Practice** Programs with their school partners have designed, implemented, and evaluated field experiences and clinical practica sufficient for prospective special educators to develop and apply knowledge, skills, and dispositions essential to the roles for which they are being prepared.

   (5) **Diversity** Programs with their school partners have designed, implemented, and evaluated curriculum and experiences sufficient for prospective special educators to develop and apply their knowledge, skills, and dispositions necessary to help all individuals with exceptional learning needs learn. The curricula and experiences include working with diverse faculty, candidates, and P-12 individuals with exceptional learning needs.

   (6) **Faculty Qualification, Performance, and Development** The program faculty is qualified and model best professional practice in their scholarship, service, and teaching.

   (7) **Program Governance and Resources** The program has appropriate leadership, authority, budget, facilities, and resources to address professional, institutional, and state standards.

CEC Policy
Approved October 2004

Section 5: Initial and Advanced Professional Content Standards and Knowledge and Skill Sets

This section includes the Initial Content Standards and the Advanced Content Standards. These two sets of standards broadly describe the knowledge and skill that all special educators bring to initial and advanced roles. These broad content standards are informed by the elements delineated in the CEC knowledge and skill sets. They provide both context and content for a variety of special education specialty disciplines. The Knowledge and Skill sets are included for candidates preparing for their first special education position, as well as for special educators preparing to move into advanced classroom-based and other advanced roles.

They are the knowledge and skills that professionals entering initial practice or assuming advanced roles should possess to practice safely and effectively.

Finally, CEC standards for Mentorship and for Continuing Education are included. Please note that CEC has not included information in this section to support faculty in preparing for CEC performance-based national recognition. In order to ensure that faculty receive the most accurate and up-to-date guidance, all information has been placed on the CEC Web site www.cec.sped.org.

INITIAL LEVEL CONTENT STANDARDS

Initial Content Standard 1: Foundations[6]

Special educators understand the field as an evolving and changing discipline based on philosophies, evidence-based **principles and theories**, relevant **laws and policies,** diverse and **historical** points of view, and **human issues** that have historically influenced and continue to influence the field of special education and the education and treatment of individuals with exceptional needs in both school and society. Special educators understand how these **influence professional practice**, including assessment, instructional planning, implementation, and program evaluation. Special educators understand how **issues of human diversity** can impact families, cultures, and schools, and how these complex human issues can interact with issues in the delivery of special education services. They understand the **relationships of organizations** of **special education** to the organizations and functions of schools, school systems, and other agencies. Special educators use this knowledge as a ground upon which to construct their own personal understandings and philosophies of special education.

Beginning special educators demonstrate their mastery of this standard through the mastery of the CEC Common Core Knowledge and Skills, as well as through the appropriate CEC Specialty Area(s) Knowledge and Skills for which the program is preparing candidates.

Initial Content Standard 2: Development and Characteristics of Learners

Special educators know and **demonstrate respect** for their students first as unique human beings. Special educators understand the **similarities and differences in human development** and the characteristics between and among individuals with and without exceptional learning needs.

Moreover, special educators understand how **exceptional conditions** can **interact** with the domains of human development and they **use this knowledge to respond to the varying abilities and behaviors of individuals** with exceptional learning needs. Special educators understand how the experiences of indi-

---

[6] Each of the content standards describes in rich narrative the skills and responsibilities of all special education specialists. The bolded phrases are critical elements of the standards identified to provide guidance to preparation program developers.

viduals with exceptional learning needs can impact families, as well as the individual's ability to learn, interact socially, and live as fulfilled contributing members of the community.

Beginning special educators demonstrate their mastery of this standard through the mastery of the CEC Common Core Knowledge and Skills, as well as through the appropriate CEC Specialty Area(s) Knowledge and Skills for which the program is preparing candidates.

Initial Content Standard 3: Individual Learning Differences

Special educators understand the **effects that an exceptional condition** can have **on an individual's learning** in school and throughout life. Special educators understand that the beliefs, traditions, and values across and within cultures can affect relationships among and between students, their families, and the school community. Moreover, special educators are **active and resourceful in seeking to understand how primary language, culture, and familial backgrounds interact with the individual's exceptional condition** to impact the individual's academic and social abilities, attitudes, values, interests, and career options. The understanding of these learning differences and their possible interactions **provides the foundation** upon which **special educators individualize instruction** to provide meaningful and challenging learning for individuals with exceptional learning needs.

Beginning special educators demonstrate their mastery of this standard through the mastery of the CEC Common Core Knowledge and Skills, as well as through the appropriate CEC Specialty Area(s) Knowledge and Skills for which the program is preparing candidates.

Initial Content Standard 4: Instructional Strategies

Special educators possess a repertoire of evidence-based **instructional strategies to individualize instruction** for individuals with exceptional learning needs. Special educators select, adapt, and use these instructional strategies to promote **positive learning results in general and special curricula** and to **modify learning environments** appropriately for individuals with exceptional learning needs. They enhance the **learning of critical thinking, problem-solving, and performance skills** of individuals with exceptional learning needs, and increase their self-awareness, self-management, self-control, self-reliance, and

self-esteem. Moreover, special educators emphasize the **development, maintenance, and generalization** of knowledge and skills across environments, settings, and the life span. Beginning special educators demonstrate their mastery of this standard through the mastery of the CEC Common Core Knowledge and Skills, as well as through the appropriate CEC Specialty Area(s) Knowledge and Skills for which the program is preparing candidates.

Initial Content Standard 5: Learning Environments and Social Interactions

Special educators actively **create learning environments** for individuals with exceptional learning needs that foster cultural understanding, safety and emotional well-being, positive social interactions, and **active engagement** of individuals with exceptional learning needs. In addition, special educators **foster environments in which diversity is valued** and individuals are taught to live harmoniously and productively in a culturally diverse world. Special educators shape **environments to encourage the independence,** self-motivation, self-direction, personal empowerment, and self-advocacy of individuals with exceptional learning needs. Special educators **help their general education colleagues integrate individuals** with exceptional learning needs in general education environments and engage them in meaningful learning activities and interactions. Special educators use **direct motivational and instructional interventions** with individuals with exceptional learning needs to teach them to respond effectively to current expectations. When necessary, special educators can safely **intervene with individuals with exceptional learning needs in crisis.** Special educators coordinate all these efforts and **provide guidance and direction to paraeducators and others,** such as classroom volunteers and tutors.

Beginning special educators demonstrate their mastery of this standard through the mastery of the CEC Common Core Knowledge and Skills, as well as through the appropriate CEC Specialty Area(s) Knowledge and Skills for which the program is preparing candidates.

Initial Content Standard 6: Language

Special educators understand **typical and atypical language development** and the ways in which exceptional conditions can interact with an individual's experience with and use of language. Special educators use individualized strategies to **enhance language development** and **teach communication skills** to individuals with exceptional learning needs. Special educators are familiar with **augmentative, alternative, and assistive technologies** to support and enhance communication of individuals with exceptional needs. Special educators match their communication methods to an individual's language proficiency and cultural and linguistic differences. Special educators provide **effective language models** and they use communication strategies and resources to **facilitate understanding of subject matter for individuals with exceptional learning needs whose primary language is not English.**

Beginning special educators demonstrate their mastery of this standard through the mastery of the CEC Common Core Knowledge and Skills, as well as through the appropriate CEC Specialty Area(s) Knowledge and Skills for which the program is preparing candidates.

Initial Content Standard 7: Instructional Planning

Individualized decision making and instruction is at the center of special education practice. Special educators develop **long-range individualized instructional plans** anchored in both general and special education curricula. In addition, special educators systematically translate these individualized plans into carefully selected **shorter-range goals and objectives** taking into consideration an individual's abilities and needs, the learning environment, and a myriad of cultural and linguistic factors. Individualized instructional plans emphasize **explicit modeling** and **efficient guided practice** to assure acquisition and fluency through maintenance and generalization. Understanding of these factors as well as the implications of an individual's exceptional condition, guides the special educator's selection, adaptation, and creation of materials, and the use of powerful instructional variables. Instructional plans are **modified based on ongoing analysis of the individual's learning progress.** Moreover, special educators facilitate this instructional planning in a **collaborative context** including the individuals with exceptionalities, families, professional colleagues, and personnel from other agencies as appropriate. Special educators also develop a variety of **individualized transition plans,** such as transitions from preschool to elementary school and from secondary settings to a variety of postsecondary work and learning contexts. Special educators are comfortable using **appropriate technologies** to support instructional planning and individualized instruction.

Beginning special educators demonstrate their mastery of this standard through the mastery of the

CEC Common Core Knowledge and Skills, as well as through the appropriate CEC Specialty Area(s) Knowledge and Skills for which the program is preparing candidates.

Initial Content Standard 8: Assessment

Assessment is integral to the decision making and teaching of special educators and special educators use **multiple types of assessment information** for a variety of educational decisions. Special educators use the results of assessments to help identify exceptional learning needs and to develop and implement individualized instructional programs, as well as to adjust instruction in response to ongoing learning progress. Special educators understand the **legal policies and ethical principles of measurement and assessment** related to referral, eligibility, program planning, instruction, and placement for individuals with exceptional learning needs, including those from culturally and linguistically diverse backgrounds. Special educators understand **measurement theory and practices** for addressing issues of validity, reliability, norms, bias, and interpretation of assessment results. In addition, special educators understand the appropriate **use and limitations** of various types of assessments. Special educators collaborate with families and other colleagues to assure **nonbiased, meaningful assessments and decision making.** Special educators conduct **formal and informal assessments** of behavior, learning, achievement, and environments to design learning experiences that support the growth and development of individuals with exceptional learning needs. Special educators use assessment information to **identify supports and adaptations** required for individuals with exceptional learning needs to access the general curriculum and to participate in school, system, and statewide assessment programs. Special educators **regularly monitor the progress** of individuals with exceptional learning needs in general and special curricula. Special educators **use appropriate technologies** to support their assessments.

Beginning special educators demonstrate their mastery of this standard through the mastery of the CEC Common Core Knowledge and Skills, as well as through the appropriate CEC Specialty Area(s) Knowledge and Skills for which the program is preparing candidates.

Initial Content Standard 9: Professional and Ethical Practice

Special educators are guided by the profession's ethical and professional practice standards. Special educators practice in multiple roles and complex situations across wide age and developmental ranges. Their practice requires ongoing attention to **legal matters** along with serious professional and **ethical considerations.** Special educators engage in **professional activities** and participate in learning communities that benefit individuals with exceptional learning needs, their families, colleagues, and their own professional growth. Special educators view themselves as **lifelong learners** and regularly reflect on and adjust their practice. Special educators are aware of how their own and others' attitudes, behaviors, and ways of communicating can influence their practice. Special educators understand that culture and language can interact with exceptionalities, and are **sensitive to the many aspects of diversity** of individuals with exceptional learning needs and their families. Special educators actively plan and engage in activities that foster their professional growth and keep them **current with evidence-based best practices.** Special educators know their own limits of practice and practice within them.

Beginning special educators demonstrate their mastery of this standard through the mastery of the CEC Common Core Knowledge and Skills, as well as through the appropriate CEC Specialty Area(s) Knowledge and Skills for which the program is preparing candidates.

Initial Content Standard 10: Collaboration

Special educators routinely and effectively **collaborate with families, other educators, related service providers, and personnel from community agencies in culturally responsive ways.** This collaboration assures that the needs of individuals with exceptional learning needs are addressed throughout schooling. Moreover, special educators embrace their special role as advocate for individuals with exceptional learning needs. Special educators promote and advocate the learning and well-being of individuals with exceptional learning needs across a wide range of settings and a range of different learning experiences. Special educators are viewed as specialists by a myriad of people who actively seek their collaboration to effectively include and teach individuals with exceptional learning needs. Special educators are a **resource to their colleagues** in understanding the laws and policies relevant to individuals with exceptional learning needs. Special educators use collaboration to **facilitate the successful transitions** of individuals with exceptional learning needs across settings and services.

Beginning special educators demonstrate their mastery of this standard through the mastery of the CEC Common Core Knowledge and Skills, as well as through the appropriate CEC Specialty Area(s) Knowledge and Skills for which the program is preparing candidates.

NOTES:

Individual with exceptional learning needs is used throughout to include individuals with disabilities and individuals with exceptional gifts and talents.

The Initial Content Standards for Educators of Individuals With Exceptional Gifts and Talents were developed by CEC in collaboration with the National Association for Gifted Children and the CEC Association for the Gifted. CEC acknowledges the service provided in the validation study by Dr. Margie Kitano, Dr. Diane Montgomery, Dr. Joyce VanTassel-Baska, Dr. Ann Robinson, Dr. Rick Olenchak, Jane Clarenbach, and Nancy Green.

Initial Content Standard 1: Foundations

Educators of the gifted understand the field as an evolving and changing discipline based on philosophies, evidence-based principles and theories, relevant laws and policies, diverse and historical points of view, and human issues. These perspectives continue to influence the field of gifted education and the education and treatment of individuals with gifts and talents both in school and society. They recognize how foundational influences affect professional practice, including assessment, instructional planning, delivery, and program evaluation. They further understand how issues of human diversity impact families, cultures, and schools, and how these complex human issues can interact in the delivery of gifted and talented education services.

Initial Content Standard 2: Development and Characteristics of Learners

Educators of the gifted know and demonstrate respect for their students as unique human beings. They understand variations in characteristics and development between and among individuals with and without exceptional learning needs and capacities. Educators of the gifted can express how different characteristics interact with the domains of human development and use this knowledge to describe the varying abilities and behaviors of individuals with gifts and talents. Educators of the gifted also understand how families and communities contribute to the development of individuals with gifts and talents.

Initial Content Standard 3: Individual Learning Differences

Educators of the gifted understand the effects that gifts and talents can have on an individual's learning in school and throughout life. Moreover, educators of the gifted are active and resourceful in seeking to understand how language, culture, and family background interact with an individual's predispositions to impact academic and social behavior, attitudes, values, and interests. The understanding of these learning differences and their interactions provides the foundation upon which educators of the gifted plan instruction to provide meaningful and challenging learning.

Initial Content Standard 4: Instructional Strategies

Educators of the gifted possess a repertoire of evidence-based curriculum and instructional strategies to differentiate for individuals with gifts and talents. They select, adapt, and use these strategies to promote challenging learning opportunities in general and special curricula and to modify learning environments to enhance self-awareness and self-efficacy for individuals with gifts and talents. They enhance the learning of critical and creative thinking, problem solving, and performance skills in specific domains. Moreover, educators of the gifted emphasize the development, practice, and transfer of advanced knowledge and skills across environments throughout the lifespan leading to creative, productive careers in society for individuals with gifts and talents.

Initial Content Standard 5: Learning Environments and Social Interactions

Educators of the gifted actively create learning environments for individuals with gifts and talents that foster cultural understanding, safety and emotional well being, positive social interactions, and active engagement. In addition, educators of the gifted foster environments in which diversity is valued and individuals are taught to live harmoniously and productively in a culturally diverse world. Educators of the gifted shape environments to encourage independence, motivation, and self-advocacy of individuals with gifts and talents.

Initial Content Standard 6: Language and Communication

Educators of the gifted understand the role of language and communication in talent development and the

---

[7] *Exceptional condition* is used throughout to include both single and co-existing conditions. These may be two or more disabling conditions or exceptional gifts or talents co-existing with one or more disabling conditions. *Special curricula* is used throughout to denote curricular areas not routinely emphasized or addressed in general curricula; (e.g., social, communication, motor, independence, self-advocacy).

ways in which exceptional conditions can hinder or facilitate such development. They use relevant strategies to teach oral and written communication skills to individuals with gifts and talents. Educators of the gifted are familiar with assistive technologies to support and enhance communication of individuals with exceptional needs. They match their communication methods to an individual's language proficiency and cultural and linguistic differences. Educators of the gifted use communication strategies and resources to facilitate understanding of subject matter for individuals with gifts and talents who are English language learners.

Initial Content Standard 7: Instructional Planning

Curriculum and instructional planning is at the center of gifted and talented education. Educators of the gifted develop long-range plans anchored in both general and special curricula. They systematically translate shorter-range goals and objectives that take into consideration an individual's abilities and needs, the learning environment, and cultural and linguistic factors. Understanding of these factors, as well as the implications of being gifted and talented, guides the educator's selection, adaptation, and creation of materials, and use of differentiated instructional strategies. Learning plans are modified based on ongoing assessment of the individual's progress. Moreover, educators of the gifted facilitate these actions in a collaborative context that includes individuals with gifts and talents, families, professional colleagues, and personnel from other agencies as appropriate. Educators of the gifted are comfortable using technologies to support instructional planning and individualized instruction.

Initial Content Standard 8: Assessment

Assessment is integral to the decision making and teaching of educators of the gifted as multiple types of assessment information are required for both identification and learning progress decisions. Educators of the gifted use the results of such assessments to adjust instruction and to enhance ongoing learning progress. Educators of the gifted understand the process of identification, legal policies, and ethical principles of measurement and assessment related to referral, eligibility, program planning, instruction, and placement for individuals with gifts and talents, including those from culturally and linguistically diverse backgrounds. They understand measurement theory and practices for addressing the interpretation of assessment results. In addition, educators of the gifted understand the appropriate use and limitations of various types of assessments. To ensure the use of nonbiased and equitable identification and learning progress models, educators of the gifted employ alternative assessments such as performance-based assessment, portfolios, and computer simulations.

Initial Content Standard 9: Professional and Ethical Practice

Educators of the gifted are guided by the profession's ethical and professional practice standards. They practice in multiple roles and complex situations across wide age and developmental ranges. Their practice requires ongoing attention to professional and ethical considerations. They engage in professional activities that promote growth in individuals with gifts and talents and update themselves on evidence-based best practices. Educators of the gifted view themselves as lifelong learners and regularly reflect on and adjust their practice. They are aware of how attitudes, behaviors, and ways of communicating can influence their practice. Educators of the gifted understand that culture and language interact with gifts and talents and are sensitive to the many aspects of the diversity of individuals with gifts and talents and their families.

Initial Content Standard 10: Collaboration

Educators of the gifted effectively collaborate with families, other educators, and related service providers. This collaboration enhances comprehensive articulated program options across educational levels and engagement of individuals with gifts and talents in meaningful learning activities and interactions. Moreover, educators of the gifted embrace their special role as advocate for individuals with gifts and talents. They promote and advocate for the learning and well-being of individuals with gifts and talents across settings and diverse learning experiences.

Initial Special Education Teachers of Individuals With Exceptional Learning Needs in Individualized General Education Curricula (IGC)

Standard 1: Foundations	
Knowledge	
ICC1K1	Models, theories, philosophies, and research methods that form the basis for special education practice
ICC1K2	Laws, policies, and ethical principles regarding behavior management planning and implementation
ICC1K3	Relationship of special education to the organization and function of educational agencies
ICC1K4	Rights and responsibilities of individuals with exceptional learning needs, parents, teachers, and other professionals, and schools related to exceptional learning needs[8]
ICC1K5	Issues in definition and identification of individuals with exceptional learning needs, including those from culturally and linguistically diverse backgrounds
ICC1K6	Issues, assurances and due process rights related to assessment, eligibility, and placement within a continuum of services
ICC1K7	Family systems and the role of families in the educational process
ICC1K8	Historical points of view and contribution of culturally diverse groups
ICC1K9	Impact of the dominant culture on shaping schools and the individuals who study and work in them
ICC1K10	Potential impact of differences in values, languages, and customs that can exist between the home and school
IGC1K1	Definitions and issues related to the identification of individuals with exceptional learning needs
IGC1K2	Models and theories of deviance and behavior problems
IGC1K3	Historical foundations, classic studies, major contributors, major legislation, and current issues related to knowledge and practice
IGC1K4	The legal, judicial, and educational systems to assist individuals with exceptional learning needs
IGC1K5	Continuum of placement and services available for individuals with exceptional learning needs
IGC1K6	Laws and policies related to provision of specialized health care in educational settings
IGC1K7	Factors that influence the over-representation of culturally/linguistically diverse individuals with exceptional learning needs in programs for individuals with exceptional learning needs
IGC1K8	Principles of normalization and concept of least restrictive environment

---

[8] Implicit to all of the knowledge and skills is the focus on individuals with exceptionalities whose education focuses on an individualized general curriculum

IGC1K9	Theory of reinforcement techniques in serving individuals with exceptional learning needs

Skills

ICC1S1	Articulate personal philosophy of special education
	None in addition to Common Core

Standard 2: Development and Characteristics of Learners

Knowledge

ICC2K1	Typical and atypical human growth and development
ICC2K2	Educational implications of characteristics of various exceptionalities
ICC2K3	Characteristics and effects of the cultural and environmental milieu of the individual with exceptional learning needs and the family
ICC2K4	Family systems and the role of families in supporting development
ICC2K5	Similarities and differences of individuals with and without exceptional learning needs
ICC2K6	Similarities and differences among individuals with exceptional learning needs
ICC2K7	Effects of various medications on individuals with exceptional learning needs
IGC2K1	Etiology and diagnosis related to various theoretical approaches
IGC2K2	Impact of sensory impairments, physical and health exceptional learning needs on individuals, families, and society
IGC2K3	Etiologies and medical aspects of conditions affecting individuals with exceptional learning needs
IGC2K4	Psychological and social-emotional characteristics of individuals with exceptional learning needs
IGC2K5	Common etiologies and the impact of sensory exceptional learning needs on learning and experience
IGC2K6	Types and transmission routes of infectious disease

Skills

	None in addition to Common Core

Standard 3: Individual Learning Differences

Knowledge

ICC3K1	Effects an exceptional condition(s) can have on an individual's life
ICC3K2	Impact of learners' academic and social abilities, attitudes, interests, and values on instruction and career development

ICC3K3	Variations in beliefs, traditions, and values across and within cultures and their effects on relationships among individuals with exceptional learning needs, family, and schooling
IGC3K1	Complications and implications of medical support services
IGC3K2	Impact disabilities may have on auditory and information processing skills
IGC3K3	Impact of multiple disabilities on behavior

Skills

IGC3S1	Relate levels of support to the needs of the individual

Standard 4: Instructional Strategies

Knowledge

ICC4K1	Evidence-based practices validated for specific characteristics of learners and settings
IGC4K1	Sources of specialized materials, curricula, and resources for individuals with exceptional learning needs
IGC4K2	Strategies to prepare for and take tests
IGC4K3	Advantages and limitations of instructional strategies and practices for teaching individuals with exceptional learning needs
IGC4K4	Prevention and intervention strategies for individuals at risk for a disability
IGC4K5	Strategies for integrating student initiated learning experiences into ongoing instruction
IGC4K6	Methods for increasing accuracy and proficiency in math calculations and applications
IGC4K7	Methods for guiding individuals in identifying and organizing critical content

Skills

ICC4S1	Use strategies to facilitate integration into various settings
ICC4S2	Teach individuals to use self-assessment, problem-solving, and other cognitive strategies to meet their needs
ICC4S3	Select, adapt, and use instructional strategies and materials according to characteristics of the individual with exceptional learning needs
ICC4S4	Use strategies to facilitate maintenance and generalization of skills across learning environments
ICC4S5	Use procedures to increase the individual's self-awareness, self-management, self-control, self-reliance, and self-esteem
ICC4S6	Use strategies that promote successful transitions for individuals with exceptional learning needs
IGC4S1	Use research-supported methods for academic and nonacademic instruction of individuals with exceptional learning needs
IGC4S2	Use strategies from multiple theoretical approaches for individuals with exceptional learning needs

IGC4S3	Teach learning strategies and study skills to acquire academic content
IGC4S4	Use reading methods appropriate to individuals with exceptional learning needs
IGC4S5	Use methods to teach mathematics appropriate to the individuals with exceptional learning needs
IGC4S6	Modify pace of instruction and provide organizational cures
IGC4S7	Use appropriate adaptations and technology for all individuals with exceptional learning needs
IGC4S8	Resources, and techniques used to transition individuals with exceptional learning needs into and out of school and postschool environments
IGC4S9	Use a variety of nonaversive techniques to control targeted behavior and maintain attention of individuals with exceptional learning needs
IGC4S10	Identify and teach basic structures and relationships within and across curricula
IGC4S11	Use instructional methods to strengthen and compensate for deficits in perception, comprehension, memory, and retrieval
IGC4S12	Use responses and errors to guide instructional decisions and provide feedback to learners
IGC4S13	Identify and teach essential concepts, vocabulary, and content across the general curriculum
IGC4S14	Implement systematic instruction in teaching reading comprehension and monitoring strategies
IGC4S15	Teach strategies for organizing and composing written products
IGC4S16	Implement systematic instruction to teach accuracy, fluency, and comprehension in content area reading and written language

Standard 5: Learning Environments/Social Interactions

Knowledge

ICC5K1	Demands of learning environments
ICC5K2	Basic classroom management theories and strategies for individuals with exceptional learning needs
ICC5K3	Effective management of teaching and learning
ICC5K4	Teacher attitudes and behaviors that influence behavior of individuals with exceptional learning needs
ICC5K5	Social skills needed for educational and other environments
ICC5K6	Strategies for crisis prevention and intervention
ICC5K7	Strategies for preparing individuals to live harmoniously and productively in a culturally diverse world
ICC5K8	Ways to create learning environments that allow individuals to retain and appreciate their own and each other's respective language and cultural heritage
ICC5K9	Ways specific cultures are negatively stereotyped

ICC5K10	Strategies used by diverse populations to cope with a legacy of former and continuing racism
IGC5K1	Barriers to accessibility and acceptance of individuals with exceptional learning needs
IGC5K2	Adaptation of the physical environment to provide optimal learning opportunities for individuals with exceptional learning needs
IGC5K3	Methods for ensuring individual academic success in one-to-one, small-group, and large-group settings

Skills

ICC5S1	Create a safe, equitable, positive, and supportive learning environment in which diversities are valued
ICC5S2	Identify realistic expectations for personal and social behavior in various settings
ICC5S3	Identify supports needed for integration into various program placements
ICC5S4	Design learning environments that encourage active participation in individual and group activities
ICC5S5	Modify the learning environment to manage behaviors
ICC5S6	Use performance data and information from all stakeholders to make or suggest modifications in learning environments
ICC5S7	Establish and maintain rapport with individuals with and without exceptional learning needs
ICC5S8	Teach self-advocacy
ICC5S9	Create an environment that encourages self-advocacy and increased independence
ICC5S10	Use effective and varied behavior management strategies
ICC5S11	Use the least intensive behavior management strategy consistent with the needs of the individual with exceptional learning needs
ICC5S12	Design and manage daily routines
ICC5S13	Organize, develop, and sustain learning environments that support positive intracultural and intercultural experiences
ICC5S14	Mediate controversial intercultural issues among individuals with exceptional learning needs within the learning environment in ways that enhance any culture, group, or person
ICC5S15	Structure, direct, and support the activities of paraeducators, volunteers, and tutors
ICC5S16	Use universal precautions
IGC5S1	Provide instruction in community-based settings
IGC5S2	Use and maintain assistive technologies
IGC5S3	Plan instruction in a variety of educational settings
IGC5S4	Teach individuals with exceptional learning needs to give and receive meaningful feedback from peers and adults

IGC5S5	Use skills in problem-solving and conflict resolution
IGC5S6	Establish a consistent classroom routine for individuals with exceptional learning needs

Standard 6: Language

Knowledge

ICC6K1	Effects of cultural and linguistic differences on growth and development
ICC6K2	Characteristics of one's own culture and use of language and the ways in which these can differ from other cultures and uses of languages
ICC6K3	Ways of behaving and communicating among cultures that can lead to misinterpretation and misunderstanding
ICC6K4	Augmentative and assistive communication strategies
IGC6K1	Impact of language development and listening comprehension on academic and non-academic learning of individuals with exceptional learning needs
IGC6K2	Communication and social interaction alternatives for individuals who are nonspeaking
IGC6K3	Typical language development and how that may differ for individuals with learning exceptional learning needs

Skills

ICC6S1	Use strategies to support and enhance communication skills of individuals with exceptional learning needs
ICC6S2	Use communication strategies and resources to facilitate understanding of subject matter for individuals with exceptional learning needs whose primary language is not the dominant language
IGC6S1	Enhance vocabulary development
IGC6S2	Teach strategies for spelling accuracy and generalization
IGC6S3	Teach individuals with exceptional learning needs to monitor for errors in oral and written language
IGC6S4	Teach methods and strategies for producing legible documents
IGC6S5	Plan instruction on the use of alternative and augmentative communication systems

Standard 7: Instructional Planning

Knowledge

ICC7K1	Theories and research that form the basis of curriculum development and instructional practice
ICC7K2	Scope and sequences of general and special curricula
ICC7K3	National, state or provincial, and local curricula standards

ICC7K4	Technology for planning and managing the teaching and learning environment
ICC7K5	Roles and responsibilities of the paraeducator related to instruction, intervention, and direct service
IGC7K1	Integrate academic instruction and behavior management for individuals and groups with exceptional learning needs
IGC7K2	Model career, vocational, and transition programs for individuals with exceptional learning needs
IGC7K3	Interventions and services for children who may be at risk for learning exceptional learning needs
IGC7K4	Relationships among exceptional learning needs and reading instruction

Skills

ICC7S1	Identify and prioritize areas of the general curriculum and accommodations for individuals with exceptional learning needs
ICC7S2	Develop and implement comprehensive, longitudinal individualized programs in collaboration with team members
ICC7S3	Involve the individual and family in setting instructional goals and monitoring progress
ICC7S4	Use functional assessments to develop intervention plans
ICC7S5	Use task analysis
ICC7S6	Sequence, implement, and evaluate individualized learning objectives
ICC7S7	Integrate affective, social, and life skills with academic curricula
ICC7S8	Develop and select instructional content, resources, and strategies that respond to cultural, linguistic, and gender differences
ICC7S9	Incorporate and implement instructional and assistive technology into the educational program
ICC7S10	Prepare lesson plans
ICC7S11	Prepare and organize materials to implement daily lesson plans
ICC7S12	Use instructional time effectively
ICC7S13	Make responsive adjustments to instruction based on continual observations
ICC7S14	Prepare individuals to exhibit self-enhancing behavior in response to societal attitudes and actions
ICC7S15	Evaluate and modify instructional practices in response to ongoing assessment data
IGC7S1	Plan and implement individualized reinforcement systems and environmental modifications at levels equal to the intensity of the behavior
IGC7S2	Select and use specialized instructional strategies appropriate to the abilities and needs of the individual

IGC7S3	Plan and implement age and ability appropriate instruction for individuals with exceptional learning needs
IGC7S4	Select, design, and use technology, materials and resources required to educate individuals whose exceptional learning needs interfere with communication
IGC7S5	Interpret sensory, mobility, reflex, and perceptual information to create or adapt appropriate learning plans
IGC7S6	Design and implement instructional programs that address independent living and career education for individuals
IGC7S7	Design and implement curriculum and instructional strategies for medical self-management procedures
IGC7S8	Design, implement, and evaluate instructional programs that enhance social participation across environments

Standard 8: Assessment

Knowledge

ICC8K1	Basic terminology used in assessment
ICC8K2	Legal provisions and ethical principles regarding assessment of individuals
ICC8K3	Screening, prereferral, referral, and classification procedures
ICC8K4	Use and limitations of assessment instruments
ICC8K5	National, state or provincial, and local accommodations and modifications
IGC8K1	Specialized terminology used in the assessment of individuals with exceptional learning needs
IGC8K2	Laws and policies regarding referral and placement procedures for individuals with exceptional learning needs
IGC8K3	Types and importance of information concerning individuals with exceptional learning needs available from families and public agencies
IGC8K4	Procedures for early identification of young children who may be at risk for exceptional learning needs

Skills

ICC8S1	Gather relevant background information
ICC8S2	Administer nonbiased formal and informal assessments
ICC8S3	Use technology to conduct assessments
ICC8S4	Develop or modify individualized assessment strategies
ICC8S5	Interpret information from formal and informal assessments
ICC8S6	Use assessment information in making eligibility, program, and placement decisions for individuals with exceptional learning needs, including those from culturally and/or linguistically diverse backgrounds

ICC8S7	Report assessment results to all stakeholders using effective communication skills
ICC8S8	Evaluate instruction and monitor progress of individuals with exceptional learning needs
ICC8S9	Create and maintain records
IGC8S1	Implement procedures for assessing and reporting both appropriate and problematic social behaviors of individuals with exceptional learning needs
IGC8S2	Use exceptionality-specific assessment instruments with individuals with exceptional learning needs
IGC8S3	Select, adapt, and modify assessments to accommodate the unique abilities and needs of individuals with exceptional learning needs
IGC8S4	Assess reliable method(s) of response of individuals who lack typical communication and performance abilities
IGC8S5	Monitor intragroup behavior changes across subjects and activities

Standard 9: Professional And Ethical Practice

Knowledge

ICC9K1	Personal cultural biases and differences that affect one's teaching
ICC9K2	Importance of the teacher serving as a model for individuals with exceptional learning needs
ICC9K3	Continuum of lifelong professional development
ICC9K4	Methods to remain current regarding research-validated practice
IGC9K1	Sources of unique services, networks, and organizations for individuals with exceptional learning needs
IGC9K2	Organizations and publications relevant to individuals with exceptional learning needs

Skills

ICC9S1	Practice within the CEC Code of Ethics and other standards of the profession
ICC9S2	Uphold high standards of competence and integrity and exercise sound judgment in the practice of the profession
ICC9S3	Act ethically in advocating for appropriate services
ICC9S4	Conduct professional activities in compliance with applicable laws and policies
ICC9S5	Demonstrate commitment to developing the highest education and quality-of-life potential of individuals with exceptional learning needs
ICC9S6	Demonstrate sensitivity for the culture, language, religion, gender, disability, socioeconomic status, and sexual orientation of individuals
ICC9S7	Practice within one's skill limits and obtain assistance as needed

ICC9S8	Use verbal, nonverbal, and written language effectively
ICC9S9	Conduct self-evaluation of instruction
ICC9S10	Access information on exceptionalities
ICC9S11	Reflect on one's practice to improve instruction and guide professional growth
ICC9S12	Engage in professional activities that benefit individuals with exceptional learning needs, their families, and one's colleagues
ICC9S13	Demonstrate commitment to engage in evidence-based practices
IGC9S1	Participate in the activities of professional organizations relevant to individuals with exceptional learning needs
IGC9S2	Ethical responsibility to advocate for appropriate services for individuals with exceptional learning needs

Standard 10: Collaboration

Knowledge

ICC10K1	Models and strategies of consultation and collaboration
ICC10K2	Roles of individuals with exceptional learning needs, families, and school and community personnel in planning of an individualized program
ICC10K3	Concerns of families of individuals with exceptional learning needs and strategies to help address these concerns
ICC10K4	Culturally responsive factors that promote effective communication and collaboration with individuals with exceptional learning needs, families, school personnel, and community members
IGC10K1	Parent education programs and behavior management guides that address severe behavior problems and facilitation communication for individuals with exceptional learning needs
IGC10K2	Collaborative and/or consultative role of the special education teacher in the reintegration of individuals with exceptional learning needs
IGC10K3	Roles of professional groups and referral agencies in identifying, assessing, and providing services to individuals with exceptional learning needs
IGC10K4	Co-planning and co-teaching methods to strengthen content acquisition of individuals with learning exceptional learning needs

Skills

ICC10S1	Maintain confidential communication about individuals with exceptional learning needs
ICC10S2	Collaborate with families and others in assessment of individuals with exceptional learning needs
ICC10S3	Foster respectful and beneficial relationships between families and professionals

ICC10S4	Assist individuals with exceptional learning needs and their families in becoming active participants in the educational team
ICC10S5	Plan and conduct collaborative conferences with individuals with exceptional learning needs and their families
ICC10S6	Collaborate with school personnel and community members in integrating individuals with exceptional learning needs into various settings
ICC10S7	Use group problem-solving skills to develop, implement, and evaluate collaborative activities
ICC10S8	Model techniques and coach others in the use of instructional methods and accommodations
ICC10S9	Communicate with school personnel about the characteristics and needs of individuals with exceptional learning needs
ICC10S10	Communicate effectively with families of individuals with exceptional learning needs from diverse backgrounds
ICC10S11	Observe, evaluate, and provide feedback to paraeducators
IGC10S1	Use local community, and state and provincial resources to assist in programming with individuals with exceptional learning needs
IGC10S2	Select, plan, and coordinate activities of related services personnel to maximize direct instruction for individuals with exceptional learning needs
IGC10S3	Teach parents to use appropriate behavior management and counseling techniques
IGC10S4	Collaborate with team members to plan transition to adulthood that encourages full community participation

Initial Special Education Teachers of Individuals With Exceptional Learning Needs in Individualized Independence Curricula (IIC)

Standard 1: Foundations	
Knowledge	
ICC1K1	Models, theories, philosophies, and research methods that form the basis for special education practice
ICC1K2	Laws, policies, and ethical principles regarding behavior management planning and implementation
ICC1K3	Relationship of special education to the organization and function of educational agencies
ICC1K4	Rights and responsibilities of individuals with exceptional learning needs, parents, teachers, and other professionals, and schools related to exceptional learning needs[8]
ICC1K5	Issues in definition and identification of individuals with exceptional learning needs, including those from culturally and linguistically diverse backgrounds
ICC1K6	Issues, assurances and due process rights related to assessment, eligibility, and placement within a continuum of services
ICC1K7	Family systems and the role of families in the educational process
ICC1K8	Historical points of view and contribution of culturally diverse groups
ICC1K9	Impact of the dominant culture on shaping schools and the individuals who study and work in them
ICC1K10	Potential impact of differences in values, languages, and customs that can exist between the home and school
IIC1K1	Definitions and issues related to the identification of individuals with exceptional learning needs
IIC1K2	Historical foundations, classic studies, major contributors, major legislation, and current issues related to knowledge and practice
IIC1K3	The legal, judicial, and educational systems to assist individuals with exceptional learning needs
IIC1K4	Continuum of placement and services available for individuals with exceptional learning needs
IIC1K5	Laws and policies related to provision of specialized health care in educational settings
IIC1K6	Principles of normalization and concept of least restrictive environment
IIC1K7	Theory of reinforcement techniques in serving individuals with exceptional learning needs
IIC1K8	Theories of behavior problems of individuals with exceptional learning needs

---

[8] Implicit to all of the knowledge and skills is the focus on individuals with exceptionalities whose education focuses on an individualized general curriculum

Skills	
ICC1S1	Articulate personal philosophy of special education
	None in addition to Common Core

Standard 2: Development and Characteristics of Learners

Knowledge

ICC2K1	Typical and atypical human growth and development
ICC2K2	Educational implications of characteristics of various exceptionalities
ICC2K3	Characteristics and effects of the cultural and environmental milieu of the individual with exceptional learning needs and the family
ICC2K4	Family systems and the role of families in supporting development
ICC2K5	Similarities and differences of individuals with and without exceptional learning needs
ICC2K6	Similarities and differences among individuals with exceptional learning needs
ICC2K7	Effects of various medications on individuals with exceptional learning needs
IIC2K1	Etiology and diagnosis related to various theoretical approaches
IIC2K2	Impact of sensory impairments, physical and health exceptional learning needs on individuals, families and society
IIC2K3	Etiologies and medical aspects of conditions affecting individuals with exceptional learning needs
IIC2K4	Psychological and social-emotional characteristics of individuals with exceptional learning needs
IIC2K5	Types and transmission routes of infectious disease

Skills

	None in addition to Common Core

Standard 3: Individual Learning Differences

Knowledge

ICC3K1	Effects an exceptional condition(s) can have on an individual's life
ICC3K2	Impact of learners' academic and social abilities, attitudes, interests, and values on instruction and career development
ICC3K3	Variations in beliefs, traditions, and values across and within cultures and their effects on relationships among individuals with exceptional learning needs, family, and schooling
ICC3K4	Cultural perspectives influencing the relationships among families, schools, and communities as related to instruction

ICC3K5	Differing ways of learning of individuals with exceptional learning needs, including those from culturally diverse backgrounds and strategies for addressing these differences
IIC3K1	Complications and implications of medical support services
IIC3K2	Impact disabilities may have on auditory and information processing skills
IIC3K3	Impact of multiple disabilities on behavior

Skills

IIC3S1	Relate levels of support to the needs of the individual

Standard 4: Instructional Strategies

Knowledge

ICC4K1	Evidence-based practices validated for specific characteristics of learners and settings
IIC4K1	Specialized materials for individuals with exceptional learning needs
IIC4K2	Prevention and intervention strategies for individuals with exceptional learning needs
IIC4K3	Strategies for integrating student-initiated learning experiences into ongoing instruction
IIC4K4	Resources, and techniques used to transition individuals with exceptional learning needs into and out of school and postschool environments

Skills

ICC4S1	Use strategies to facilitate integration into various settings
ICC4S2	Teach individuals to use self-assessment, problem-solving, and other cognitive strategies to meet their needs
ICC4S3	Select, adapt, and use instructional strategies and materials according to characteristics of the individual with exceptional learning needs
ICC4S4	Use strategies to facilitate maintenance and generalization of skills across learning environments
ICC4S5	Use procedures to increase the individual's self-awareness, self-management, self-control, self-reliance, and self-esteem
ICC4S6	Use strategies that promote successful transitions for individuals with exceptional learning needs
IIC4S1	Use research-supported instructional strategies and practices
IIC4S2	Use appropriate adaptations and assistive technology for all individuals with exceptional learning needs
IIC4S3	Use a variety of nonaversive techniques to control targeted behavior and maintain attention of individuals with exceptional learning needs
IIC4S4	Identify and teach basic structures and relationships within and across curricula

IIC4S5	Use instructional methods to strengthen and compensate for deficits in perception, comprehension, memory, and retrieval
IIC4S6	Use responses and errors to guide instructional decisions and provide feedback to learners

Standard 5: Learning Environments/Social Interactions

Knowledge

ICC5K1	Demands of learning environments
ICC5K2	Basic classroom management theories and strategies for individuals with exceptional learning needs
ICC5K3	Effective management of teaching and learning
ICC5K4	Teacher attitudes and behaviors that influence behavior of individuals with exceptional learning needs
ICC5K5	Social skills needed for educational and other environments
ICC5K6	Strategies for crisis prevention and intervention
ICC5K7	Strategies for preparing individuals to live harmoniously and productively in a culturally diverse world
ICC5K8	Ways to create learning environments that allow individuals to retain and appreciate their own and each other's respective language and cultural heritage
ICC5K9	Ways specific cultures are negatively stereotyped
ICC5K10	Strategies used by diverse populations to cope with a legacy of former and continuing racism
IIC5K1	Specialized health care interventions for individuals with physical and health exceptional learning needs educational settings
IIC5K2	Barriers to accessibility and acceptance of individuals with exceptional learning needs
IIC5K3	Adaptation of the physical environment to provide optimal learning opportunities for individuals with exceptional learning needs
IIC5K4	Methods for ensuring individual academic success in one-to-one, small-group, and large-group settings
IIC5K5	Advantages and disadvantages of placement options and programs on the continuum of services for individuals with exceptional learning needs

Skills

ICC5S1	Create a safe, equitable, positive, and supportive learning environment in which diversities are valued
ICC5S2	Identify realistic expectations for personal and social behavior in various settings
ICC5S3	Identify supports needed for integration into various program placements
ICC5S4	Design learning environments that encourage active participation in individual and group activities
ICC5S5	Modify the learning environment to manage behaviors

ICC5S6	Use performance data and information from all stakeholders to make or suggest modifications in learning environments
ICC5S7	Establish and maintain rapport with individuals with and without exceptional learning needs
ICC5S8	Teach self-advocacy
ICC5S9	Create an environment that encourages self-advocacy and increased independence
ICC5S10	Use effective and varied behavior management strategies
ICC5S11	Use the least intensive behavior management strategy consistent with the needs of the individual with exceptional learning needs
ICC5S12	Design and manage daily routines
ICC5S13	Organize, develop, and sustain learning environments that support positive intracultural and intercultural experiences
ICC5S14	Mediate controversial intercultural issues among individuals with exceptional learning needs within the learning environment in ways that enhance any culture, group, or person
ICC5S15	Structure, direct, and support the activities of paraeducators, volunteers, and tutors
ICC5S16	Use universal precautions
IIC5S1	Provide instruction in community-based settings
IIC5S2	Use and maintain assistive technologies
IIC5S3	Structure the educational environment to provide optimal learning opportunities for individuals with exceptional learning needs
IIC5S4	Plan instruction in a variety of educational settings
IIC5S5	Teach individuals with exceptional learning needs to give and receive meaningful feedback from peers and adults
IIC5S6	Design learning environments that are multisensory and that facilitate active participation self-advocacy, and independence of individuals with exceptional learning needs in a variety of group and individual learning activities
IIC5S7	Use techniques of physical positioning and management of individuals with exceptional learning needs to ensure participation in academic and social environments
IIC5S8	Demonstrate appropriate body mechanics to ensure student and teacher safety in transfer, lifting, positioning, and seating
IIC5S9	Use positioning techniques that decrease inappropriate tone and facilitate appropriate postural reactions to enhance participation
IIC5S10	Use skills in problem solving and conflict resolution
IIC5S11	Design and implement sensory stimulation programs

IIC5S12	Plan instruction for independent functional life skills relevant to the community, personal living, sexuality, and employment

Standard 6: Language

Knowledge

ICC6K1	Effects of cultural and linguistic differences on growth and development
ICC6K2	Characteristics of one's own culture and use of language and the ways in which these can differ from other cultures and uses of languages
ICC6K3	Ways of behaving and communicating among cultures that can lead to misinterpretation and misunderstanding
ICC6K4	Augmentative and assistive communication strategies
IIC6K1	Impact of language development and listening comprehension on academic and nonacademic learning of individuals with exceptional learning needs
IIC6K2	Communication and social interaction alternatives for individuals who are nonspeaking

Skills

ICC6S1	Use strategies to support and enhance communication skills of individuals with exceptional learning needs
ICC6S2	Use communication strategies and resources to facilitate understanding of subject matter for individuals with exceptional learning needs whose primary language is not the dominant language
IIC6S1	Teach individuals with exceptional learning needs to monitor for errors in oral and written language
IIC6S2	Teach methods and strategies for producing legible documents
IIC6S3	Plan instruction on the use of alternative and augmentative communication systems

Standard 7: Instructional Planning

Knowledge

ICC7K1	Theories and research that form the basis of curriculum development and instructional practice
ICC7K2	Scope and sequences of general and special curricula
ICC7K3	National, state or provincial, and local curricula standards
ICC7K4	Technology for planning and managing the teaching and learning environment
ICC7K5	Roles and responsibilities of the paraeducator related to instruction, intervention, and direct service
IIC7K1	Model career, vocational, and transition programs for individuals with exceptional learning needs

Skills	
ICC7S1	Identify and prioritize areas of the general curriculum and accommodations for individuals with exceptional learning needs
ICC7S2	Develop and implement comprehensive, longitudinal individualized programs in collaboration with team members
ICC7S3	Involve the individual and family in setting instructional goals and monitoring progress
ICC7S4	Use functional assessments to develop intervention plans
ICC7S5	Use task analysis
ICC7S6	Sequence, implement, and evaluate individualized learning objectives
ICC7S7	Integrate affective, social, and life skills with academic curricula
ICC7S8	Develop and select instructional content, resources, and strategies that respond to cultural, linguistic, and gender differences
ICC7S9	Incorporate and implement instructional and assistive technology into the educational program
ICC7S10	Prepare lesson plans
ICC7S11	Prepare and organize materials to implement daily lesson plans
ICC7S12	Use instructional time effectively
ICC7S13	Make responsive adjustments to instruction based on continual observations
ICC7S14	Prepare individuals to exhibit self-enhancing behavior in response to societal attitudes and actions
ICC7S15	Evaluate and modify instructional practices in response to ongoing assessment data
IIC7S1	Plan and implement individualized reinforcement systems and environmental modifications
IIC7S2	Plan and implement age- and ability-appropriate instruction for individuals with exceptional learning needs
IIC7S3	Select and plan for integration of related services into the instructional program
IIC7S4	Select, design, and use medical materials, and resources required to educate individuals whose exceptional learning needs interfere with communications
IIC7S5	Interpret sensory and physical information to create or adapt appropriate learning plans
IIC7S6	Design and implement instructional programs that address independent living and career education
IIC7S7	Design and implement curriculum strategies for medical self-management procedures
IIC7S8	Design, implement, and evaluate instructional programs that enhance social participation across environments

Standard 8: Assessment

Knowledge

ICC8K1	Basic terminology used in assessment
ICC8K2	Legal provisions and ethical principles regarding assessment of individuals
ICC8K3	Screening, prereferral, referral, and classification procedures
ICC8K4	Use and limitations of assessment instruments
ICC8K5	National, state or provincial, and local accommodations and modifications
IIC8K1	Specialized terminology used in the assessment of individuals with exceptional learning needs
IIC8K2	Laws and policies regarding referral and placement procedures for individuals with exceptional learning needs
IIC8K3	Types and importance of information concerning individuals with exceptional learning needs available from families and public agencies

Skills

ICC8S1	Gather relevant background information
ICC8S2	Administer nonbiased formal and informal assessments
ICC8S3	Use technology to conduct assessments
ICC8S4	Develop or modify individualized assessment strategies
ICC8S5	Interpret information from formal and informal assessments
ICC8S6	Use assessment information in making eligibility, program, and placement decisions for individuals with exceptional learning needs, including those from culturally and/or linguistically diverse backgrounds
ICC8S7	Report assessment results to all stakeholders using effective communication skills
ICC8S8	Evaluate instruction and monitor progress of individuals with exceptional learning needs
ICC8S9	Create and maintain records
IIC8S1	Implement procedures for assessing and reporting both appropriate and problematic social behaviors of individuals with exceptional learning needs
IIC8S2	Use exceptionality-specific assessment instruments with individuals with exceptional learning needs
IIC8S3	Select, adapt and modify assessments to accommodate the unique abilities and needs of individuals with exceptional learning needs
IIC8S4	Adapt and modify assessments to accommodate the unique abilities and needs of individuals with exceptional learning needs

IIC8S5	Develop and use a technology plan based on adaptive technology assessment
IIC8S6	Assess reliable method(s) of response of individuals who lack typical communication and performance abilities
IIC8S7	Monitor intragroup behavior changes across subjects and activities

Standard 9: Professional and Ethical Practice

Knowledge

ICC9K1	Personal cultural biases and differences that affect one's teaching
ICC9K2	Importance of the teacher serving as a model for individuals with exceptional learning needs
ICC9K3	Continuum of lifelong professional development
ICC9K4	Methods to remain current regarding research-validated practice
IIC9K1	Sources of unique services, networks, and organizations for individuals with exceptional learning needs
IIC9K2	Organizations and publications relevant to individuals with exceptional learning needs

Skills

ICC9S1	Practice within the CEC Code of Ethics and other standards of the profession
ICC9S2	Uphold high standards of competence and integrity and exercise sound judgment in the practice of the professional
ICC9S3	Act ethically in advocating for appropriate services
ICC9S4	Conduct professional activities in compliance with applicable laws and policies
ICC9S5	Demonstrate commitment to developing the highest education and quality-of-life potential of individuals with exceptional learning needs
ICC9S6	Demonstrate sensitivity for the culture, language, religion, gender, disability, socioeconomic status, and sexual orientation of individuals
ICC9S7	Practice within one's skill limits and obtain assistance as needed
ICC9S8	Use verbal, nonverbal, and written language effectively
ICC9S9	Conduct self-evaluation of instruction
ICC9S10	Access information on exceptionalities
ICC9S11	Reflect on one's practice to improve instruction and guide professional growth
ICC9S12	Engage in professional activities that benefit individuals with exceptional learning needs, their families, and one's colleagues
ICC9S13	Demonstrate commitment to engage in evidence-based practices

IIC9S1	Participate in the activities of professional organizations relevant to individuals with exceptional learning needs
IIC9S2	Ethical responsibility to advocate for appropriate services for individuals with exceptional learning needs
IIC9S3	Seek information regarding protocols, procedural guidelines, and policies designed to assist individuals with exceptional learning needs as they participate in school and community-based activities

Standard 10: Collaboration

Knowledge

ICC10K1	Models and strategies of consultation and collaboration
ICC10K2	Roles of individuals with exceptional learning needs, families, and school and community personnel in planning of an individualized program
ICC10K3	Concerns of families of individuals with exceptional learning needs and strategies to help address these concerns
ICC10K4	Culturally responsive factors that promote effective communication and collaboration with individuals with exceptional learning needs, families, school personnel, and community members
IIC10K1	Parent education programs and behavior management guides that address severe behavior problems and facilitation communication for individuals with exceptional learning needs
IIC10K2	Collaborative and/or consultative role of the special education teacher in the reintegration of individuals with exceptional learning needs
IIC10K3	Roles of professional groups and referral agencies in identifying, assessing, and providing services to individuals with exceptional learning needs

Skills

ICC10S1	Maintain confidential communication about individuals with exceptional learning needs
ICC10S2	Collaborate with families and others in assessment of individuals with exceptional learning needs
ICC10S3	Foster respectful and beneficial relationships between families and professionals
ICC10S4	Assist individuals with exceptional learning needs and their families in becoming active participants in the educational team
ICC10S5	Plan and conduct collaborative conferences with individuals with exceptional learning needs and their families
ICC10S6	Collaborate with school personnel and community members in integrating individuals with exceptional learning needs into various settings
ICC10S7	Use group problem-solving skills to develop, implement, and evaluate collaborative activities
ICC10S8	Model techniques and coach others in the use of instructional methods and accommodations

ICC10S9	Communicate with school personnel about the characteristics and needs of individuals with exceptional learning needs
ICC10S10	Communicate effectively with families of individuals with exceptional learning needs from diverse backgrounds
ICC10S11	Observe, evaluate, and provide feedback to paraeducators
IIC10S1	Participate in the selection and implementation of augmentative or alternative communication systems
IIC10S2	Use local community, and state and provincial resources to assist in programming with individuals with exceptional learning needs
IIC10S3	Select, plan, and coordinate activities of related services personnel to maximize direct instruction for individuals with exceptional learning needs
IIC10S4	Collaborate with team members to plan transition to adulthood that encourages full community participation
IIC10S5	Collaborate with families of and service providers to individuals who are chronically or terminally ill

Initial Special Education Teachers of Individuals With Exceptional Learning Needs Who Are Deaf or Hard of Hearing

Standard 1: Foundations	
Knowledge	
ICC1K1	Models, theories, philosophies, and research methods that form the basis for special education practice
ICC1K2	Laws, policies, and ethical principles regarding behavior management planning and implementation
ICC1K3	Relationship of special education to the organization and function of educational agencies
ICC1K4	Rights and responsibilities of individuals with exceptional learning needs, parents, teachers and other professionals, and schools related to exceptional learning needs
ICC1K5	Issues in definition and identification of individuals with exceptional learning needs, including those from culturally and/or linguistically diverse backgrounds
ICC1K6	Issues, assurances, and due process rights related to assessment, eligibility, and placement within a continuum of services
ICC1K7	Family systems and the role of families in the educational process
ICC1K8	Historical points of view and contribution of culturally diverse groups
ICC1K9	Impact of the dominant culture on shaping schools and the individuals who study and work in them
ICC1K10	Potential impact of differences in values, languages, and customs that can exist between the home and school
D&HH1K1	Incidence and prevalence figures for individuals who are deaf and hard of hearing
D&HH1K2	Sociocultural, historical, and political forces unique to deaf education
D&HH1K3	Etiologies of hearing loss that can result in additional learning challenges
D&HH1K4	Historical foundations and research evidence upon which educational practice is based
Skills	
ICC1S1	Articulate personal philosophy of special education
D&HH1S1	Develop and enrich cultural competence relative to the deaf community
Standard 2: Development and Characteristics of Learners	
Knowledge	
ICC2K1	Typical and atypical human growth and development
ICC2K2	Educational implications of characteristics of various exceptionalities

ICC2K3	Characteristics and effects of the cultural and environmental milieu of the individual with exceptional learning needs and the family
ICC2K4	Family systems and the role of families in supporting development
ICC2K5	Similarities and differences of individuals with and without exceptional learning needs
ICC2K6	Similarities and differences among individuals with exceptional learning needs
ICC2K7	Effects of various medications on individuals with exceptional learning needs
D&HH2K1	Cognitive and language development of individuals who are deaf and hard of hearing
D&HH2K2	Effects of the interrelationship among onset of hearing loss, age of identification, and provision of services on the development of the individuals who are deaf or hard of hearing

Skills

	None in addition to the Common Core

Standard 3: Individual Learning Differences

Knowledge

ICC3K1	Effects an exceptional condition(s) can have on an individual's life
ICC3K2	Impact of learners' academic and social abilities, attitudes, interests, and values on instruction and career development
ICC3K3	Variations in beliefs, traditions, and values across and within cultures and their effects on relationships among individuals with exceptional learning needs, family, and schooling
ICC3K4	Cultural perspectives influencing the relationships among families, schools, and communities as related to instruction
ICC3K5	Differing ways of learning of individuals with exceptional learning needs, including those from culturally diverse backgrounds and strategies for addressing these differences
D&HH3K1	Influence of experience and educational placement on all developmental domains
D&HH3K2	Influence of cultural identity and language on all developmental domains

Skills

	None in addition to the Common Core

Standard 4: Instructional Strategies

Knowledge

ICC4K1	Evidence-based practices validated for specific characteristics of learners and settings
D&HH4K1	Visual tools and organizers that support content mastery and retention by individuals who are deaf or hard of hearing

Skills	
ICC4S1	Use strategies to facilitate integration into various settings
ICC4S2	Teach individuals to use self-assessment, problem-solving, and other cognitive strategies to meet their needs
ICC4S3	Select, adapt, and use instructional strategies and materials according to characteristics of the individual with exceptional learning needs
ICC4S4	Use strategies to facilitate maintenance and generalization of skills across learning environments
ICC4S5	Use procedures to increase the individual's self-awareness, self-management, self-control, self-reliance, and self-esteem
ICC4S6	Use strategies that promote successful transitions for individuals with exceptional learning needs
D&HH4S1	Develop proficiency in the languages used to teach individuals who are deaf or hard of hearing
D&HH4S2	Provide activities to promote print literacy and content area reading and writing through instruction via spoken language and/or the signed language indigenous to the deaf community
D&HH4S3	Apply first and second language teaching strategies to the instruction of the individual
D&HH4S4	Provide balance among explicit instruction, guided instruction, peer learning, and reflection

Standard 5: Learning Environments/Social Interactions

Knowledge	
ICC5K1	Demands of learning environments
ICC5K2	Basic classroom management theories and strategies for individuals with exceptional learning needs
ICC5K3	Effective management of teaching and learning
ICC5K4	Teacher attitudes and behaviors that influence behavior of individuals with exceptional learning needs
ICC5K5	Social skills needed for educational and other environments
ICC5K6	Strategies for crisis prevention and intervention
ICC5K7	Strategies for preparing individuals to live harmoniously and productively in a culturally diverse world
ICC5K8	Ways to create learning environments that allow individuals to retain and appreciate their own and each other's respective language and cultural heritage
ICC5K9	Ways specific cultures are negatively stereotyped
ICC5K10	Strategies used by diverse populations to cope with a legacy of former and continuing racism
D&HH5K1	Influence of family communication and culture on all developmental domains

	Skills
ICC5S1	Create a safe, equitable, positive, and supportive learning environment in which diversities are valued
ICC5S2	Identify realistic expectations for personal and social behavior in various settings
ICC5S3	Identify supports needed for integration into various program placements
ICC5S4	Design learning environments that encourage active participation in individual and group activities
ICC5S5	Modify the learning environment to manage behaviors
ICC5S6	Use performance data and information from all stakeholders to make or suggest modifications in learning environments
ICC5S7	Establish and maintain rapport with individuals with and without exceptional learning needs
ICC5S8	Teach self-advocacy
ICC5S9	Create an environment that encourages self-advocacy and increased independence
ICC5S10	Use effective and varied behavior management strategies
ICC5S11	Use the least intensive behavior management strategy consistent with the needs of the individual with exceptional learning needs
ICC5S12	Design and manage daily routines
ICC5S13	Organize, develop, and sustain learning environments that support positive intracultural and intercultural experiences
ICC5S14	Mediate controversial intercultural issues among individuals with exceptional learning needs within the learning environment in ways that enhance any culture, group, or person
ICC5S15	Structure, direct, and support the activities of paraeducators, volunteers, and tutors
ICC5S16	Use universal precautions
D&HH5S1	Provide ongoing opportunities for interactions between individuals who are deaf or hard of hearing with peers and role models who are deaf or hard of hearing
D&HH5S2	Provide access to incidental language experiences
D&HH5S3	Prepare individuals who are deaf or hard of hearing to use interpreters
D&HH5S4	Manage assistive technology for individuals who are deaf or hard of hearing
D&HH5S5	Design a classroom environment that maximizes opportunities for visual and/or auditory learning and meets developmental and learning needs

Standard 6: Language

	Knowledge
ICC6K1	Effects of cultural and linguistic differences on growth and development

ICC6K2	Characteristics of one's own culture and use of language and the ways in which these can differ from other cultures and uses of languages
ICC6K3	Ways of behaving and communicating among cultures that can lead to misinterpretation and misunderstanding
ICC6K4	Augmentative and assistive communication strategies
D&HH6K1	Components of linguistic and nonlinguistic communication
D&HH6K2	Importance of early intervention to language development
D&HH6K3	Effects of sensory input on the development of language and learning
D&HH6K4	Spoken and visual communication modes
D&HH6K5	Current theories of the development of spoken language and signed languages

Skills

ICC6S1	Use strategies to support and enhance communication skills of individuals with exceptional learning needs
ICC6S2	Use communication strategies and resources to facilitate understanding of subject matter for individuals with exceptional learning needs whose primary language is not the dominant language
D&HH6S1	Apply strategies to facilitate cognitive and communicative development
D&HH6S2	Implement strategies for stimulating and using residual hearing
D&HH6S3	Facilitate independent communication in all contexts
D&HH6S4	Communicate proficiently in spoken language or the sign language indigenous to the deaf community
D&HH6S5	Implement strategies for developing spoken language in orally communicating individuals with exceptional learning needs and sign language proficiency in signing individuals with exceptional learning needs

Standard 7: Instructional Planning

Knowledge

ICC7K1	Theories and research that form the basis of curriculum development and instructional practice
ICC7K2	Scope and sequences of general and special curricula
ICC7K3	National, state or provincial, and local curricula standards
ICC7K4	Technology for planning and managing the teaching and learning environment
ICC7K5	Roles and responsibilities of the paraeducator related to instruction, intervention, and direct service
D&HH7K1	Model programs for individuals who are deaf or hard of hearing

Skills		
ICC7S1	Identify and prioritize areas of the general curriculum and accommodations for individuals with exceptional learning needs	
ICC7S2	Develop and implement comprehensive, longitudinal individualized programs in collaboration with team members	
ICC7S3	Involve the individual and family in setting instructional goals and monitoring progress	
ICC7S4	Use functional assessments to develop intervention plans	
ICC7S5	Use task analysis	
ICC7S6	Sequence, implement, and evaluate individualized learning objectives	
ICC7S7	Integrate affective, social, and life skills with academic curricula	
ICC7S8	Develop and select instructional content, resources, and strategies that respond to cultural, linguistic, and gender differences	
ICC7S9	Incorporate and implement instructional and assistive technology into the educational program	
ICC7S10	Prepare lesson plans	
ICC7S11	Prepare and organize materials to implement daily lesson plans	
ICC7S12	Use instructional time effectively	
ICC7S13	Make responsive adjustments to instruction based on continual observations	
ICC7S14	Prepare individuals to exhibit self-enhancing behavior in response to societal attitudes and actions	
ICC7S15	Evaluate and modify instructional practices in response to ongoing assessment data	
D&HH7S1	Use specialized technologies, resources, and instructional strategies unique to individuals with exceptional learning needs who are deaf or hard of hearing	
D&HH7S2	Plan and implement transitions across service continuums	
D&HH7S3	Integrate language instruction into academic areas	
D&HH7S4	Develop successful inclusion experiences	

Standard 8: Assessment

Knowledge		
ICC8K1	Basic terminology used in assessment	
ICC8K2	Legal provisions and ethical principles regarding assessment of individuals	
ICC8K3	Screening, prereferral, referral, and classification procedures	

ICC8K4	Use and limitations of assessment instruments
ICC8K5	National, state or provincial, and local accommodations and modifications
D&HH8K1	Specialized terminology used in assessing individuals who are deaf or hard of hearing

Skills	
ICC8S1	Gather relevant background information
ICC8S2	Administer nonbiased formal and informal assessments
ICC8S3	Use technology to conduct assessments
ICC8S4	Develop or modify individualized assessment strategies
ICC8S5	Interpret information from formal and informal assessments
ICC8S6	Use assessment information in making eligibility, program, and placement decisions for individuals with exceptional learning needs, including those from culturally and/or linguistically diverse backgrounds
ICC8S7	Report assessment results to all stakeholders using effective communication skills
ICC8S8	Evaluate instruction and monitor progress of individuals with exceptional learning needs
ICC8S9	Create and maintain records
D&HH8S1	Administer assessment tools using the individuals with exceptional learning needs preferred mode and language of communication
D&HH8S2	Develop specialized assessment procedures that allow for alternative forms of expression
D&HH8S3	Collect and analyze spoken, signed, or written communication samples

Standard 9: Professional And Ethical Practice

Knowledge	
ICC9K1	Personal cultural biases and differences that affect one's teaching
ICC9K2	Importance of the teacher serving as a model for individuals with exceptional learning needs
ICC9K3	Continuum of lifelong professional development
ICC9K4	Methods to remain current regarding research-validated practice
D&HH9K1	Roles and responsibilities of teachers and support personnel in educational practice for individuals who are deaf or hard of hearing
D&HH9K2	Professional resources relevant to the field of education of individuals who are deaf or hard of hearing
D&HH9K3	Knowledge of professional organizations in the field of deaf education

Skills	
ICC9S1	Practice within the CEC Code of Ethics and other standards of the profession
ICC9S2	Uphold high standards of competence and integrity and exercise sound judgment in the practice of the profession
ICC9S3	Act ethically in advocating for appropriate services
ICC9S4	Conduct professional activities in compliance with applicable laws and policies
ICC9S5	Demonstrate commitment to developing the highest education and quality-of-life potential of individuals with exceptional learning needs
ICC9S6	Demonstrate sensitivity for the culture, language, religion, gender, disability, socioeconomic status, and sexual orientation of individuals
ICC9S7	Practice within one's skill limits and obtain assistance as needed
ICC9S8	Use verbal, nonverbal, and written language effectively
ICC9S9	Conduct self-evaluation of instruction
ICC9S10	Access information on exceptionalities
ICC9S11	Reflect on one's practice to improve instruction and guide professional growth
ICC9S12	Engage in professional activities that benefit individuals with exceptional learning needs, their families, and one's colleagues
ICC9S13	Demonstrate commitment to engage in evidence-based practices
D&HH9S1	Increase proficiency and sustain a life-long commitment to maintaining instructional language competence

Standard 10: Collaboration

Knowledge	
ICC10K1	Models and strategies of consultation and collaboration
ICC10K2	Roles of individuals with exceptional learning needs, families, and school and community personnel in planning of an individualized program
ICC10K3	Concerns of families of individuals with exceptional learning needs and strategies to help address these concerns
ICC10K4	Culturally responsive factors that promote effective communication and collaboration with individuals with exceptional learning needs, families, school personnel, and community members
D&HH10K1	Services, organizations, and networks that support individuals who are deaf or hard of hearing

Skills	
ICC10S1	Maintain confidential communication about individuals with exceptional learning needs
ICC10S2	Collaborate with families and others in assessment of individuals with exceptional learning needs
ICC10S3	Foster respectful and beneficial relationships between families and professionals
ICC10S4	Assist individuals with exceptional learning needs and their families in becoming active participants in the educational team
ICC10S5	Plan and conduct collaborative conferences with individuals with exceptional learning needs and their families
ICC10S6	Collaborate with school personnel and community members in integrating individuals with exceptional learning needs into various settings
ICC10S7	Use group problem-solving skills to develop, implement, and evaluate collaborative activities
ICC10S8	Model techniques and coach others in the use of instructional methods and accommodations
ICC10S9	Communicate with school personnel about the characteristics and needs of individuals with exceptional learning needs
ICC10S10	Communicate effectively with families of individuals with exceptional learning needs from diverse backgrounds
ICC10S11	Observe, evaluate, and provide feedback to paraeducators
D&HH10S1	Provide families with support to make informed choices regarding communication modes, philosophies, and educational options

Initial Special Education Professionals in Early Childhood Special Education/ Early Intervention (Birth to Eight)[9]

Standard 1: Foundations	
Knowledge	
ICC1K1	Models, theories, philosophies, and research methods that form the basis for special education practice
ICC1K2	Laws, policies, and ethical principles regarding behavior management planning and implementation
ICC1K3	Relationship of special education to the organization and function of educational agencies
ICC1K4	Rights and responsibilities of individuals with exceptional learning needs, parents, teachers, and other professionals, and schools related to exceptional learning needs
ICC1K5	Issues in definition and identification of individuals with exceptional learning needs, including those from culturally and/or linguistically diverse backgrounds
ICC1K6	Issues, assurances, and due process rights related to assessment, eligibility, and placement within a continuum of services
ICC1K7	Family systems and the role of families in the educational process
ICC1K8	Historical points of view and contribution of culturally diverse groups
ICC1K9	Impact of the dominant culture on shaping schools and the individuals who study and work in them
ICC1K10	Potential impact of differences in values, languages, and customs that can exist between the home and school
ECSEK1	Historical, philosophical foundations, and legal basis of services for infants and young children both with and without exceptional needs

[9] Terminology specific to Initial Special Education Professionals in Early Childhood Special Education/Early Intervention (Birth to Eight) standards:

- Infants and Young Children: all children birth to age 8 years
- Exceptional Needs: in response to Exceptional Learning Needs (ELN) specified in the CEC standards, "infants and young children with exceptional needs" will be used, and not Exceptional Learning Needs, because infants and young children have developmental needs as well as learning needs
- Infants and Young Children with Exceptional Needs: refers to infants and young children, birth to age 8 years, who have, or are at risk for, developmental delays and disabilities
- Development and Learning: terms to be used, and in that order, to convey the focus of the following knowledge and skills for personnel – to support the developmental and learning needs of infants and young children, and their families
- Individualized family services plan/Individualized education program: The language of the standards requires spelling out IFSP and IEP. K&S suggests using "family or educational plan" to (a) simplify the expressions and (b) include Canadian terminology in the standards. Division for Early Childhood respectfully requests the use of "individualized plan" to simplify the language since the IFSP is an educational plan, too
- Developmental Domains: Term to be used to simplify the listing of the five developmental domains specified in federal law – cognitive, communicative, social-emotional, motor, and adaptive development
- Settings for Infants and Young Children: to avoid lists, these settings refer to home, community-based, and school-based settings
- Developmental and academic content refers to curriculum

ECSE1K2	Trends and issues in early childhood education, early childhood special education, and early intervention

Skills

ICC1S1	Articulate personal philosophy of special education
ECSE1S1	Implement family services consistent with due process safeguards

Standard 2: Development and Characteristics of Learners

Knowledge

ICC2K1	Typical and atypical human growth and development
ICC2K2	Educational implications of characteristics of various exceptionalities
ICC2K3	Characteristics and effects of the cultural and environmental milieu of the individual with exceptional learning needs and the family
ICC2K4	Family systems and the role of families in supporting development
ICC2K5	Similarities and differences of individuals with and without exceptional learning needs
ICC2K6	Similarities and differences among individuals with exceptional learning needs
ICC2K7	Effects of various medications on individuals with exceptional learning needs
ECSE2K1	Theories of typical and atypical early childhood development
ECSE2K2	Biological and environmental factors that affect pre-, peri-, and postnatal development and learning
ECSE2K3	Specific disabilities, including the etiology, characteristics, and classification of common disabilities in infants and young children, and specific implications for development and learning in the first years of life
ECSE2K4	Impact of medical conditions and related care on development and learning
ECSE2K5	Impact of medical conditions on family concerns, resources, and priorities
ECSE2K6	Factors that affect the mental health and social-emotional development of infants and young children
ECSE2K7	Infants and young children develop and learn at varying rates

Skills

ECSE2S1	Apply current research to the five developmental domains, play and temperament in learning situations

Standard 3: Individual Learning Differences

Knowledge

ICC3K1	Effects an exceptional condition(s) can have on an individual's life

ICC3K2	Impact of learners' academic and social abilities, attitudes, interests, and values on instruction and career development
ICC3K3	Variations in beliefs, traditions, and values across and within cultures and their effects on relationships among individuals with exceptional learning needs, family, and schooling
ICC3K4	Cultural perspectives influencing the relationships among families, schools, and communities as related to instruction
ICC3K5	Differing ways of learning of individuals with exceptional learning needs, including those from culturally diverse backgrounds and strategies for addressing these differences
ECSE3K1	Impact of child's abilities, needs, and characteristics on development and learning
ECSE3K2	Impact of social and physical environments on development and learning

Skills

ECSE3S1	Develop, implement, and evaluate learning experiences and strategies that respect the diversity of infants and young children, and their families
ECSE3S2	Develop and match learning experiences and strategies to characteristics of infants and young children

Standard 4: Instructional Strategies

Knowledge

ICC4K1	Evidence-based practices validated for specific characteristics of learners and settings
ECSE4K1	Concept of universal design for learning

Skills

ICC4S1	Use strategies to facilitate integration into various settings
ICC4S2	Teach individuals to use self-assessment, problem-solving, and other cognitive strategies to meet their needs
ICC4S3	Select, adapt, and use instructional strategies and materials according to characteristics of the individual with exceptional learning needs
ICC4S4	Use strategies to facilitate maintenance and generalization of skills across learning environments
ICC4S5	Use procedures to increase the individual's self-awareness, self-management, self-control, self-reliance, and self-esteem
ICC4S6	Use strategies that promote successful transitions for individuals with exceptional learning needs
ECSE4S1	Plan, implement, and evaluate developmentally appropriate curricula, instruction, and adaptations based on knowledge of individual children, the family, and the community
ECSE4S2	Facilitate child-initiated development and learning
ECSE4S3	Use teacher-scaffolded and initiated instruction to complement child-initiated learning

ECSE4S4	Link development, learning experiences, and instruction to promote educational transitions
ECSE4S5	Use individual and group guidance and problem-solving techniques to develop supportive relationships with and among children
ECSE4S6	Use strategies to teach social skills and conflict resolution
ECSE4S7	Use a continuum of intervention strategies to support access of young children in the general curriculum and daily routines
ECSE4S8	Implement and evaluate preventative and reductive strategies to address challenging behaviors

Standard 5: Learning Environments/Social Interactions

Knowledge

ICC5K1	Demands of learning environments
ICC5K2	Basic classroom management theories and strategies for individuals with exceptional learning needs
ICC5K3	Effective management of teaching and learning
ICC5K4	Teacher attitudes and behaviors that influence behavior of individuals with exceptional learning needs
ICC5K5	Social skills needed for educational and other environments
ICC5K6	Strategies for crisis prevention and intervention
ICC5K7	Strategies for preparing individuals to live harmoniously and productively in a culturally diverse world
ICC5K8	Ways to create learning environments that allow individuals to retain and appreciate their own and each other's respective language and cultural heritage
ICC5K9	Ways specific cultures are negatively stereotyped
ICC5K10	Strategies used by diverse populations to cope with a legacy of former and continuing racism
	None in addition to Common Core

Skills

ICC5S1	Create a safe, equitable, positive, and supportive learning environment in which diversities are valued
ICC5S2	Identify realistic expectations for personal and social behavior in various settings
ICC5S3	Identify supports needed for integration into various program placements
ICC5S4	Design learning environments that encourage active participation in individual and group activities
ICC5S5	Modify the learning environment to manage behaviors
ICC5S6	Use performance data and information from all stakeholders to make or suggest modifications in learning environments

ICC5S7	Establish and maintain rapport with individuals with and without exceptional learning needs
ICC5S8	Teach self-advocacy
ICC5S9	Create an environment that encourages self-advocacy and increased independence
ICC5S10	Use effective and varied behavior management strategies
ICC5S11	Use the least intensive behavior management strategy consistent with the needs of the individual with exceptional learning needs
ICC5S12	Design and manage daily routines
ICC5S13	Organize, develop, and sustain learning environments that support positive intracultural and intercultural experiences
ICC5S14	Mediate controversial intercultural issues among individuals with exceptional learning needs within the learning environment in ways that enhance any culture, group, or person
ICC5S15	Structure, direct, and support the activities of paraeducators, volunteers, and tutors
ICC5S16	Use universal precautions
ECSE5S1	Select, develop, and evaluate developmentally and functionally appropriate materials, equipment, and environments
ECSE5S2	Organize space, time, materials, peers, and adults to maximize progress in natural and structured environments
ECSE5S3	Embed learning opportunities in everyday routines, relationships, activities, and places
ECSE5S4	Structure social environments, using peer models and proximity, and responsive adults, to promote interactions among peers, parents, and caregivers
ECSE5S5	Provide a stimulus-rich indoor and outdoor environment that employs materials, media, and adaptive and assistive technology, responsive to individual differences
ECSE5S6	Implement basic health, nutrition and safety management procedures for infants and young children
ECSE5S7	Use evaluation procedures and recommend referral with ongoing follow-up to community health and social services

Standard 6: Language

Knowledge

ICC6K1	Effects of cultural and linguistic differences on growth and development
ICC6K2	Characteristics of one's own culture and use of language and the ways in which these can differ from other cultures and uses of languages
ICC6K3	Ways of behaving and communicating among cultures that can lead to misinterpretation and misunderstanding
ICC6K4	Augmentative and assistive communication strategies

ECSE6K1	Impact of language delays on cognitive, social-emotional, adaptive, play, temperament and motor development
ECSE6K2	Impact of language delays on behavior

Skills

ICC6S1	Use strategies to support and enhance communication skills of individuals with exceptional learning needs
ICC6S2	Use communication strategies and resources to facilitate understanding of subject matter for individuals with exceptional learning needs whose primary language is not the dominant language
ECSE6S1	Support and facilitate family and child interactions as primary contexts for development and learning
ECSE6S2	Support caregivers to respond to child's cues and preferences, establish predictable routines and turn-taking, and facilitate communicative initiations
ECSE6S3	Establish communication systems for young children that support self-advocacy

Standard 7: Instructional Planning

Knowledge

ICC7K1	Theories and research that form the basis of curriculum development and instructional practice
ICC7K2	Scope and sequences of general and special curricula
ICC7K3	National, state or provincial, and local curricula standards
ICC7K4	Technology for planning and managing the teaching and learning environment
ICC7K5	Roles and responsibilities of the paraeducator related to instruction, intervention, and direct service
ECSE7K1	Theories and research that form the basis of developmental and academic curricula and instructional strategies for infants and young children
ECSE7K2	Developmental and academic content
ECSE7K3	Connection of curriculum to assessment and progress monitoring activities

Skills

ICC7S1	Identify and prioritize areas of the general curriculum and accommodations for individuals with exceptional learning needs
ICC7S2	Develop and implement comprehensive, longitudinal individualized programs in collaboration with team members
ICC7S3	Involve the individual and family in setting instructional goals and monitoring progress
ICC7S4	Use functional assessments to develop intervention plans
ICC7S5	Use task analysis

ICC7S6	Sequence, implement, and evaluate individualized learning objectives
ICC7S7	Integrate affective, social, and life skills with academic curricula
ICC7S8	Develop and select instructional content, resources, and strategies that respond to cultural, linguistic, and gender differences
ICC7S9	Incorporate and implement instructional and assistive technology into the educational program
ICC7S10	Prepare lesson plans
ICC7S11	Prepare and organize materials to implement daily lesson plans
ICC7S12	Use instructional time effectively
ICC7S13	Make responsive adjustments to instruction based on continual observations
ICC7S14	Prepare individuals to exhibit self-enhancing behavior in response to societal attitudes and actions
ICC7S15	Evaluate and modify instructional practices in response to ongoing assessment data
ECSE7S1	Develop, implement, and evaluate individualized plans, with family members and other professionals, as a member of a team
ECSE7S2	Plan and implement developmentally and individually appropriate curriculum
ECSE7S3	Design intervention strategies incorporating information from multiple disciplines
ECSE7S4	Implement developmentally and functionally appropriate activities, using a variety of formats, based on systematic instruction
ECSE7S5	Align individualized goals with developmental and academic content
ECSE7S6	Develop individualized plans that support development and learning as well as caregiver responsiveness
ECSE7S7	Develop an individualized plan that supports the child's independent functioning in the child's natural environments
ECSE7S8	Make adaptations for the unique developmental and learning needs of children, including those from diverse backgrounds

Standard 8: Assessment

Knowledge

ICC8K1	Basic terminology used in assessment
ICC8K2	Legal provisions and ethical principles regarding assessment of individuals
ICC8K3	Screening, prereferral, referral, and classification procedures
ICC8K4	Use and limitations of assessment instruments

ICC8K5	National, state or provincial, and local accommodations and modifications
ECSE8K1	Role of the family in the assessment process
ECSE8K2	Legal requirements that distinguish among at-risk, developmental delay and disability
ECSE8K3	Alignment of assessment with curriculum, content standards, and local, state, and federal regulations
Skills	
ICC8S1	Gather relevant background information
ICC8S2	Administer nonbiased formal and informal assessments
ICC8S3	Use technology to conduct assessments
ICC8S4	Develop or modify individualized assessment strategies
ICC8S5	Interpret information from formal and informal assessments
ICC8S6	Use assessment information in making eligibility, program, and placement decisions for individuals with exceptional learning needs, including those from culturally and/or linguistically diverse backgrounds
ICC8S7	Report assessment results to all stakeholders using effective communication skills
ICC8S8	Evaluate instruction and monitor progress of individuals with exceptional learning needs
ICC8S9	Create and maintain records
ECSE8S1	Assist families in identifying their concerns, resources, and priorities
ECSE8S2	Integrate family priorities and concerns in the assessment process
ECSE8S3	Assess progress in the five developmental domains, play, and temperament
ECSE8S4	Select and administer assessment instruments in compliance with established criteria
ECSE8S5	Use informal and formal assessment to make decisions about infants and young children's development and learning
ECSE8S6	Gather information from multiple sources and environments
ECSE8S7	Use a variety of materials and contexts to maintain the interest of infants and young children in the assessment process
ECSE8S8	Participate as a team member to integrate assessment results in the development and implementation of individualized plans
ECSE8S9	Emphasize child's strengths and needs in assessment reports
ECSE8S10	Produce reports that focus on developmental domains and functional concerns
ECSE8S11	Conduct ongoing formative child, family, and setting assessments to monitor instructional effectiveness

Standard 9: Professional And Ethical Practice

Knowledge

ICC9K1	Personal cultural biases and differences that affect one's teaching
ICC9K2	Importance of the teacher serving as a model for individuals with exceptional learning needs
ICC9K3	Continuum of lifelong professional development
ICC9K4	Methods to remain current regarding research-validated practice
ECSE9K1	Legal, ethical, and policy issues related to educational, developmental, and medical services for infants and young children, and their families
ECSE9K2	Advocacy for professional status and working conditions for those who serve infants and young children, and their families

Skills

ICC9S1	Practice within the CEC Code of Ethics and other standards of the profession
ICC9S2	Uphold high standards of competence and integrity and exercise sound judgment in the practice of the professional
ICC9S3	Act ethically in advocating for appropriate services
ICC9S4	Conduct professional activities in compliance with applicable laws and policies
ICC9S5	Demonstrate commitment to developing the highest education and quality-of-life potential of individuals with exceptional learning needs
ICC9S6	Demonstrate sensitivity for the culture, language, religion, gender, disability, socioeconomic status, and sexual orientation of individuals
ICC9S7	Practice within one's skill limits and obtain assistance as needed
ICC9S8	Use verbal, nonverbal, and written language effectively
ICC9S9	Conduct self-evaluation of instruction
ICC9S10	Access information on exceptionalities
ICC9S11	Reflect on one's practice to improve instruction and guide professional growth
ICC9S12	Engage in professional activities that benefit individuals with exceptional learning needs, their families, and one's colleagues
ICC9S13	Demonstrate commitment to engage in evidence-based practices
ECSE9S1	Recognize signs of emotional distress, neglect, and abuse, and follow reporting procedures
ECSE9S2	Integrate family systems theories and principles into professional practice

ECSE9S3	Respect family choices and goals
ECSE9S4	Apply models of team process in early childhood
ECSE9S5	Participate in activities of professional organizations relevant to early childhood special education and early intervention
ECSE9S6	Apply evidence-based and recommended practices for infants and young children including those from diverse backgrounds
ECSE9S7	Advocate on behalf of infants and young children and their families

Standard 10: Collaboration

Knowledge

ICC10K1	Models and strategies of consultation and collaboration
ICC10K2	Roles of individuals with exceptional learning needs, families, and school personnel, and community members in planning of an individualized program
ICC10K3	Concerns of families of individuals with exceptional learning needs and strategies to help address these concerns
ICC10K4	Culturally responsive factors that promote effective communication and collaboration with individuals with exceptional learning needs, families, school personnel, and community members
ECSE10K1	Structures supporting interagency collaboration, including interagency agreements, referral, and consultation

Skills

ICC10S1	Maintain confidential communication about individuals with exceptional learning needs
ICC10S2	Collaborate with families and others in assessment of individuals with exceptional learning needs
ICC10S3	Foster respectful and beneficial relationships between families and professionals
ICC10S4	Assist individuals with exceptional learning needs and their families in becoming active participants in the educational team
ICC10S5	Plan and conduct collaborative conferences with individuals with exceptional learning needs and their families
ICC10S6	Collaborate with school personnel and community members in integrating individuals with exceptional learning needs into various settings
ICC10S7	Use group problem-solving skills to develop, implement, and evaluate collaborative activities
ICC10S8	Model techniques and coach others in the use of instructional methods and accommodations
ICC10S9	Communicate with school personnel about the characteristics and needs of individuals with exceptional learning needs

ICC10S10	Communicate effectively with families of individuals with exceptional learning needs from diverse backgrounds
ICC10S11	Observe, evaluate, and provide feedback to paraeducators
ECSE10S1	Collaborate with caregivers, professionals, and agencies to support children's development and learning
ECSE10S2	Support families' choices and priorities in the development of goals and intervention strategies
ECSE10S3	Implement family-oriented services based on the family's identified resources, priorities, and concerns
ECSE10S4	Provide consultation in settings serving infants and young children
ECSE10S5	Involve families in evaluation of services
ECSE10S6	Participate as a team member to identify and enhance team roles, communication, and problem-solving
ECSE10S7	Employ adult learning principles in consulting and training family members and service providers
ECSE10S8	Assist the family in planning for transition
ECSE10S9	Implement processes and strategies that support transitions among settings for infants and young children

Initial Special Education Teachers of Individuals With Exceptional Learning Needs With Emotional and/or Behavioral Disorders

Standard 1: Foundations	
Knowledge	
ICC1K1	Models, theories, philosophies, and research methods that form the basis for special education practice
ICC1K2	Laws, policies, and ethical principles regarding behavior management planning and implementation
ICC1K3	Relationship of special education to the organization and function of educational agencies
ICC1K4	Rights and responsibilities of individuals with exceptional learning needs, parents, teachers and other professionals, and schools related to exceptional learning needs
ICC1K5	Issues in definition and identification of individuals with exceptional learning needs, including those from culturally and linguistically diverse backgrounds
ICC1K6	Issues, assurances and due process rights related to assessment, eligibility, and placement within a continuum of services
ICC1K7	Family systems and the role of families in the educational process
ICC1K8	Historical points of view and contribution of culturally and/or linguistically diverse groups
ICC1K9	Impact of the dominant culture on shaping schools and the individuals who study and work in them
ICC1K10	Potential impact of differences in values, languages, and customs that can exist between the home and school
BD1K1	Specialized terminology in the area of emotional and/or behavioral disorders
BD1K2	Impacts of the legal, judicial, and educational systems serving individuals with emotional and/or behavioral disorders
BD1K3	Principles of reinforcement theory in serving individuals with emotional and/or behavioral disorders
BD1K4	Principles of least restrictive environment for individuals with emotional and/or behavioral disorders
Skills	
ICC1S1	Articulate personal philosophy of special education
	None in addition to the initial common core
Standard 2: Development and Characteristics of Learners	
Knowledge	
ICC2K1	Typical and atypical human growth and development
ICC2K2	Educational implications of characteristics of various exceptionalities

ICC2K3	Characteristics and effects of the cultural and environmental milieu of the individual with exceptional learning needs and the family
ICC2K4	Family systems and the role of families in supporting development
ICC2K5	Similarities and differences of individuals with and without exceptional learning needs
ICC2K6	Similarities and differences among individuals with exceptional learning needs
ICC2K7	Effects of various medications on individuals with exceptional learning needs
BD2K1	Range of characteristics within and among individuals with emotional and/or behavioral disorders
BD2K2	Co-occurrence of emotional and/or behavioral disorders with other exceptionalities

Skills

	None in addition to the initial common core

Standard 3: Individual Learning Differences

Knowledge

ICC3K1	Effects an exceptional condition(s) can have on an individual's life
ICC3K2	Impact of learners' academic and social abilities, attitudes, interests, and values on instruction and career development
ICC3K3	Variations in beliefs, traditions, and values across and within cultures and their effects on relationships among individuals with exceptional learning needs, family, and schooling
ICC3K4	Cultural perspectives influencing the relationships among families, schools, and communities as related to instruction
ICC3K5	Differing ways of learning of individuals with exceptional learning needs, including those from culturally diverse backgrounds and strategies for addressing these differences
BD3K1	Performance issues in the core academic content for individuals with emotional and/or behavioral disorders
BD3K2	Impact of emotional factors on the learning process

Skills

	None in addition to the initial common core

Standard 4: Instructional Strategies

Knowledge

ICC4K1	Evidence-based practices validated for specific characteristics of learners and settings
	None in addition to the Initial Common Core

Skills

ICC4S1	Use strategies to facilitate integration into various settings
ICC4S2	Teach individuals to use self-assessment, problem-solving, and other cognitive strategies to meet their needs
ICC4S3	Select, adapt, and use instructional strategies and materials according to characteristics of the individual with exceptional learning needs
ICC4S4	Use strategies to facilitate maintenance and generalization of skills across learning environments
ICC4S5	Use procedures to increase the individual's self-awareness, self-management, self-control, self-reliance, and self-esteem
ICC4S6	Use strategies that promote successful transitions for individuals with exceptional learning needs
BD4S1	Use nonaversive techniques to support targeted behavior and maintain attention of individuals with emotional and/or behavioral disorders
BD4S2	Use evidence-based practices to enhance academic and social competence
BD4S3	Use prevention and intervention strategies for individuals at risk for emotional and/or behavioral disorders
BD4S4	Use strategies to teach alternative behaviors

Standard 5: Learning Environments/Social Interactions

Knowledge

ICC5K1	Demands of learning environments
ICC5K2	Basic classroom management theories and strategies for individuals with exceptional learning needs
ICC5K3	Effective management of teaching and learning
ICC5K4	Teacher attitudes and behaviors that influence behavior of individuals with exceptional learning needs
ICC5K5	Social skills needed for educational and other environments
ICC5K6	Strategies for crisis prevention and intervention
ICC5K7	Strategies for preparing individuals to live harmoniously and productively in a culturally diverse world
ICC5K8	Ways to create learning environments that allow individuals to retain and appreciate their own and each other's respective language and cultural heritage
ICC5K9	Ways specific cultures are negatively stereotyped
ICC5K10	Strategies used by diverse populations to cope with a legacy of former and continuing racism
BD5K1	Advantages and disadvantages of placement options for individuals with emotional and/or behavior disorders

Skills	
ICC5S1	Create a safe, equitable, positive, and supportive learning environment in which diversities are valued
ICC5S2	Identify realistic expectations for personal and social behavior in various settings
ICC5S3	Identify supports needed for integration into various program placements
ICC5S4	Design learning environments that encourage active participation in individual and group activities
ICC5S5	Modify the learning environment to manage behaviors
ICC5S6	Use performance data and information from all stakeholders to make or suggest modifications in learning environments
ICC5S7	Establish and maintain rapport with individuals with and without exceptional learning needs
ICC5S8	Teach self-advocacy
ICC5S9	Create an environment that encourages self-advocacy and increased independence
ICC5S10	Use effective and varied behavior management strategies
ICC5S11	Use the least intensive behavior management strategy consistent with the needs of the individual with exceptional learning needs
ICC5S12	Design and manage daily routines
ICC5S13	Organize, develop, and sustain learning environments that support positive intracultural and intercultural experiences
ICC5S14	Mediate controversial intercultural issues among individuals with exceptional learning needs within the learning environment in ways that enhance any culture, group, or person
ICC5S15	Structure, direct, and support the activities of paraeducators, volunteers, and tutors
ICC5S16	Use universal precautions
	None in addition to the Initial Common Core

Standard 6: Language

Knowledge	
ICC6K1	Effects of cultural and linguistic differences on growth and development
ICC6K2	Characteristics of one's own culture and use of language and the ways in which these can differ from other cultures and uses of languages
ICC6K3	Ways of behaving and communicating among cultures that can lead to misinterpretation and misunderstanding
ICC6K4	Augmentative and assistive communication strategies
	None in addition to the Initial Common Core

ICC6S1	Use strategies to support and enhance communication skills of individuals with exceptional learning needs
ICC6S2	Use communication strategies and resources to facilitate understanding of subject matter for individuals with exceptional learning needs whose primary language is not the dominant language
	None in addition to the Initial Common Core

Standard 7: Instructional Planning

Knowledge

ICC7K1	Theories and research that form the basis of curriculum development and instructional practice
ICC7K2	Scope and sequences of general and special curricula
ICC7K3	National, state or provincial, and local curricula standards
ICC7K4	Technology for planning and managing the teaching and learning environment
ICC7K5	Roles and responsibilities of the paraeducator related to instruction, intervention, and direct service
	None in addition to the Initial Common Core

Skills

ICC7S1	Identify and prioritize areas of the general curriculum and accommodations for individuals with exceptional learning needs
ICC7S2	Develop and implement comprehensive, longitudinal individualized programs in collaboration with team members
ICC7S3	Involve the individual and family in setting instructional goals and monitoring progress
ICC7S4	Use functional assessments to develop intervention plans
ICC7S5	Use task analysis
ICC7S6	Sequence, implement, and evaluate individualized learning objectives
ICC7S7	Integrate affective, social, and life skills with academic curricula
ICC7S8	Develop and select instructional content, resources, and strategies that respond to cultural, linguistic, and gender differences
ICC7S9	Incorporate and implement instructional and assistive technology into the educational program
ICC7S10	Prepare lesson plans
ICC7S11	Prepare and organize materials to implement daily lesson plans
ICC7S12	Use instructional time effectively

ICC7S13	Make responsive adjustments to instruction based on continual observations
ICC7S14	Prepare individuals to exhibit self-enhancing behavior in response to societal attitudes and actions
ICC7S15	Evaluate and modify instructional practices in response to ongoing assessment data
BD7S1	Plan and implement individualized reinforcement systems and environmental modifications at levels equal to the intensity of the behavior
BD7S2	Integrate academic and affective instruction with behavior management for individuals and groups with emotional/behavioral disorders

Standard 8: Assessment

Knowledge

ICC8K1	Basic terminology used in assessment
ICC8K2	Legal provisions and ethical principles regarding assessment of individuals
ICC8K3	Screening, prereferral, referral, and classification procedures
ICC8K4	Use and limitations of assessment instruments
ICC8K5	National, state or provincial, and local accommodations and modifications
	None in addition to the Initial Common Core

Skills

ICC8S1	Gather relevant background information
ICC8S2	Administer nonbiased formal and informal assessments
ICC8S3	Use technology to conduct assessments
ICC8S4	Develop or modify individualized assessment strategies
ICC8S5	Interpret information from formal and informal assessments
ICC8S6	Use assessment information in making eligibility, program, and placement decisions for individuals with exceptional learning needs, including those from culturally and/or linguistically diverse backgrounds
ICC8S7	Report assessment results to all stakeholders using effective communication skills
ICC8S8	Evaluate instruction and monitor progress of individuals with exceptional learning needs
ICC8S9	Create and maintain records
BD8S1	Conduct functional behavior assessments
BD8S2	Assess social behaviors of individuals with emotional and/or behavioral disorders
BD8S3	Prepare functional behavior assessment reports on individuals with emotional and/or behavioral disorders

Standard 9: Professional And Ethical Practice

Knowledge

ICC9K1	Personal cultural biases and differences that affect one's teaching
ICC9K2	Importance of the teacher serving as a model for individuals with exceptional learning needs
ICC9K3	Continuum of lifelong professional development
ICC9K4	Methods to remain current regarding research-validated practice
	None in addition to the Initial Common Core

Skills

ICC9S1	Practice within the CEC Code of Ethics and other standards of the profession
ICC9S2	Uphold high standards of competence and integrity and exercise sound judgment in the practice of the professional
ICC9S3	Act ethically in advocating for appropriate services
ICC9S4	Conduct professional activities in compliance with applicable laws and policies
ICC9S5	Demonstrate commitment to developing the highest education and quality-of-life potential of individuals with exceptional learning needs
ICC9S6	Demonstrate sensitivity for the culture, language, religion, gender, disability, socioeconomic status, and sexual orientation of individuals
ICC9S7	Practice within one's skill limits and obtain assistance as needed
ICC9S8	Use verbal, nonverbal, and written language effectively
ICC9S9	Conduct self-evaluation of instruction
ICC9S10	Access information on exceptionalities
ICC9S11	Reflect on one's practice to improve instruction and guide professional growth
ICC9S12	Engage in professional activities that benefit individuals with exceptional learning needs, their families, and one's colleagues
ICC9S13	Demonstrate commitment to engage in evidence-based practices
	None in addition to the Initial Common Core

Standard 10: Collaboration

Knowledge

ICC10K1	Models and strategies of consultation and collaboration
ICC10K2	Roles of individuals with exceptional learning needs, families, and school and community personnel in planning of an individualized program
ICC10K3	Concerns of families of individuals with exceptional learning needs and strategies to help address these concerns
ICC10K4	Culturally responsive factors that promote effective communication and collaboration with individuals with exceptional learning needs, families, school personnel, and community members
	None in addition to the Initial Common Core

Skills

ICC10S1	Maintain confidential communication about individuals with exceptional learning needs
ICC10S2	Collaborate with families and others in assessment of individuals with exceptional learning needs
ICC10S3	Foster respectful and beneficial relationships between families and professionals
ICC10S4	Assist individuals with exceptional learning needs and their families in becoming active participants in the educational team
ICC10S5	Plan and conduct collaborative conferences with individuals with exceptional learning needs and their families
ICC10S6	Collaborate with school personnel and community members in integrating individuals with exceptional learning needs into various settings
ICC10S7	Use group problem-solving skills to develop, implement, and evaluate collaborative activities
ICC10S8	Model techniques and coach others in the use of instructional methods and accommodations
ICC10S9	Communicate with school personnel about the characteristics and needs of individuals with exceptional learning needs
ICC10S10	Communicate effectively with families of individuals with exceptional learning needs from diverse backgrounds
ICC10S11	Observe, evaluate, and provide feedback to paraeducators
BD10S1	Share effective behavior management techniques with families

Initial Special Education Teachers of Individuals With Exceptional Learning Needs With Gifts and Talents

Standard 1: Foundations	
Knowledge	
GT1K1	Historical foundations of gifted and talented education including points of view and contributions of individuals from diverse backgrounds
GT1K2	Key philosophies, theories, models, and research supporting gifted and talented education
GT1K3	Local, state/provincial and federal laws and policies related to gifted and talented education
GT1K4	Issues in conceptions, definitions, and identification of gifts and talents, including those of individuals from diverse backgrounds
GT1K5	Impact of the dominant culture's role in shaping schools and the differences in values, languages, and customs between school and home
GT1K6	Societal, cultural, and economic factors, including anti-intellectualism and equity vs. excellence, enhancing or inhibiting the development of gifts and talents
GT1K7	Key issues and trends, including diversity and inclusion, connecting general, special, and gifted and talented education
Skills	
	None

Standard 2: Development and Characteristics of Learners	
Knowledge	
GT2K1	Cognitive and affective characteristics of individuals with gifts and talents, including those from diverse backgrounds, in intellectual, academic, creative, leadership, and artistic domains
GT2K2	Characteristics and effects of culture and environment on the development of individuals with gifts and talents
GT2K3	Role of families and communities in supporting the development of individuals with gifts and talents
GT2K4	Advanced developmental milestones of individuals with gifts and talents from early childhood through adolescence
GT2K5	Similarities and differences within the group of individuals with gifts and talents as compared to the general population
Skills	
	None

Standard 3: Individual Learning Differences

Knowledge

GT3K1	Influences of diversity factors on individuals with exceptional learning needs
GT3K2	Academic and affective characteristics and learning needs of individuals with gifts, talents, and disabilities
GT3K3	Idiosyncratic learning patterns of individuals with gifts and talents, including those from diverse backgrounds
GT3K4	Influences of different beliefs, traditions, and values across and within diverse groups on relationships among individuals with gifts and talents, their families, schools, and communities

Skills

GT3S1	Integrate perspectives of diverse groups into planning instruction for individuals with gifts and talents

Standard 4: Instructional Strategies

Knowledge

GT4K1	School and community resources, including content specialists, which support differentiation
GT4K2	Curricular, instructional, and management strategies effective for individuals with exceptional learning needs

Skills

GT4S1	Apply pedagogical content knowledge to instructing learners with gifts and talents
GT4S2	Apply higher-level thinking and metacognitive models to content areas to meet the needs of individuals with gifts and talents
GT4S3	Provide opportunities for individuals with gifts and talents to explore, develop, or research their areas of interest or talent
GT4S4	Pre-assess the learning needs of individuals with gifts and talents in various domains and adjust instruction based on continual assessment
GT4S5	Pace delivery of curriculum and instruction consistent with needs of individuals with gifts and talents
GT4S6	Engage individuals with gifts and talents from all backgrounds in challenging, multicultural curricula
GT4S7	Use information and/or assistive technologies to meet the needs of individuals with exceptional learning needs

Standard 5: Learning Environments/Social Interactions

Knowledge

GT5K1	Ways in which groups are stereotyped and experience historical and current discrimination and implications for gifted and talented education

GT5K2	Influence of social and emotional development on interpersonal relationships and learning of individuals with gifts and talents

Skills

GT5S1	Design learning opportunities for individuals with gifts and talents that promote self-awareness, positive peer relationships, intercultural experiences, and leadership
GT5S2	Create learning environments for individuals with gifted and talents that promote self-awareness, self-efficacy, leadership, and lifelong learning
GT5S3	Create safe learning environments for individuals with gifts and talents that encourage active participation in individual and group activities to enhance independence, interdependence, and positive peer-relationships
GT5S4	Create learning environments and intercultural experiences that allow individuals with gifts and talents to appreciate their own and others' language and cultural heritage
GT5S5	Develop social interaction and coping skills in individuals with gifts and talents to address personal and social issues, including discrimination and stereotyping

Standard 6: Language

Knowledge

GT6K1	Forms and methods of communication essential to the education of individuals with gifts and talents, including those from diverse backgrounds
GT6K2	Impact of diversity on communication
GT6K3	Implications of culture, behavior, and language on the development of individuals with gifts and talents

Skills

GT6S1	Access resources and develop strategies to enhance communication skills for individuals with gifts and talents including those with advanced communication and/or English language learners
GT6S2	Use advanced oral and written communication tools, including assistive technologies, to enhance the learning experiences of individuals with exceptional learning needs

Standard 7: Instructional Planning

Knowledge

GT7K1	Theories and research models that form the basis of curriculum development and instructional practice for individuals with gifts and talents
GT7K2	Features that distinguish differentiated curriculum from general curricula for individuals with exceptional learning needs
GT7K3	Curriculum emphases for individuals with gifts and talents within cognitive, affective, aesthetic, social, and linguistic domains

Skills	
GT7S1	Align differentiated instructional plans with local, state or provincial, and national curricular standards
GT7S2	Design differentiated learning plans for individuals with gifts and talents, including individuals from diverse backgrounds
GT7S3	Develop scope and sequence plans for individuals with gifts and talents
GT7S4	Select curriculum resources, strategies, and product options that respond to cultural, linguistic, and intellectual differences among individuals with gifts and talents
GT7S5	Select and adapt a variety of differentiated curricula that incorporate advanced, conceptually challenging, in-depth, distinctive, and complex content
GT7S6	Integrate academic and career guidance experiences into the learning plan for individuals with gifts and talents

Standard 8: Assessment

Knowledge	
GT8K1	Processes and procedures for the identification of individuals with gifts and talents
GT8K2	Uses, limitations, and interpretation of multiple assessments in different domains for identifying individuals with exceptional learning needs, including those from diverse backgrounds
GT8K3	Uses and limitations of assessments documenting academic growth of individuals with gifts and talents
Skills	
GT8S1	Use nonbiased and equitable approaches for identifying individuals with gifts and talents, including those from diverse backgrounds
GT8S2	Use technically adequate qualitative and quantitative assessments for identifying and placing individuals with gifts and talents
GT8S3	Develop differentiated curriculum-based assessments for use in instructional planning and delivery for individuals with gifts and talents
GT8S4	Use alternative assessments and technologies to evaluate learning of individuals with gifts and talents

Standard 9: Professional and Ethical Practice

Knowledge	
GT9K1	Personal and cultural frames of reference that affect one's teaching of individuals with gifts and talents, including biases about individuals from diverse backgrounds
GT9K2	Organizations and publications relevant to the field of gifted and talented education
Skills	
GT9S1	Assess personal skills and limitations in teaching individuals with exceptional learning needs

GT9S2	Maintain confidential communication about individuals with gifts and talents
GT9S3	Encourage and model respect for the full range of diversity among individuals with gifts and talents
GT9S4	Conduct activities in gifted and talented education in compliance with laws, policies, and standards of ethical practice
GT9S5	Improve practice through continuous research-supported professional development in gifted education and related fields
GT9S6	Participate in the activities of professional organizations related to gifted and talented education
GT9S7	Reflect on personal practice to improve teaching and guide professional growth in gifted and talented education

Standard 10: Collaboration

Knowledge

GT10K1	Culturally responsive behaviors that promote effective communication and collaboration with individuals with gifts and talents, their families, school personnel, and community members

Skills

GT10S1	Respond to concerns of families of individuals with gifts and talents
GT10S2	Collaborate with stakeholders outside the school setting who serve individuals with exceptional learning needs and their families
GT10S3	Advocate for the benefit of individuals with gifts and talents and their families
GT10S4	Collaborate with individuals with gifts and talents, their families, general, and special educators, and other school staff to articulate a comprehensive preschool through secondary educational program
GT10S5	Collaborate with families, community members, and professionals in assessment of individuals with gifts and talents
GT10S6	Communicate and consult with school personnel about the characteristics and needs of individuals with gifts and talents, including individuals from diverse backgrounds

Initial Special Education Teachers of Individuals With Exceptional Learning Needs With Developmental Disabilities and/or Autism

Standard 1: Foundations

Knowledge

ICC1K1	Models, theories, philosophies, and research methods that form the basis for special education practice
ICC1K2	Laws, policies, and ethical principles regarding behavior management planning and implementation
ICC1K3	Relationship of special education to the organization and function of educational agencies
ICC1K4	Rights and responsibilities of individuals with exceptional learning needs, parents, teachers, and other professionals, and schools related to exceptional learning needs
ICC1K5	Issues in definition and identification of individuals with exceptional learning needs, including those from culturally and linguistically diverse backgrounds
ICC1K6	Issues, assurances and due process rights related to assessment, eligibility, and placement within a continuum of services
ICC1K7	Family systems and the role of families in the educational process
ICC1K8	Historical points of view and contribution of culturally diverse groups
ICC1K9	Impact of the dominant culture on shaping schools and the individuals who study and work in them
ICC1K10	Potential impact of differences in values, languages, and customs that can exist between the home and school
DD1K1	Definitions and issues related to the identification of individuals with developmental disabilities
DD1K2	Continuum of placement and services available for individuals with developmental disabilities
DD1K3	Historical foundations and classic studies of developmental disabilities
DD1K4	Trends and practices in the field of developmental disabilities
DD1K5	Theories of behavior problems of individuals with developmental disabilities

Skills

ICC1S1	Articulate personal philosophy of special education

Standard 2: Development and Characteristics of Learners

Knowledge

ICC2K1	Typical and atypical human growth and development
ICC2K2	Educational implications of characteristics of various exceptionalities

ICC2K3	Characteristics and effects of the cultural and environmental milieu of the individual with exceptional learning needs and the family
ICC2K4	Family systems and the role of families in supporting development
ICC2K5	Similarities and differences of individuals with and without exceptional learning needs
ICC2K6	Similarities and differences among individuals with exceptional learning needs
ICC2K7	Effects of various medications on individuals with exceptional learning needs
DD2K1	Medical aspects of developmental disabilities and their implications for learning
DD2K2	Psychological, social/emotional, and motor characteristics of individuals with developmental disabilities
DD2K3	Identification of significant core deficit areas for individuals with pervasive developmental disabilities, autism, and autism spectrum disorder
DD2K4	Factors that influence overrepresentation of culturally and/or linguistically diverse individuals
DD2K5	Complications and implications of medical support services

Skills	
	None

Standard 3: Individual Learning Differences

Knowledge	
ICC3K1	Effects an exceptional condition(s) can have on an individual's life
ICC3K2	Impact of learners' academic and social abilities, attitudes, interests, and values on instruction and career development
ICC3K3	Variations in beliefs, traditions, and values across and within cultures and their effects on relationships among individuals with exceptional learning needs, family, and schooling
ICC3K4	Cultural perspectives influencing the relationships among families, schools, and communities as related to instruction
ICC3K5	Differing ways of learning of individuals with exceptional learning needs, including those from culturally diverse backgrounds and strategies for addressing these differences
DD3K1	Impact of multiple disabilities on behavior

Skills	
	None

Standard 4: Instructional Strategies

Knowledge

ICC4K1	Evidence-based practices validated for specific characteristics of learners and settings
DD4K1	Specialized materials for individuals with developmental disabilities
DD4K2	Evidence-based practices for teaching individuals with pervasive developmental disabilities, autism, and autism spectrum disorders
DD4K3	Specialized curriculum specifically designed to meet the needs of individuals with pervasive developmental disabilities, autism, and autism spectrum disorders

Skills

ICC4S1	Use strategies to facilitate integration into various settings
ICC4S2	Teach individuals to use self-assessment, problem-solving, and other cognitive strategies to meet their needs
ICC4S3	Select, adapt, and use instructional strategies and materials according to characteristics of the individual with exceptional learning needs
ICC4S4	Use strategies to facilitate maintenance and generalization of skills across learning environments
ICC4S5	Use procedures to increase the individual's self-awareness, self-management, self-control, self-reliance, and self-esteem
ICC4S6	Use strategies that promote successful transitions for individuals with exceptional learning needs
DD4S1	Use specialized teaching strategies matched to the need of the learner
DD4S2	Relate levels of support to the needs of the individual

Standard 5: Learning Environments/Social Interactions

Knowledge

ICC5K1	Demands of learning environments
ICC5K2	Basic classroom management theories and strategies for individuals with exceptional learning needs
ICC5K3	Effective management of teaching and learning
ICC5K4	Teacher attitudes and behaviors that influence behavior of individuals with exceptional learning needs
ICC5K5	Social skills needed for educational and other environments
ICC5K6	Strategies for crisis prevention and intervention
ICC5K7	Strategies for preparing individuals to live harmoniously and productively in a culturally diverse world

ICC5K8	Ways to create learning environments that allow individuals to retain and appreciate their own and each other's respective language and cultural heritage
ICC5K9	Ways specific cultures are negatively stereotyped
ICC5K10	Strategies used by diverse populations to cope with a legacy of former and continuing racism

Skills

ICC5S1	Create a safe, equitable, positive, and supportive learning environment in which diversities are valued
ICC5S2	Identify realistic expectations for personal and social behavior in various settings
ICC5S3	Identify supports needed for integration into various program placements
ICC5S4	Design learning environments that encourage active participation in individual and group activities
ICC5S5	Modify the learning environment to manage behaviors
ICC5S6	Use performance data and information from all stakeholders to make or suggest modifications in learning environments
ICC5S7	Establish and maintain rapport with individuals with and without exceptional learning needs
ICC5S8	Teach self-advocacy
ICC5S9	Create an environment that encourages self-advocacy and increased independence
ICC5S10	Use effective and varied behavior management strategies
ICC5S11	Use the least intensive behavior management strategy consistent with the needs of the individual with exceptional learning needs
ICC5S12	Design and manage daily routines
ICC5S13	Organize, develop, and sustain learning environments that support positive intracultural and intercultural experiences
ICC5S14	Mediate controversial intercultural issues among individuals with exceptional learning needs within the learning environment in ways that enhance any culture, group, or person
ICC5S15	Structure, direct, and support the activities of paraeducators, volunteers, and tutors
ICC5S16	Use universal precautions
DD5S1	Provide instruction in community-based settings
DD5S2	Demonstrate transfer, lifting and positioning techniques
DD5S3	Use and maintain assistive technologies
DD5S4	Structure the physical environment to provide optimal learning for individuals with developmental disabilities

DD5S5	Plan instruction for individuals with developmental disabilities in a variety of placement settings

Standard 6: Language

Knowledge

ICC6K1	Effects of cultural and linguistic differences on growth and development
ICC6K2	Characteristics of one's own culture and use of language and the ways in which these can differ from other cultures and uses of languages
ICC6K3	Ways of behaving and communicating among cultures that can lead to misinterpretation and misunderstanding
ICC6K4	Augmentative and assistive communication strategies

Skills

ICC6S1	Use strategies to support and enhance communication skills of individuals with exceptional learning needs
ICC6S2	Use communication strategies and resources to facilitate understanding of subject matter for individuals with exceptional learning needs whose primary language is not the dominant language
DD6S1	Plan instruction on the use of alternative and augmentative communication systems
DD6S2	Use pragmatic language instruction to facilitate ongoing social skills instruction

Standard 7: Instructional Planning

Knowledge

ICC7K1	Theories and research that form the basis of curriculum development and instructional practice
ICC7K2	Scope and sequences of general and special curricula
ICC7K3	National, state or provincial, and local curricula standards
ICC7K4	Technology for planning and managing the teaching and learning environment
ICC7K5	Roles and responsibilities of the paraeducator related to instruction, intervention, and direct service
DD7K1	Model career/vocational transition programs for individuals with developmental disabilities including career/vocational transition

Skills

ICC7S1	Identify and prioritize areas of the general curriculum and accommodations for individuals with exceptional learning needs
ICC7S2	Develop and implement comprehensive, longitudinal individualized programs in collaboration with team members

ICC7S3	Involve the individual and family in setting instructional goals and monitoring progress
ICC7S4	Use functional assessments to develop intervention plans
ICC7S5	Use task analysis
ICC7S6	Sequence, implement, and evaluate individualized learning objectives
ICC7S7	Integrate affective, social, and life skills with academic curricula
ICC7S8	Develop and select instructional content, resources, and strategies that respond to cultural, linguistic, and gender differences
ICC7S9	Incorporate and implement instructional and assistive technology into the educational program
ICC7S10	Prepare lesson plans
ICC7S11	Prepare and organize materials to implement daily lesson plans
ICC7S12	Use instructional time effectively
ICC7S13	Make responsive adjustments to instruction based on continual observations
ICC7S14	Prepare individuals to exhibit self-enhancing behavior in response to societal attitudes and actions
ICC7S15	Evaluate and modify instructional practices in response to ongoing assessment data
DD7S1	Plan instruction for independent functional life skills relevant to the community, personal living, sexuality, and employment
DD7S2	Plan and implement instruction for individuals with developmental disabilities that is both age-appropriate and ability-appropriate
DD7S3	Select and plan for integration of related services into the instructional program for individuals with developmental disabilities
DD7S4	Design, implement, and evaluate specialized instructional programs for persons with developmental disabilities that enhance social participation across environments

Standard 8: Assessment

Knowledge

ICC8K1	Basic terminology used in assessment
ICC8K2	Legal provisions and ethical principles regarding assessment of individuals
ICC8K3	Screening, prereferral, referral, and classification procedures
ICC8K4	Use and limitations of assessment instruments
ICC8K5	National, state or provincial, and local accommodations and modifications
DD8K1	Specialized terminology used in the assessment of individuals with developmental disabilities

DD8K2	Environmental assessment conditions that promote maximum performance of individuals with developmental disabilities
DD8K3	Adaptive behavior assessment
DD8K4	Laws and policies regarding referral and placement procedures for individuals with developmental disabilities

Skills

ICC8S1	Gather relevant background information
ICC8S2	Administer nonbiased formal and informal assessments
ICC8S3	Use technology to conduct assessments
ICC8S4	Develop or modify individualized assessment strategies
ICC8S5	Interpret information from formal and informal assessments
ICC8S6	Use assessment information in making eligibility, program, and placement decisions for individuals with exceptional learning needs, including those from culturally and/or linguistically diverse backgrounds
ICC8S7	Report assessment results to all stakeholders using effective communication skills
ICC8S8	Evaluate instruction and monitor progress of individuals with exceptional learning needs
ICC8S9	Create and maintain records
DD8S1	Select, adapt, and use instructional assessment tools and methods to accommodate the abilities and needs of individuals with mental retardation and developmental disabilities

Standard 9: Professional And Ethical Practice

Knowledge

ICC9K1	Personal cultural biases and differences that affect one's teaching
ICC9K2	Importance of the teacher serving as a model for individuals with exceptional learning needs
ICC9K3	Continuum of lifelong professional development
ICC9K4	Methods to remain current regarding research-validated practice
DD9K1	Organizations and publications in the field of developmental disabilities

Skills

ICC9S1	Practice within the CEC Code of Ethics and other standards of the profession
ICC9S2	Uphold high standards of competence and integrity and exercise sound judgment in the practice of the professional
ICC9S3	Act ethically in advocating for appropriate services

ICC9S4	Conduct professional activities in compliance with applicable laws and policies
ICC9S5	Demonstrate commitment to developing the highest education and quality-of-life potential of individuals with exceptional learning needs
ICC9S6	Demonstrate sensitivity for the culture, language, religion, gender, disability, socioeconomic status, and sexual orientation of individuals
ICC9S7	Practice within one's skill limits and obtain assistance as needed
ICC9S8	Use verbal, nonverbal, and written language effectively
ICC9S9	Conduct self-evaluation of instruction
ICC9S10	Access information on exceptionalities
ICC9S11	Reflect on one's practice to improve instruction and guide professional growth
ICC9S12	Engage in professional activities that benefit individuals with exceptional learning needs, their families, and one's colleagues
ICC9S13	Demonstrate commitment to engage in evidence-based practices
DD9S1	Participate in the activities of professional organizations in the field of developmental disabilities

Standard 10: Collaboration

Knowledge

ICC10K1	Models and strategies of consultation and collaboration
ICC10K2	Roles of individuals with exceptional learning needs, families, and school and community personnel in planning of an individualized program
ICC10K3	Concerns of families of individuals with exceptional learning needs and strategies to help address these concerns
ICC10K4	Culturally responsive factors that promote effective communication and collaboration with individuals with exceptional learning needs, families, school personnel, and community members
DD10K1	Services, networks, and organizations for individuals with developmental disabilities

Skills

ICC10S1	Maintain confidential communication about individuals with exceptional learning needs
ICC10S2	Collaborate with families and others in assessment of individuals with exceptional learning needs
ICC10S3	Foster respectful and beneficial relationships between families and professionals
ICC10S4	Assist individuals with exceptional learning needs and their families in becoming active participants in the educational team

ICC10S5	Plan and conduct collaborative conferences with individuals with exceptional learning needs and their families
ICC10S6	Collaborate with school personnel and community members in integrating individuals with exceptional learning needs into various settings
ICC10S7	Use group problem-solving skills to develop, implement, and evaluate collaborative activities
ICC10S8	Model techniques and coach others in the use of instructional methods and accommodations
ICC10S9	Communicate with school personnel about the characteristics and needs of individuals with exceptional learning needs
ICC10S10	Communicate effectively with families of individuals with exceptional learning needs from diverse backgrounds
ICC10S11	Observe, evaluate, and provide feedback to paraeducators
DD10S1	Collaborate with team members to plan transition to adulthood that encourages full community participation

Initial Special Education Teachers of Individuals With Exceptional Learning Needs With Learning Disabilities

Standard 1: Foundations	
Knowledge	
ICC1K1	Models, theories, philosophies, and research methods that form the basis for special education practice
ICC1K2	Laws, policies, and ethical principles regarding behavior management planning and implementation
ICC1K3	Relationship of special education to the organization and function of educational agencies
ICC1K4	Rights and responsibilities of individuals with exceptional learning needs, parents, teachers and other professionals, and schools related to exceptional learning needs
ICC1K5	Issues in definition and identification of individuals with exceptional learning needs, including those from culturally and/or linguistically diverse backgrounds
ICC1K6	Issues, assurances and due process rights related to assessment, eligibility, and placement within a continuum of services
ICC1K7	Family systems and the role of families in the educational process
ICC1K8	Historical points of view and contribution of culturally diverse groups
ICC1K9	Impact of the dominant culture on shaping schools and the individuals who study and work in them
ICC1K10	Potential impact of differences in values, languages, and customs that can exist between the home and school
LD1K1	Historical foundations, classical studies, and major contributors in the field of learning disabilities
LD1K2	Philosophies, theories, models, and issues related to individuals with learning disabilities.
LD1K3	Impact of legislation on the education of individuals with learning disabilities
LD1K4	Laws and policies regarding pre-referral, referral, and placement procedures for individuals who may have learning disabilities
LD1K5	Current definitions and issues related to the identification of individuals with learning disabilities.
Skills	
ICC1S1	Articulate personal philosophy of special education
	None in addition to Common Core
Standard 2: Development and Characteristics of Learners	
Knowledge	
ICC2K1	Typical and atypical human growth and development

ICC2K2	Educational implications of characteristics of various exceptionalities
ICC2K3	Characteristics and effects of the cultural and environmental milieu of the individual with exceptional learning needs and the family
ICC2K4	Family systems and the role of families in supporting development
ICC2K5	Similarities and differences of individuals with and without exceptional learning needs
ICC2K6	Similarities and differences among individuals with exceptional learning needs
ICC2K7	Effects of various medications on individuals with exceptional learning needs
LD2K1	Etiologies of learning disabilities
LD2K2	Neurobiological and medical factors that may impact the learning of individuals with learning disabilities
LD2K3	Psychological, social, and emotional characteristics of individuals with learning disabilities

Skills

	None in addition to Common Core

Standard 3: Individual Learning Differences

Knowledge

ICC3K1	Effects an exceptional condition(s) can have on an individual's life
ICC3K2	Impact of learners' academic and social abilities, attitudes, interests, and values on instruction and career development
ICC3K3	Variations in beliefs, traditions, and values across and within cultures and their effects on relationships among individuals with exceptional learning needs, family, and schooling
ICC3K4	Cultural perspectives influencing the relationships among families, schools, and communities as related to instruction
ICC3K5	Differing ways of learning of individuals with exceptional learning needs, including those from culturally diverse backgrounds and strategies for addressing these differences
LD3K1	Impact of co-existing conditions and exceptionalities on individuals with learning disabilities
LD3K2	Effects of phonological awareness on the reading abilities of individuals with learning disabilities
LD3K3	Impact learning disabilities may have on auditory and information processing skills

Skills

	None in addition to Initial Common Core

Standard 4: Instructional Strategies

Knowledge

ICC4K1	Evidence-based practices validated for specific characteristics of learners and settings
LD4K1	Strategies to prepare for and take tests
LD4K2	Methods for ensuring individual academic success in one-to-one, small-group, and large-group settings
LD4K3	Methods for increasing accuracy and proficiency in math calculations and applications
LD4K4	Methods for teaching individuals to independently use cognitive processing to solve problems
LD4K5	Methods for guiding individuals in identifying and organizing critical content

Skills

ICC4S1	Use strategies to facilitate integration into various settings
ICC4S2	Teach individuals to use self-assessment, problem-solving, and other cognitive strategies to meet their needs
ICC4S3	Select, adapt, and use instructional strategies and materials according to characteristics of the individual with exceptional learning needs
ICC4S4	Use strategies to facilitate maintenance and generalization of skills across learning environments
ICC4S5	Use procedures to increase the individual's self-awareness, self-management, self-control, self-reliance, and self-esteem
ICC4S6	Use strategies that promote successful transitions for individuals with exceptional learning needs
LD4S1	Use research-supported methods for academic and nonacademic instruction of individuals with learning disabilities
LD4S2	Use specialized methods for teaching basic skills
LD4S3	Modify the pace of instruction and provide organizational cues
LD4S4	Identify and teach basic structures and relationships within and across curricula
LD4S5	Use instructional methods to strengthen and compensate for deficits in perception, comprehension, memory, and retrieval
LD4S6	Use responses and errors to guide instructional decisions and provide feedback to learners
LD4S7	Identify and teach essential concepts, vocabulary, and content across the general curriculum
LD4S8	Use reading methods appropriate to the individual with learning disabilities
LD4S9	Implement systematic instruction in teaching reading comprehension and monitoring strategies
LD4S10	Teach strategies for organizing and composing written products

LD4S11	Implement systematic instruction to teach accuracy, fluency, and comprehension in content area reading and written language
LD4S12	Use methods to teach mathematics appropriate to the individual with learning disabilities
LD4S13	Teach learning strategies and study skills to acquire academic content

Standard 5: Learning Environments/Social Interactions

Knowledge

ICC5K1	Demands of learning environments
ICC5K2	Basic classroom management theories and strategies for individuals with exceptional learning needs
ICC5K3	Effective management of teaching and learning
ICC5K4	Teacher attitudes and behaviors that influence behavior of individuals with exceptional learning needs
ICC5K5	Social skills needed for educational and other environments
ICC5K6	Strategies for crisis prevention and intervention
ICC5K7	Strategies for preparing individuals to live harmoniously and productively in a culturally diverse world
ICC5K8	Ways to create learning environments that allow individuals to retain and appreciate their own and each other's respective language and cultural heritage
ICC5K9	Ways specific cultures are negatively stereotyped
ICC5K10	Strategies used by diverse populations to cope with a legacy of former and continuing racism
	None in addition to Initial Common Core

Skills

ICC5S1	Create a safe, equitable, positive, and supportive learning environment in which diversities are valued
ICC5S2	Identify realistic expectations for personal and social behavior in various settings
ICC5S3	Identify supports needed for integration into various program placements
ICC5S4	Design learning environments that encourage active participation in individual and group activities
ICC5S5	Modify the learning environment to manage behaviors
ICC5S6	Use performance data and information from all stakeholders to make or suggest modifications in learning environments
ICC5S7	Establish and maintain rapport with individuals with and without exceptional learning needs
ICC5S8	Teach self-advocacy
ICC5S9	Create an environment that encourages self-advocacy and increased independence

ICC5S10	Use effective and varied behavior management strategies
ICC5S11	Use the least intensive behavior management strategy consistent with the needs of the individual with exceptional learning needs
ICC5S12	Design and manage daily routines
ICC5S13	Organize, develop, and sustain learning environments that support positive intracultural and intercultural experiences
ICC5S14	Mediate controversial intercultural issues among individuals with exceptional learning needs within the learning environment in ways that enhance any culture, group, or person
ICC5S15	Structure, direct, and support the activities of paraeducators, volunteers, and tutors
ICC5S16	Use universal precautions
LD5S1	Teach individuals with learning disabilities to give and receive meaningful feedback from peers and adults

Standard 6: Language

Knowledge

ICC6K1	Effects of cultural and linguistic differences on growth and development
ICC6K2	Characteristics of one's own culture and use of language and the ways in which these can differ from other cultures and uses of languages
ICC6K3	Ways of behaving and communicating among cultures that can lead to misinterpretation and misunderstanding
ICC6K4	Augmentative and assistive communication strategies
LD6K1	Typical language development and how that may differ for individuals with learning disabilities
LD6K2	Impact of language development and listening comprehension on academic and nonacademic learning of individuals with learning disabilities

Skills

ICC6S1	Use strategies to support and enhance communication skills of individuals with exceptional learning needs
ICC6S2	Use communication strategies and resources to facilitate understanding of subject matter for individuals with exceptional learning needs whose primary language is not the dominant language
LD6S1	Enhance vocabulary development
LD6S2	Teach strategies for spelling accuracy and generalization
LD6S3	Teach methods and strategies for producing legible documents
LD6S4	Teach individuals with learning disabilities to monitor for errors in oral and written communications

Standard 7: Instructional Planning

Knowledge

ICC7K1	Theories and research that form the basis of curriculum development and instructional practice
ICC7K2	Scope and sequences of general and special curricula
ICC7K3	National, state or provincial, and local curricula standards
ICC7K4	Technology for planning and managing the teaching and learning environment
ICC7K5	Roles and responsibilities of the paraeducator related to instruction, intervention, and direct service
LD7K1	Relationships among reading instruction methods and learning disabilities
LD7K2	Sources of specialized curricula, materials, and resources for individuals with learning disabilities
LD7K3	Interventions and services for children who may be at risk for learning disabilities

Skills

ICC7S1	Identify and prioritize areas of the general curriculum and accommodations for individuals with exceptional learning needs
ICC7S2	Develop and implement comprehensive, longitudinal individualized programs in collaboration with team members
ICC7S3	Involve the individual and family in setting instructional goals and monitoring progress
ICC7S4	Use functional assessments to develop intervention plans
ICC7S5	Use task analysis
ICC7S6	Sequence, implement, and evaluate individualized learning objectives
ICC7S7	Integrate affective, social, and life skills with academic curricula
ICC7S8	Develop and select instructional content, resources, and strategies that respond to cultural, linguistic, and gender differences
ICC7S9	Incorporate and implement instructional and assistive technology into the educational program
ICC7S10	Prepare lesson plans
ICC7S11	Prepare and organize materials to implement daily lesson plans
ICC7S12	Use instructional time effectively
ICC7S13	Make responsive adjustments to instruction based on continual observations
ICC7S14	Prepare individuals to exhibit self-enhancing behavior in response to societal attitudes and actions
ICC7S15	Evaluate and modify instructional practices in response to ongoing assessment data

	None in addition to Initial Common Core

Standard 8: Assessment

Knowledge

ICC8K1	Basic terminology used in assessment
ICC8K2	Legal provisions and ethical principles regarding assessment of individuals
ICC8K3	Screening, prereferral, referral, and classification procedures
ICC8K4	Use and limitations of assessment instruments
ICC8K5	National, state or provincial, and local accommodations and modifications
LD8K1	Terminology and procedures used in the assessment of individuals with learning disabilities
LD8K2	Factors that could lead to misidentification of individuals as having learning disabilities
LD8K3	Procedures to identify young children who may be at risk for learning disabilities

Skills

ICC8S1	Gather relevant background information
ICC8S2	Administer nonbiased formal and informal assessments
ICC8S3	Use technology to conduct assessments
ICC8S4	Develop or modify individualized assessment strategies
ICC8S5	Interpret information from formal and informal assessments
ICC8S6	Use assessment information in making eligibility, program, and placement decisions for individuals with exceptional learning needs, including those from culturally and/or linguistically diverse backgrounds
ICC8S7	Report assessment results to all stakeholders using effective communication skills
ICC8S8	Evaluate instruction and monitor progress of individuals with exceptional learning needs
ICC8S9	Create and maintain records
LD8S1	Choose and administer assessment instruments appropriate to the individual with learning disabilities

Standard 9: Professional and Ethical Practice

Knowledge

ICC9K1	Personal cultural biases and differences that affect one's teaching
ICC9K2	Importance of the teacher serving as a model for individuals with exceptional learning needs
ICC9K3	Continuum of lifelong professional development

ICC9K4	Methods to remain current regarding research-validated practice
LD9K1	Ethical responsibility to advocate for appropriate services for individuals with learning disabilities
LD9K2	Professional organizations and sources of information relevant to the field of learning disabilities

Skills

ICC9S1	Practice within the CEC Code of Ethics and other standards of the profession
ICC9S2	Uphold high standards of competence and integrity and exercise sound judgment in the practice of the professional
ICC9S3	Act ethically in advocating for appropriate services
ICC9S4	Conduct professional activities in compliance with applicable laws and policies
ICC9S5	Demonstrate commitment to developing the highest education and quality-of-life potential of individuals with exceptional learning needs
ICC9S6	Demonstrate sensitivity for the culture, language, religion, gender, disability, socioeconomic status, and sexual orientation of individuals
ICC9S7	Practice within one's skill limits and obtain assistance as needed
ICC9S8	Use verbal, nonverbal, and written language effectively
ICC9S9	Conduct self-evaluation of instruction
ICC9S10	Access information on exceptionalities
ICC9S11	Reflect on one's practice to improve instruction and guide professional growth
ICC9S12	Engage in professional activities that benefit individuals with exceptional learning needs, their families, and one's colleagues
ICC9S13	Demonstrate commitment to engage in evidence-based practices
LD9S1	Participate in the activities of professional organizations relevant to individuals with exceptional learning needs
LD9S2	Ethical responsibility to advocate for appropriate services for individuals with exceptional learning needs

Standard 10: Collaboration

Knowledge

ICC10K1	Models and strategies of consultation and collaboration
ICC10K2	Roles of individuals with exceptional learning needs, families, and school and community personnel in planning of an individualized program

ICC10K3	Concerns of families of individuals with exceptional learning needs and strategies to help address these concerns
ICC10K4	Culturally responsive factors that promote effective communication and collaboration with individuals with exceptional learning needs, families, school personnel, and community members
LD10K1	Co-planning and co-teaching methods to strengthen content acquisition of individuals with learning disabilities
LD10K2	Services, networks, and organizations that provide support across the life span for individuals with learning disabilities
Skills	
ICC10S1	Maintain confidential communication about individuals with exceptional learning needs
ICC10S2	Collaborate with families and others in assessment of individuals with exceptional learning needs
ICC10S3	Foster respectful and beneficial relationships between families and professionals
ICC10S4	Assist individuals with exceptional learning needs and their families in becoming active participants in the educational team
ICC10S5	Plan and conduct collaborative conferences with individuals with exceptional learning needs and their families
ICC10S6	Collaborate with school personnel and community members in integrating individuals with exceptional learning needs into various settings
ICC10S7	Use group problem-solving skills to develop, implement, and evaluate collaborative activities
ICC10S8	Model techniques and coach others in the use of instructional methods and accommodations
ICC10S9	Communicate with school personnel about the characteristics and needs of individuals with exceptional learning needs
ICC10S10	Communicate effectively with families of individuals with exceptional learning needs from diverse backgrounds
ICC10S11	Observe, evaluate, and provide feedback to paraeducators
	None in addition to Common Core

Initial Special Education Teachers of Individuals With Exceptional Learning Needs With Physical and Health Disabilities

Standard 1: Foundations

Knowledge

ICC1K1	Models, theories, philosophies, and research methods that form the basis for special education practice
ICC1K2	Laws, policies, and ethical principles regarding behavior management planning and implementation
ICC1K3	Relationship of special education to the organization and function of educational agencies
ICC1K4	Rights and responsibilities of individuals with exceptional learning needs, parents, teachers, and other professionals, and schools related to exceptional learning needs
ICC1K5	Issues in definition and identification of individuals with exceptional learning needs, including those from culturally and linguistically diverse backgrounds
ICC1K6	Issues, assurances and due process rights related to assessment, eligibility, and placement within a continuum of services
ICC1K7	Family systems and the role of families in the educational process
ICC1K8	Historical points of view and contribution of culturally and/or linguistically diverse groups
ICC1K9	Impact of the dominant culture on shaping schools and the individuals who study and work in them
ICC1K10	Potential impact of differences in values, languages, and customs that can exist between the home and school
PH1K1	Issues and educational definitions of individuals with physical and health disabilities
PH1K2	Historical foundations related to knowledge and practices in physical and health disabilities.
PH1K3	Laws and policies related to the provision of specialized health care in the educational setting.

Skills

ICC1S1	Articulate personal philosophy of special education
PH1S1	Articulate key elements of service delivery for individual with physical and health disabilities.

Standard 2: Development and Characteristics of Learners

Knowledge

ICC2K1	Typical and atypical human growth and development
ICC2K2	Educational implications of characteristics of various exceptionalities
ICC2K3	Characteristics and effects of the cultural and environmental milieu of the individual with exceptional learning needs and the family

ICC2K4	Family systems and the role of families in supporting development
ICC2K5	Similarities and differences of individuals with and without exceptional learning needs
ICC2K6	Similarities and differences among individuals with exceptional learning needs
ICC2K7	Effects of various medications on individuals with exceptional learning needs
PH2K1	Characteristics, treatment, and course of physical and health disabilities
PH2K2	Secondary conditions and treatment options that accompany physical and health disabilities
PH2K3	Implications of physical and health disabilities on development and learning
PH2K4	Medical terminology related to physical and health disabilities
PH2K5	Types and transmission routes of infectious and communicable diseases
PH2K6	Progression of degenerative diseases and the impact on educational performance
PH2K7	Issues related to children's perceptions of death and dying

Skills

PH2S1	Apply knowledge of characteristics of individual's physical and health disabilities to their treatment interventions
PH2S2	Monitor the effects of medication on individual performance

Standard 3: Individual Learning Differences

Knowledge

ICC3K1	Effects an exceptional condition(s) can have on an individual's life
ICC3K2	Impact of learners' academic and social abilities, attitudes, interests, and values on instruction and career development
ICC3K3	Variations in beliefs, traditions, and values across and within cultures and their effects on relationships among individuals with exceptional learning needs, family, and schooling
ICC3K4	Cultural perspectives influencing the relationships among families, schools, and communities as related to instruction
ICC3K5	Differing ways of learning of individuals with exceptional learning needs, including those from culturally diverse backgrounds and strategies for addressing these differences
PH3K1	Effects of physical disabilities on the way information is processed
PH3K2	Functional effects of the type and severity of physical and health disabilities on individual performance
PH3K3	Psychosocial effects of physical and health disabilities

Skills	
PH3S1	Address learned helplessness in individuals with physical and health disabilities

Standard 4: Instructional Strategies

Knowledge	
ICC4K1	Evidence-based practices validated for specific characteristics of learners and settings
PH4K1	Adaptations and assistive technology necessary to accommodate the unique characteristics of individuals with physical and health disabilities
PH4K2	Strategies for teaching organization and study skills
PH4K3	Strategies for teaching adapted physical education and recreational skills
PH4K4	Techniques for teaching human sexuality

Skills	
ICC4S1	Use strategies to facilitate integration into various settings
ICC4S2	Teach individuals to use self-assessment, problem-solving, and other cognitive strategies to meet their needs
ICC4S3	Select, adapt, and use instructional strategies and materials according to characteristics of the individual with exceptional learning needs
ICC4S4	Use strategies to facilitate maintenance and generalization of skills across learning environments
ICC4S5	Use procedures to increase the individual's self-awareness, self-management, self-control, self-reliance, and self-esteem
ICC4S6	Use strategies that promote successful transitions for individuals with exceptional learning needs
PH4S1	Use specialized instructional strategies for academic and functional tasks for individuals with physical and health disabilities
PH4S2	Use adaptations and assistive technology to provide access to and participation in the general curriculum
PH4S3	Individualize instructional strategies to minimize the functional effects of the disability
PH4S4	Teach how to manage and document personal health care procedures in a safe healthy environment
PH4S5	Teach use and management of technology
PH4S6	Identify sources of specialized materials, equipment, and assistive technology for individuals with physical and health disabilities
PH4S7	Demonstrate techniques for teaching literacy skills to individuals who are nonverbal

Standard 5: Learning Environments/Social Interactions

Knowledge

ICC5K1	Demands of learning environments
ICC5K2	Basic classroom management theories and strategies for individuals with exceptional learning needs
ICC5K3	Effective management of teaching and learning
ICC5K4	Teacher attitudes and behaviors that influence behavior of individuals with exceptional learning needs
ICC5K5	Social skills needed for educational and other environments
ICC5K6	Strategies for crisis prevention and intervention
ICC5K7	Strategies for preparing individuals to live harmoniously and productively in a culturally diverse world
ICC5K8	Ways to create learning environments that allow individuals to retain and appreciate their own and each other's respective language and cultural heritage
ICC5K9	Ways specific cultures are negatively stereotyped
ICC5K10	Strategies used by diverse populations to cope with a legacy of former and continuing racism
PH5K1	Adaptations of educational environments to enhance the potential of individuals with physical and health disabilities
PH5K2	Barriers to accessibility by individuals with physical and health disabilities
PH5K3	Evacuation plans and emergency plans for individuals with physical and health disabilities

Skills

ICC5S1	Create a safe, equitable, positive, and supportive learning environment in which diversities are valued
ICC5S2	Identify realistic expectations for personal and social behavior in various settings
ICC5S3	Identify supports needed for integration into various program placements
ICC5S4	Design learning environments that encourage active participation in individual and group activities
ICC5S5	Modify the learning environment to manage behaviors
ICC5S6	Use performance data and information from all stakeholders to make or suggest modifications in learning environments
ICC5S7	Establish and maintain rapport with individuals with and without exceptional learning needs
ICC5S8	Teach self-advocacy
ICC5S9	Create an environment that encourages self-advocacy and increased independence
ICC5S10	Use effective and varied behavior management strategies

ICC5S11	Use the least intensive behavior management strategy consistent with the needs of the individual with exceptional learning needs
ICC5S12	Design and manage daily routines
ICC5S13	Organize, develop, and sustain learning environments that support positive intracultural and intercultural experiences
ICC5S14	Mediate controversial intercultural issues among individuals with exceptional learning needs within the learning environment in ways that enhance any culture, group, or person
ICC5S15	Structure, direct, and support the activities of paraeducators, volunteers, and tutors
ICC5S16	Use universal precautions
PH5S1	Use proper positioning techniques and equipment to promote participation in academic and social environments
PH5S2	Demonstrate proper body mechanics to promote individual and teacher safety in transfer, lifting, positioning, and seating
PH5S3	Arrange equipment and materials to provide a safe and healthy environment
PH5S4	Provide information that promotes sensitivity towards, and acceptance of, those who have physical and health disabilities including communicable diseases
PH5S5	Create learning environments to develop self-advocacy and independence when working with personal assistants

Standard 6: Language

Knowledge

ICC6K1	Effects of cultural and linguistic differences on growth and development
ICC6K2	Characteristics of one's own culture and use of language and the ways in which these can differ from other cultures and uses of languages
ICC6K3	Ways of behaving and communicating among cultures that can lead to misinterpretation and misunderstanding
ICC6K4	Augmentative and assistive communication strategies
PH6K1	Continuum of nonsymbolic to symbolic forms of communication

Skills

ICC6S1	Use strategies to support and enhance communication skills of individuals with exceptional learning needs
ICC6S2	Use communication strategies and resources to facilitate understanding of subject matter for individuals with exceptional learning needs whose primary language is not the dominant language
PH6S1	Support the use of primary and secondary forms of communication across environments

PH6S2	Suggest data driven adjustments to communication systems

Standard 7: Instructional Planning

Knowledge

ICC7K1	Theories and research that form the basis of curriculum development and instructional practice
ICC7K2	Scope and sequences of general and special curricula
ICC7K3	National, state or provincial, and local curricula standards
ICC7K4	Technology for planning and managing the teaching and learning environment
ICC7K5	Roles and responsibilities of the paraeducator related to instruction, intervention, and direct service
PH7K1	Incorporation of augmentative and assistive communication into instruction and daily living activities

Skills

ICC7S1	Identify and prioritize areas of the general curriculum and accommodations for individuals with exceptional learning needs
ICC7S2	Develop and implement comprehensive, longitudinal individualized programs in collaboration with team members
ICC7S3	Involve the individual and family in setting instructional goals and monitoring progress
ICC7S4	Use functional assessments to develop intervention plans
ICC7S5	Use task analysis
ICC7S6	Sequence, implement, and evaluate individualized learning objectives
ICC7S7	Integrate affective, social, and life skills with academic curricula
ICC7S8	Develop and select instructional content, resources, and strategies that respond to cultural, linguistic, and gender differences
ICC7S9	Incorporate and implement instructional and assistive technology into the educational program
ICC7S10	Prepare lesson plans
ICC7S11	Prepare and organize materials to implement daily lesson plans
ICC7S12	Use instructional time effectively
ICC7S13	Make responsive adjustments to instruction based on continual observations
ICC7S14	Prepare individuals to exhibit self-enhancing behavior in response to societal attitudes and actions
ICC7S15	Evaluate and modify instructional practices in response to ongoing assessment data
PH7S1	Use assistive technology assessment to plan adaptations

PH7S2	Integrate individualized health care plan into daily programming
PH7S3	Pace instruction based on individual characteristics and health factors
PH7S4	Implement data-driven progress monitoring to document and guide instruction
PH7S5	Include independent living and postsecondary needs in instructional programming and transitional planning

Standard 8: Assessment

Knowledge

ICC8K1	Basic terminology used in assessment
ICC8K2	Legal provisions and ethical principles regarding assessment of individuals
ICC8K3	Screening, prereferral, referral, and classification procedures
ICC8K4	Use and limitations of assessment instruments
ICC8K5	National, state or provincial, and local accommodations and modifications
PH8K1	Valid and reliable assessment instruments for individuals who have poor motor skills and/or are nonverbal

Skills

ICC8S1	Gather relevant background information
ICC8S2	Administer nonbiased formal and informal assessments
ICC8S3	Use technology to conduct assessments
ICC8S4	Develop or modify individualized assessment strategies
ICC8S5	Interpret information from formal and informal assessments
ICC8S6	Use assessment information in making eligibility, program, and placement decisions for individuals with exceptional learning needs, including those from culturally and/or linguistically diverse backgrounds
ICC8S7	Report assessment results to all stakeholders using effective communication skills
ICC8S8	Evaluate instruction and monitor progress of individuals with exceptional learning needs
ICC8S9	Create and maintain records
PH8S1	Teach response modes to establish accuracy in the assessment of individuals with physical and health disabilities
PH8S2	Select, adapt, and use assessment information when tests are not validated on individuals with physical and health disabilities
PH8S3	Modify and adapt tools and procedures within the confines of the standardization process

Standard 9: Professional And Ethical Practice

Knowledge

ICC9K1	Personal cultural biases and differences that affect one's teaching
ICC9K2	Importance of the teacher serving as a model for individuals with exceptional learning needs
ICC9K3	Continuum of lifelong professional development
ICC9K4	Methods to remain current regarding research-validated practice
	None in addition to the Initial Common Core

Skills

ICC9S1	Practice within the CEC Code of Ethics and other standards of the profession
ICC9S2	Uphold high standards of competence and integrity and exercise sound judgment in the practice of the professional
ICC9S3	Act ethically in advocating for appropriate services
ICC9S4	Conduct professional activities in compliance with applicable laws and policies
ICC9S5	Demonstrate commitment to developing the highest education and quality-of-life potential of individuals with exceptional learning needs
ICC9S6	Demonstrate sensitivity for the culture, language, religion, gender, disability, socioeconomic status, and sexual orientation of individuals
ICC9S7	Practice within one's skill limits and obtain assistance as needed
ICC9S8	Use verbal, nonverbal, and written language effectively
ICC9S9	Conduct self-evaluation of instruction
ICC9S10	Access information on exceptionalities
ICC9S11	Reflect on one's practice to improve instruction and guide professional growth
ICC9S12	Engage in professional activities that benefit individuals with exceptional learning needs, their families, and one's colleagues
ICC9S13	Demonstrate commitment to engage in evidence-based practices
PH9S1	Participate in the activities of professional organizations in the field of physical and health disabilities

Standard 10: Collaboration

Knowledge

ICC10K1	Models and strategies of consultation and collaboration

ICC10K2	Roles of individuals with exceptional learning needs, families, and school personnel and community members in planning of an individualized program
ICC10K3	Concerns of families of individuals with exceptional learning needs and strategies to help address these concerns
ICC10K4	Culturally responsive factors that promote effective communication and collaboration with individuals with exceptional learning needs, families, school personnel, and community members
PH10K1	Roles and responsibilities of schools and community-based medical and related services personnel

Skills

ICC10S1	Maintain confidential communication about individuals with exceptional learning needs
ICC10S2	Collaborate with families and others in assessment of individuals with exceptional learning needs
ICC10S3	Foster respectful and beneficial relationships between families and professionals
ICC10S4	Assist individuals with exceptional learning needs and their families in becoming active participants in the educational team
ICC10S5	Plan and conduct collaborative conferences with individuals with exceptional learning needs and their families
ICC10S6	Collaborate with school personnel and community members in integrating individuals with exceptional learning needs into various settings
ICC10S7	Use group problem-solving skills to develop, implement, and evaluate collaborative activities
ICC10S8	Model techniques and coach others in the use of instructional methods and accommodations
ICC10S9	Communicate with school personnel about the characteristics and needs of individuals with exceptional learning needs
ICC10S10	Communicate effectively with families of individuals with exceptional learning needs from diverse backgrounds
ICC10S11	Observe, evaluate, and provide feedback to paraeducators
PH10S1	Collaborate in the selection and implementation of augmentative and alternative communication and assistive technology
PH10S2	Use available resources to assist with planning and design of programs for individuals with physical and health disabilities
PH10S3	Support individuals with exceptional learning needs as members of augmentative and assistive communication and assistive technology selection teams
PH10S4	Coordinate with related service personnel to maximize direct instruction time for individuals with physical and health disabilities
PH10S5	Collaborate with service providers, general education teachers, and families to provide integrated services
PH10S6	Participate in transdisciplinary teams

Initial Special Education Teachers of Individuals With Exceptional Learning Needs Who Are Blind and/or Visually Impaired

Standard 1: Foundations	
Knowledge	
ICC1K1	Models, theories, philosophies, and research methods that form the basis for special education practice
ICC1K2	Laws, policies, and ethical principles regarding behavior management planning and implementation
ICC1K3	Relationship of special education to the organization and function of educational agencies
ICC1K4	Rights and responsibilities of individuals with exceptional learning needs, parents, teachers, and other professionals, and schools related to exceptional learning needs
ICC1K5	Issues in definition and identification of individuals with exceptional learning needs, including those from culturally and linguistically diverse backgrounds
ICC1K6	Issues, assurances and due process rights related to assessment, eligibility, and placement within a continuum of services
ICC1K7	Family systems and the role of families in the educational process
ICC1K8	Historical points of view and contribution of culturally diverse groups
ICC1K9	Impact of the dominant culture on shaping schools and the individuals who study and work in them
ICC1K10	Potential impact of differences in values, languages, and customs that can exist between the home and school
B&VI1K1	Access rights to specialized equipment and materials for individuals with visual impairments
B&VI1K2	Historical foundations of education of individuals with visual impairments as related to traditional roles of specialized and public schools around the world
B&VI1K3	Incidence and prevalence for individuals with visual impairments
B&VI1K4	Basic terminology related to the function of the human visual system
Skills	
ICC1S1	Articulate personal philosophy of special education
B&VI1S1	Articulate an instructional philosophy that responds to the specific implications of visual impairment within the general curriculum
B&VI1S2	Articulate a professional philosophy that draws on specialized knowledge of visual impairment within the continuum of instructional options
Standard 2: Development and Characteristics of Learners	
Knowledge	
ICC2K1	Typical and atypical human growth and development

ICC2K2	Educational implications of characteristics of various exceptionalities
ICC2K3	Characteristics and effects of the cultural and environmental milieu of the individual with exceptional learning needs and the family
ICC2K4	Family systems and the role of families in supporting development
ICC2K5	Similarities and differences of individuals with and without exceptional learning needs
ICC2K6	Similarities and differences among individuals with exceptional learning needs
ICC2K7	Effects of various medications on individuals with exceptional learning needs
B&VI2K1	Development of the human visual system
B&VI2K2	Development of secondary senses when vision is impaired
B&VI2K3	Effects of visual impairment on development
B&VI2K4	Impact of visual impairment on learning and experience
B&VI2K5	Psychosocial aspects of visual impairment and cultural identity

Skills

B&VI2S1	Select and develop teaching strategies addressing age, visual impairment and visual prognosis

Standard 3: Individual Learning Differences

Knowledge

ICC3K1	Effects an exceptional condition(s) can have on an individual's life
ICC3K2	Impact of learners' academic and social abilities, attitudes, interests, and values on instruction and career development
ICC3K3	Variations in beliefs, traditions, and values across and within cultures and their effects on relationships among individuals with exceptional learning needs, family, and schooling
ICC3K4	Cultural perspectives influencing the relationships among families, schools, and communities as related to instruction
ICC3K5	Differing ways of learning of individuals with exceptional learning needs, including those from culturally diverse backgrounds and strategies for addressing these differences
B&VI3K1	Effects of visual impairment on receptive and expressive literacy and communication

Skills

B&VI3S1	Use strategies to address the effects of visual impairment on the family and the reciprocal impact on the individuals' self-esteem
B&VI3S2	Select, adapt and use instructional strategies to address the impact of additional exceptionalities

Standard 4: Instructional Strategies

Knowledge

ICC4K1	Evidence-based practices validated for specific characteristics of learners and settings
B&VI4K1	Strategies for teaching new concepts
B&VI4K2	Strategies for teaching visual efficiency skills and use of print adaptations, optical devices, and nonoptical devices
B&VI4K3	Strategies for teaching organization and study skills
B&VI4K4	Strategies for teaching tactual perceptual skills
B&VI4K5	Strategies for teaching adapted physical and recreational skills
B&VI4K6	Strategies for teaching social, daily living, and functional life skills
B&VI4K7	Strategies for teaching career-vocational skills and providing vocational counseling
B&VI4K8	Strategies to prepare individuals with progressive eye conditions to achieve a positive transition to alternative skills
B&VI4K9	Techniques for teaching human sexuality

Skills

ICC4S1	Use strategies to facilitate integration into various settings
ICC4S2	Teach individuals to use self-assessment, problem-solving, and other cognitive strategies to meet their needs
ICC4S3	Select, adapt, and use instructional strategies and materials according to characteristics of the individual with exceptional learning needs
ICC4S4	Use strategies to facilitate maintenance and generalization of skills across learning environments
ICC4S5	Use procedures to increase the individual's self-awareness, self-management, self-control, self-reliance, and self-esteem
ICC4S6	Use strategies that promote successful transitions for individuals with exceptional learning needs
B&VI4S1	Select and adapt materials in Braille, accessible print, and other formats
B&VI4S2	Teach the use of braillewriter, slate and stylus, and computer technology to produce Braille materials
B&VI4S3	Teach the use of the abacus, talking calculator, tactile graphics, and adapted science equipment
B&VI4S4	Prepare individuals for sighted guide and pre-cane orientation and mobility instruction
B&VI4S5	Teach literacy skills to individuals who have vision loss as well as other disabilities

Standard 5: Learning Environments/Social Interactions

Knowledge

ICC5K1	Demands of learning environments
ICC5K2	Basic classroom management theories and strategies for individuals with exceptional learning needs
ICC5K3	Effective management of teaching and learning
ICC5K4	Teacher attitudes and behaviors that influence behavior of individuals with exceptional learning needs
ICC5K5	Social skills needed for educational and other environments
ICC5K6	Strategies for crisis prevention and intervention
ICC5K7	Strategies for preparing individuals to live harmoniously and productively in a culturally diverse world
ICC5K8	Ways to create learning environments that allow individuals to retain and appreciate their own and each other's respective language and cultural heritage
ICC5K9	Ways specific cultures are negatively stereotyped
ICC5K10	Strategies used by diverse populations to cope with a legacy of former and continuing racism
B&VI5K1	Classroom organization to accommodate materials, equipment, and technology for vision loss and other disabilities
B&VI5K2	Importance of role models with visual impairments

Skills

ICC5S1	Create a safe, equitable, positive, and supportive learning environment in which diversities are valued
ICC5S2	Identify realistic expectations for personal and social behavior in various settings
ICC5S3	Identify supports needed for integration into various program placements
ICC5S4	Design learning environments that encourage active participation in individual and group activities
ICC5S5	Modify the learning environment to manage behaviors
ICC5S6	Use performance data and information from all stakeholders to make or suggest modifications in learning environments
ICC5S7	Establish and maintain rapport with individuals with and without exceptional learning needs
ICC5S8	Teach self-advocacy
ICC5S9	Create an environment that encourages self-advocacy and increased independence
ICC5S10	Use effective and varied behavior management strategies

ICC5S11	Use the least intensive behavior management strategy consistent with the needs of the individual with exceptional learning needs
ICC5S12	Design and manage daily routines
ICC5S13	Organize, develop, and sustain learning environments that support positive intracultural and intercultural experiences
ICC5S14	Mediate controversial intercultural issues among individuals with exceptional learning needs within the learning environment in ways that enhance any culture, group, or person
ICC5S15	Structure, direct, and support the activities of paraeducators, volunteers, and tutors
ICC5S16	Use universal precautions
B&VI5S1	Design multisensory learning environments that encourage active participation in group and individual activities
B&VI5S2	Provide access to incidental learning experiences

Standard 6: Language

Knowledge

ICC6K1	Effects of cultural and linguistic differences on growth and development
ICC6K2	Characteristics of one's own culture and use of language and the ways in which these can differ from other cultures and uses of languages
ICC6K3	Ways of behaving and communicating among cultures that can lead to misinterpretation and misunderstanding
ICC6K4	Augmentative and assistive communication strategies
B&VI6K1	Strategies for responding and understanding the implications of nonverbal communication as a substructure of language
B&VI6K2	Strategies for teaching listening and compensatory auditory skills

Skills

ICC6S1	Use strategies to support and enhance communication skills of individuals with exceptional learning needs
ICC6S2	Use communication strategies and resources to facilitate understanding of subject matter for individuals with exceptional learning needs whose primary language is not the dominant language
B&VI6S1	Teach communication through technology and adaptations specific to visual impairments

Standard 7: Instructional Planning

Knowledge

ICC7K1	Theories and research that form the basis of curriculum development and instructional practice

ICC7K2	Scope and sequences of general and special curricula
ICC7K3	National, state or provincial, and local curricula standards
ICC7K4	Technology for planning and managing the teaching and learning environment
ICC7K5	Roles and responsibilities of the paraeducator related to instruction, intervention, and direct service
B&VI7K1	Relationship among assessment, development of individualized education program, and placement as they affect vision-related services
Skills	
ICC7S1	Identify and prioritize areas of the general curriculum and accommodations for individuals with exceptional learning needs
ICC7S2	Develop and implement comprehensive, longitudinal individualized programs in collaboration with team members
ICC7S3	Involve the individual and family in setting instructional goals and monitoring progress
ICC7S4	Use functional assessments to develop intervention plans
ICC7S5	Use task analysis
ICC7S6	Sequence, implement, and evaluate individualized learning objectives
ICC7S7	Integrate affective, social, and life skills with academic curricula
ICC7S8	Develop and select instructional content, resources, and strategies that respond to cultural, linguistic, and gender differences
ICC7S9	Incorporate and implement instructional and assistive technology into the educational program
ICC7S10	Prepare lesson plans
ICC7S11	Prepare and organize materials to implement daily lesson plans
ICC7S12	Use instructional time effectively
ICC7S13	Make responsive adjustments to instruction based on continual observations
ICC7S14	Prepare individuals to exhibit self-enhancing behavior in response to societal attitudes and actions
ICC7S15	Evaluate and modify instructional practices in response to ongoing assessment data
B&VI7S1	Select and use technologies to accomplish instructional objectives
B&VI7S2	Sequence, implement, and evaluate learning objectives based on the expanded core curriculum for individuals with visual impairments
B&VI7S3	Obtain and organize specialized materials to implement instructional goals
B&VI7S4	Integrate the individualized health care plan into daily programming

Standard 8: Assessment

Knowledge

ICC8K1	Basic terminology used in assessment
ICC8K2	Legal provisions and ethical principles regarding assessment of individuals
ICC8K3	Screening, prereferral, referral, and classification procedures
ICC8K4	Use and limitations of assessment instruments
ICC8K5	National, state or provincial, and local accommodations and modifications
B&VI8K1	Specialized terminology used in assessing individuals with visual impairments
B&VI8K2	Alternative assessment techniques for individuals with visual impairments

Skills

ICC8S1	Gather relevant background information
ICC8S2	Administer nonbiased formal and informal assessments
ICC8S3	Use technology to conduct assessments
ICC8S4	Develop or modify individualized assessment strategies
ICC8S5	Interpret information from formal and informal assessments
ICC8S6	Use assessment information in making eligibility, program, and placement decisions for individuals with exceptional learning needs, including those from culturally and/or linguistically diverse backgrounds
ICC8S7	Report assessment results to all stakeholders using effective communication skills
ICC8S8	Evaluate instruction and monitor progress of individuals with exceptional learning needs
ICC8S9	Create and maintain records
B&VI8S1	Administer and interpret vision-related assessments
B&VI8S2	Use functional evaluations related to the expanded core curriculum
B&VI8S3	Select, adapt, and use assessment information when tests are not validated on individuals with visual impairments
B&VI8S4	Participate in the standardization process for local and state assessments
B&VI8S5	Interpret and apply background information and family history related to the individual's visual status

Standard 9: Professional And Ethical Practice

Knowledge

ICC9K1	Personal cultural biases and differences that affect one's teaching
ICC9K2	Importance of the teacher serving as a model for individuals with exceptional learning needs
ICC9K3	Continuum of lifelong professional development
ICC9K4	Methods to remain current regarding research-validated practice
	None in addition to the Initial Common Core

Skills

ICC9S1	Practice within the CEC Code of Ethics and other standards of the profession
ICC9S2	Uphold high standards of competence and integrity and exercise sound judgment in the practice of the professional
ICC9S3	Act ethically in advocating for appropriate services
ICC9S4	Conduct professional activities in compliance with applicable laws and policies
ICC9S5	Demonstrate commitment to developing the highest education and quality-of-life potential of individuals with exceptional learning needs
ICC9S6	Demonstrate sensitivity for the culture, language, religion, gender, disability, socioeconomic status, and sexual orientation of individuals
ICC9S7	Practice within one's skill limits and obtain assistance as needed
ICC9S8	Use verbal, nonverbal, and written language effectively
ICC9S9	Conduct self-evaluation of instruction
ICC9S10	Access information on exceptionalities
ICC9S11	Reflect on one's practice to improve instruction and guide professional growth
ICC9S12	Engage in professional activities that benefit individuals with exceptional learning needs, their families, and one's colleagues
ICC9S13	Demonstrate commitment to engage in evidence-based practices
B&VI9S1	Participate in the activities of professional organizations in the field of visual impairment
B&VI9S2	Advocate for educational policy related to visual impairment

Standard 10: Collaboration

Knowledge

ICC10K1	Models and strategies of consultation and collaboration
ICC10K2	Roles of individuals with exceptional learning needs, families, and school and community personnel in planning of an individualized program
ICC10K3	Concerns of families of individuals with exceptional learning needs and strategies to help address these concerns
ICC10K4	Culturally responsive factors that promote effective communication and collaboration with individuals with exceptional learning needs, families, school personnel, and community members
B&VI10K1	Strategies for assisting families and other team members in transition planning
B&VI10K2	Services, networks, publications for and organizations of individuals with visual impairments

Skills

ICC10S1	Maintain confidential communication about individuals with exceptional learning needs
ICC10S2	Collaborate with families and others in assessment of individuals with exceptional learning needs
ICC10S3	Foster respectful and beneficial relationships between families and professionals
ICC10S4	Assist individuals with exceptional learning needs and their families in becoming active participants in the educational team
ICC10S5	Plan and conduct collaborative conferences with individuals with exceptional learning needs and their families
ICC10S6	Collaborate with school personnel and community members in integrating individuals with exceptional learning needs into various settings
ICC10S7	Use group problem-solving skills to develop, implement, and evaluate collaborative activities
ICC10S8	Model techniques and coach others in the use of instructional methods and accommodations
ICC10S9	Communicate with school personnel about the characteristics and needs of individuals with exceptional learning needs
ICC10S10	Communicate effectively with families of individuals with exceptional learning needs from diverse backgrounds
ICC10S11	Observe, evaluate, and provide feedback to paraeducators
B&VI10S1	Structure and supervise the activities of paraeducators and others who work with individuals with visual impairments
B&VI10S2	Plan and implement literacy and communication and consultative support within the general curriculum and the expanded core curriculum

After mastering initial special education professional standards, many special educators continue their professional growth toward mastery of advanced professional standards at the postbaccalaureate levels, including masters, specialists, and doctoral degree programs, as well as nondegree advanced certificate programs. For some, this means deepening their understanding and expertise and adding new responsibilities for leadership within the classroom. Some special educators choose to specialize their knowledge for educating individuals with a given disability, age-range or functional area. Others work toward assuming functions outside the classroom, moving into specializations, administering special education programs and services, or moving into teacher preparation and research roles.

At the advanced level, special educators share an array of functions and responsibilities. Reflecting this commonality, CEC has validated knowledge and skills that all special educators have mastered as a part of their preparation for advanced practice (see following Validated Advance Common Core Knowledge and Skill Set). The knowledge and skill sets are organized under six Advanced Content Standards (ARCS) that broadly describe in rich narrative what is expected of special educators preparing for an advanced role. Programs preparing special educators for advanced roles should ensure that their programs coordinate with the six ARCS as informed by the knowledge and skill sets. Although the six ARCS provide a rich narrative focus and organizing heuristic, CEC has validated specific knowledge and skills sets for each of the roles that differentiate the emphasis, focus, and contextualized skills for each role. These validated knowledge and skill sets inform and differentiate the specific skills and contextual expertise expected in the various roles. Programs preparing special educators for an advanced special education role[10] should use the appropriate knowledge and skills set(s) within the development of the preparation programs to inform the program's curriculum of study and to design the program assessment plan.

CEC uses the ARCS to organize the reviews of advanced preparation programs in partnership with the National Council for the Accreditation of Teacher Education (NCATE). Moreover, the six ARCS coordinate with the organized framework used by the National Board for Professional Teaching Standards across the five Exceptional Educator pathways. This makes it reasonable for programs that prepare NBPTS candidates to address the CEC ARCS.

Similar to the 10 CEC Special Education Content Standards for initial roles, these 6 Special Education Advanced Roles Content Standards are identical across advanced special education roles. Each Standard is based on validated knowledge and skills in the Advanced Common Core Knowledge and Skill Sets. In addition, each specific advanced role will have knowledge and skills specific to that role.

Advanced Standard 1: Leadership and Policy[11]

Special educators in advanced programs learn to use their deep understanding of the **history of special education, current legal and ethical standards, and emerging issues** to provide leadership. Special educators **promote high professional self-expectations and help others understand the needs of individuals with exceptional learning needs**. They **advocate for educational policy based on solid evidence-based knowledge** to support high quality education for individuals with exceptional learning needs. As appropriate to their role, they **advocate for appropriate resources** to ensure that all personnel involved have effective preparation. Special educators use their **knowledge of the needs of different groups in a**

---

[10] Both initial and advanced special education professional content standards are the basis for recognizing quality special education preparation programs and for developing special educator licensure frameworks. The initial special education professional standards provide a benchmark that jurisdictions can use to ensure that licensed beginning special educators can practice safely and effectively. The advanced standards provide a benchmark to ensure that experienced special education professionals are able to practice at an accomplished level of skill. Every special educator should use the special education professional standards in guiding their own professional growth and development.

Initial special education professional content standards describe the minimal knowledge, skills, and dispositions necessary for individuals to enter initial practice safely and effectively as a special education professional.

Advanced special education professional content standards describe the knowledge, skills, and dispositions necessary for individuals to practice at accomplished levels of special education and in advanced special education roles. After previously mastering initial special education professional standards, special educators work toward mastery of advanced professional standards at the post baccalaureate levels, including masters, specialists, and doctoral degree programs, as well as nondegree advanced certificate programs.

[11] The bolded phrases are important elements of the standards identified to provide guidance to performance-based program developers.

pluralistic society to promote evidence-based practices and challenging expectations for individuals with exceptional learning needs. They model respect for all individuals and ethical practice. They help to create positive and productive work environments and celebrate accomplishments with colleagues. They mentor others and promote high expectations for themselves, other professionals, and individuals with exceptional learning needs.

Advanced Standard 2: Program Development and Organization

Special educators apply their knowledge of cognitive science, learning theory, and instructional technologies to improve instructional programs. They advocate for a continuum of program options and services to ensure the appropriate instructional supports for individuals with exceptional learning needs. They help design and deliver, as appropriate to their role, ongoing results-oriented professional development designed to support the use of evidenced-based practices at all relevant organizational levels. They use their understanding of the effects of cultural, social, and economic diversity and variations of individual development to inform their development of programs and services for individuals with exceptional learning needs. Special educators continuously broaden and deepen their professional knowledge, and expand their expertise with instructional technologies, curriculum standards, effective teaching strategies, and assistive technologies to support access to learning. They use their deep understanding of how to coordinate educational standards to the needs of individuals with exceptional learning needs to help all individuals with exceptional learning needs to access challenging curriculum standards.

Advanced Standard 3: Research and Inquiry

Research and inquiry inform the decisions of special educators who have completed advanced programs in guiding professional practice. Special educators know models, theories, philosophies, and research methods that form the basis for evidence-based practices in special education. This knowledge includes information sources, data collection, and data analysis strategies. Special educators evaluate the appropriateness of research methodologies in relation to practices presented in the literature. They use educational research to improve instructional techniques, intervention strategies, and curricular

materials. They foster an environment supportive of continuous instructional improvement, and engage in the design and implementation of action research. Special educators are able to use the literature to resolve issues of professional practice, and help others to understand various evidence-based practices.

Advanced Standard 4: Individual and Program Evaluation

Evaluation is critical to advanced practice of special educators. Underlying evaluation is the knowledge of systems and theories of educational assessment and evaluation, along with skills in the implementation of evidence-based practices in assessment. Effective special educators design and implement research activities to evaluate the effectiveness of instructional practices and, as appropriate to their role, to assess progress toward the organizational vision, mission, and goals of their programs. It is critical in evaluation that nonbiased assessment procedures are used in the selection of assessment instruments, methods, and procedures for both programs and individuals.

With respect to evaluation of individuals, special educators prepared at the advanced level are able to apply their knowledge and skill to all stages and purposes of evaluation including: prereferral and screening, preplacement for special education eligibility, monitoring and reporting learning progress in the general education curriculum and other individualized educational program goals.

Advanced Standard 5: Professional Development and Ethical Practice

Special educators are guided by the professional ethics and practice standards. Special educators have responsibility for promoting the success of individuals with exceptional learning needs, their families, and colleagues. They create supportive environments that safeguard the legal rights of students and their families. They model and promote ethical and professional practice. Special educators plan, present, and evaluate professional development, as appropriate to their roles, based on models that apply adult learning theories and focus on effective practice at all organizational levels. Special educators model their own commitment to continuously improving their own professional practice by participating in professional development themselves.

Advanced Standard 6: Collaboration

Special educators prepared at the advanced level have a deep understanding of the **centrality and importance of consultation and collaboration to the roles within special education** and use this deep understanding to **integrate services for individuals with exceptional learning needs**. They also understand the significance of the role of collaboration for both internal and external stakeholders, and **apply their skill to promote understanding, resolve conflicts, and build consensus among both internal and external stakeholders** to provide services to individuals with exceptional learning needs and their families.

They possess current knowledge of research on stages and models in both collaboration and consultation and ethical and legal issues related to consultation and collaboration. Moreover, special educators prepared at the advanced level have a deep understanding of the possible interactions of language, diversity, culture and religion with contextual factors and how to **use collaboration and consultation to enhance opportunities for individuals with exceptional learning needs**.

Special Education Diagnostic Specialists

Standard 1: Leadership and Policy	
Knowledge	
ACC1K1	Needs of different groups in a pluralistic society
ACC1K2	Evidence-based theories of organizational and educational leadership
ACC1K3	Emerging issues and trends that potentially affect the school community and the mission of the school
ACC1K4	National and state education laws and regulations
ACC1K5	Current legal, regulatory, and ethical issues affecting education
ACC1K6	Responsibilities and functions of school committees and boards
ED1K1	Laws and policies related to assessing individuals with exceptional learning needs
ED1K2	Emerging issues and trends that impact assessment
ED1K3	Implication of multiple factors that impact the assessment process
ED1K4	Models, theories, and philosophies that form the basis of assessment
ED1K5	Issues in general and special education that impact placement decisions for individuals with exceptional learning needs
ED1K6	Policy and research implications that promote recommended practices in assessment
Skills	
ACC1S1	Promote a free appropriate public education in the least restrictive environment
ACC1S2	Promote high expectations for self, staff, and individuals with exceptional learning needs
ACC1S3	Advocate for educational policy within the context of evidence-based practices
ACC1S4	Mentor teacher candidates, newly certified teachers, and other colleagues
ED1S1	Design and evaluate procedures for effective participation in school, system, and statewide assessments
Standard 2: Program Development and Organization	
Knowledge	
ACC2K1	Effects of the cultural and environmental milieu of the individual and the family on behavior and learning

ACC2K2	Theories and methodologies of teaching and learning, including adaptation and modification of curriculum
ACC2K3	Continuum of program options and services available to individuals with exceptional learning needs with exceptional learning needs
ACC2K4	Prereferral intervention processes and strategies
ACC2K5	Process of developing individualized education plans
ACC2K6	Developmentally appropriate strategies for modifying instructional methods and the learning environment
ED2K1	Assessment procedures that address all disabilities
ED2K2	Variability of individuals within each category of disability
ED2K3	Over- or underrepresentation of individuals with cultural and linguistic diversity who are referred for assessment
ED2K4	Characteristics of individuals with exceptional learning needs that impact the development of programs and services

Skills

ACC2S1	Develop programs including the integration of related services for individuals based on a thorough understanding of individual differences
ACC2S2	Connect educational standards to specialized instructional services
ACC2S3	Improve instructional programs using principles of curriculum development and modification, and learning theory
ACC2S4	Incorporate essential components into individualized education plans
ED2S1	Synthesize information from multiple perspectives in developing a program assessment plan.

Standard 3: Research and Inquiry

Knowledge

ACC3K1	Evidence-based practices validated for specific characteristics of learners and settings
ED3K1	Best practices in research-based assessment
ED3K2	Resources and methods that address student learning, rates, and learning styles

Skills

ACC3S1	Identify and use the research literature to resolve issues of professional practice
ACC3S2	Evaluate and modify instructional practices in response to ongoing assessment data

ACC3S3	Use educational research to improve instruction, intervention strategies, and curricular materials
ED3S1	Evaluate assessment techniques based on learning theories

Standard 4: Individual and Program Evaluation

Knowledge

ACC4K1	Evaluation process and determination of eligibility
ACC4K2	Variety of methods for assessing and evaluating individuals with exceptional learning needs' performance
ACC4K3	Strategies for identifying individuals with exceptional learning needs
ACC4K4	Evaluate a student's success in the general education curriculum
ED4K1	Standards of reliability and validity related to individual test measures
ED4K2	Procedures used in standardizing assessment instruments
ED4K3	Standard error of measurement related to individual test measures
ED4K4	Use and limitations of portfolios in assessment
ED4K5	Sources of test error
ED4K6	Uses and limitation of assessment information
ED4K7	Achievement assessment measures
ED4K8	Cognitive assessment measures
ED4K9	Language assessment measures
ED4K10	Motor skills assessment measures
ED4K11	Social, emotional, and behavioral assessment measures
ED4K12	Vocational and career assessment measures

Skills

ACC4S1	Design and use methods for assessing and evaluating programs
ACC4S2	Design and implement research activities to examine the effectiveness of instructional practices
ACC4S3	Advocate for evidence-based practices in assessment
ACC4S4	Report the assessment of individuals with exceptional learning needs' performance and evaluation of instructional programs
ED4S1	Select and use formal and informal observation measures

ED4S2	Select and use formal and informal functional assessment measures
ED4S3	Assess basic academic skills formally and informally
ED4S4	Select, administer, and score assessment instruments accurately
ED4S5	Analyze error patterns
ED4S6	Prepare comprehensive assessment reports
ED4S7	Employ assistive technology in the assessment process
ED4S8	Select accommodations and modifications based on assessment results
ED4S9	Facilitate progress monitoring
ED4S10	Use progress monitoring data to develop and revise individual goals

Standard 5: Professional Development and Ethical Practice

Knowledge

ACC5K1	Legal rights and responsibilities of individuals with exceptional learning needs, staff, and parents/guardians
ACC5K2	Moral and ethical responsibilities of educators
ACC5K3	Human rights of individuals with exceptional learning needs and their families
ED5K1	Qualifications to administer and interpret test results
ED5K2	Organizations and publications relevant to the field of educational diagnosticians
ED5K3	Ethical considerations relative to assessment

Skills

ACC5S1	Model ethical behavior and promote professional standards
ACC5S2	Implement practices that promote success for individuals with exceptional learning needs
ACC5S3	Use ethical and legal discipline strategies
ACC5S4	Disseminate information on effective school and classroom practices
ACC5S5	Create an environment which supports continuous instructional improvement
ACC5S6	Develop and implement a personalized professional development plan
ED5S1	Respect individual privacy and confidentiality
ED5S2	Participate in professional development activities

ED5S3	Cite all sources of reported information
ED5S4	Inform individuals of the purpose of evaluation, rationale, and timelines for completion
ED5S5	Provide assessment results in a clear, cohesive, and timely manner
ED5S6	Update skills necessary to provide effective assessment

Standard 6: Collaboration

Knowledge

ACC6K1	Methods for communicating goals and plans to stakeholders
ACC6K2	Roles of educators in integrated settings
ED6K1	Roles of various agencies within the community

Skills

ACC6S1	Collaborate to enhance opportunities for learners with exceptional learning needs
ACC6S2	Apply strategies to resolve conflict and build consensus
ED6S1	Communicate with team members to determine assessment needs
ED6S2	Communicate with team members to review assessment results
ED6S3	Assist with prereferral interventions and strategies
ED6S4	Assist teachers in interpreting data including large scale and individual assessments
ED6S5	Use interagency collaboration in planning intervention

NOTES:

"Individuals with exceptional learning needs" is used throughout to include individuals with disabilities and individuals with exceptional gifts and talents

"Exceptional Condition" is used throughout to include both single and co-existing conditions These may be two or more disabling conditions or exceptional gifts or talents co-existing with one or more disabling conditions

"Special Curricula" is used throughout to denote curricular areas not routinely emphasized or addressed in general curricula; (e.g., social, communication, motor, independence, self-advocacy)

Special Education Technology Specialists

Standard 1: Leadership and Policy	
Knowledge	
ACC1K1	Needs of different groups in a pluralistic society
ACC1K2	Evidence-based theories of organizational and educational leadership
ACC1K3	Emerging issues and trends that potentially affect the school community and the mission of the school
ACC1K4	National and state education laws and regulations
ACC1K5	Current legal, regulatory, and ethical issues affecting education
ACC1K6	Responsibilities and functions of school committees and boards
TE1K1	Concepts and issues related to the use of technology in education and other aspects of our society
TE1K2	National, state, or provincial PK-12 technology standards
Skills	
ACC1S1	Promote a free appropriate public education in the least restrictive environment
ACC1S2	Promote high expectations for self, staff, and individuals with exceptional learning needs
ACC1S3	Advocate for educational policy within the context of evidence-based practices
ACC1S4	Mentor teacher candidates, newly certified teachers, and other colleagues
TE1S1	Use technology-related terminology in written and oral communication
TE1S2	Describe legislative mandates and governmental regulations and their implications for technology in special education
TE1S3	Write proposals to obtain technology funds
TE1S4	Advocate for assistive or instructional technology on individual and system change levels
Standard 2: Program Development and Organization	
Knowledge	
ACC2K1	Effects of the cultural and environmental milieu of the individual and the family on behavior and learning
ACC2K2	Theories and methodologies of teaching and learning, including adaptation and modification of curriculum
ACC2K3	Continuum of program options and services available to individuals with exceptional learning needs with exceptional learning needs
ACC2K4	Prereferral intervention processes and strategies

ACC2K5	Process of developing individualized education plans
ACC2K6	Developmentally appropriate strategies for modifying instructional methods and the learning environment
TE2K1	Impact of technology at all stages of development on individuals with exceptional learning needs
TE2K2	Issues in diversity and in the use of technology
TE2K3	Procedures for the organization, management, and security of technology
TE2S4	Identify and operate instructional and assistive hardware, software and peripherals
TE2K5	Ergonomic principles to facilitate the use of technology
TE2K6	Funding sources and processes of acquisition of assistive technology devices and services

Skills

ACC2S1	Develop programs including the integration of related services for individuals based on a thorough understanding of individual differences
ACC2S2	Connect educational standards to specialized instructional services
ACC2S3	Improve instructional programs using principles of curriculum development and modification, and learning theory
ACC2S4	Incorporate essential components into individualized education plans
TE2S1	Provide technology support to individuals with exceptional learning needs who are receiving instruction in general education settings
TE2S2	Arrange for demonstrations and trial periods with potential assistive or instructional technologies prior to making purchase decisions
TE2S3	Use technology to foster social acceptance in inclusive settings
TE2S4	Identify elements of the curriculum for which technology applications are appropriate and ways they can be implemented
TE2S5	Identify and operate software that meets educational objectives for individuals with exceptional learning needs in a variety of educational environments
TE2S6	Provide consistent, structured training to individuals with exceptional learning needs to operate instructional and adaptive equipment and software until they have achieved mastery
TE2S7	Develop and implement contingency plans in the event that assistive or instructional technology devices fail
TE2S8	Instruct others in the operation of technology, maintenance, warranties, and trouble-shooting techniques

Standard 3: Research and Inquiry

Knowledge

ACC3K1	Evidence-based practices validated for specific characteristics of learners and settings
	None in addition to the Advanced Common Core

Skills

ACC3S1	Identify and use the research literature to resolve issues of professional practice
ACC3S2	Evaluate and modify instructional practices in response to ongoing assessment data
ACC3S3	Use educational research to improve instruction, intervention strategies, and curricular materials
TE3S1	Use technology to collect, analyze, summarize, and report student performance data to aid instructional decision making

Standard 4: Individual and Program Evaluation

Knowledge

ACC4K1	Evaluation process and determination of eligibility
ACC4K2	Variety of methods for assessing and evaluating individuals with exceptional learning needs' performance
ACC4K3	Strategies for identifying individuals with exceptional learning needs
ACC4K4	Evaluate a student's success in the general education curriculum
TE4K1	Procedures for evaluation of computer software and other technology materials for their potential application in special education
TE4K2	Use of technology in the assessment, diagnosis, and evaluation of individuals with exceptional learning needs

Skills

ACC4S1	Design and use methods for assessing and evaluating programs
ACC4S2	Design and implement research activities to examine the effectiveness of instructional practices
ACC4S3	Advocate for evidence-based practices in assessment
ACC4S4	Report the assessment of individuals with exceptional learning needs' performance and evaluation of instructional programs
TE4S1	Evaluate features of technology systems
TE4S2	Identify the demands of technology on the individual with exceptional learning needs

TE4S3	Design, fabricate, and install assistive technology materials and devices to meet the needs of individuals with exceptional learning needs
TE4S4	Verify proper implementation of mechanical and electrical safety practices in the assembly and integration of the technology to meet the needs of individuals with exceptional learning needs
TE4S5	Develop specifications and/or drawings necessary for technology acquisitions
TE4S6	Match characteristics of individuals with exceptional learning needs with technology product or software features
TE4S7	Identify functional needs, screen for functional limitations and identify if the need for a comprehensive assistive or instructional technology evaluation exists
TE4S8	Monitor outcomes of technology-based interventions and reevaluate and adjust the system as needed
TE4S9	Identify placement of devices and positioning of the individual to optimize the use of assistive or instructional technology
TE4S10	Examine alternative solutions prior to making assistive or instructional technology decisions
TE4S11	Make technology decisions based on a continuum of options ranging from no technology to high technology

Standard 5: Professional Development and Ethical Practice

Knowledge

ACC5K1	Legal rights and responsibilities of individuals with exceptional learning needs, staff, and parents/guardians
ACC5K2	Moral and ethical responsibilities of educators
ACC5K3	Human rights of individuals with exceptional learning needs and their families
TE5K1	Equity, ethical, legal, and human issues related to technology use in special education
TE5K2	Organizations and publications relevant to the field of technology

Skills

ACC5S1	Model ethical behavior and promote professional standards
ACC5S2	Implement practices that promote success for individuals with exceptional learning needs
ACC5S3	Use ethical and legal discipline strategies
ACC5S4	Disseminate information on effective school and classroom practices
ACC5S5	Create an environment which supports continuous instructional improvement

ACC5S6	Develop and implement a personalized professional development plan
TE5S1	Articulate a personal philosophy and goals for using technology in special education
TE5S2	Use communication technologies to access information and resources electronically
TE5S3	Assist the individual with exceptional learning needs in clarifying and prioritizing functional intervention goals regarding technology-based evaluation results
TE5S4	Maintain ongoing professional development to acquire knowledge and skills about new developments in technology
TE5S5	Adhere to copyright laws about duplication and distribution of software and other copyrighted technology materials
TE5S6	Participate in activities of professional organizations relevant to the field of technology
TE5S7	Conduct in-service training in applications of technology in special education

Standard 6: Collaboration

Knowledge

ACC6K1	Methods for communicating goals and plans to stakeholders
ACC6K2	Roles of educators in integrated settings
TE6K1	Roles that related services personnel fulfill in providing technology services
TE6K2	Guidelines for referring individuals with exceptional learning needs to another professional

Skills

ACC6S1	Collaborate to enhance opportunities for learners with exceptional learning needs
ACC6S2	Apply strategies to resolve conflict and build consensus
TE6S1	Work with team members to identify assistive and instructional technologies that can help individuals meet the demands placed upon them in their environments
TE6S2	Refer team members and families to assistive and instructional technology resources
TE6S3	Collaborate with other team members in planning and implementing the use of assistive and adaptive devices

NOTES:

*Individuals with exceptional learning need*s is used throughout to include individuals with disabilities and individuals with exceptional gifts and talents

Exceptional Condition is used throughout to include both single and co-existing conditions These may be two or more disabling conditions or exceptional gifts or talents co-existing with one or more disabling conditions

Special Curricula is used throughout to denote curricular areas not routinely emphasized or addressed in general curricula; (e.g., social, communication, motor, independence, self-advocacy)

Special Education Transition Specialists

Standard 1: Leadership and Policy

Knowledge

ACC1K1	Needs of different groups in a pluralistic society
ACC1K2	Evidence-based theories of organizational and educational leadership
ACC1K3	Emerging issues and trends that potentially affect the school community and the mission of the school
ACC1K4	National and state education laws and regulations
ACC1K5	Current legal, regulatory, and ethical issues affecting education
ACC1K6	Responsibilities and functions of school committees and boards
TS1K1	Transition-related laws and policies
TS1K2	History of national transition initiatives

Skills

ACC1S1	Promote a free appropriate public education in the least restrictive environment
ACC1S2	Promote high expectations for self, staff, and individuals with exceptional learning needs
ACC1S3	Advocate for educational policy within the context of evidence-based practices
ACC1S4	Mentor teacher candidates, newly certified teachers, and other colleagues
	None in addition to the Advanced Common Core

Standard 2: Program Development and Organization

Knowledge

ACC2K1	Effects of the cultural and environmental milieu of the individual and the family on behavior and learning
ACC2K2	Theories and methodologies of teaching and learning, including adaptation and modification of curriculum
ACC2K3	Continuum of program options and services available to individuals with exceptional learning needs with exceptional learning needs
ACC2K4	Prereferral intervention processes and strategies
ACC2K5	Process of developing individualized education plans
ACC2K6	Developmentally appropriate strategies for modifying instructional methods and the learning environment

TS2K1	School and postschool services available to specific populations of individuals with exceptional learning needs
TS2K2	Methods for providing community-based education for individuals with exceptional learning needs
TS2K3	Methods for linking academic content to transition goals
TS2K4	Strategies for involving families and individuals with exceptional learning needs in transition planning and evaluation
TS2K5	Job seeking and job retention skills identified by employers as essential for successful employment
TS2K6	Vocational education methods, models, and curricula
TS2K7	Range of postschool options within specific outcome areas

Skills	
ACC2S1	Develop programs including the integration of related services for individuals based on a thorough understanding of individual differences
ACC2S2	Connect educational standards to specialized instructional services
ACC2S3	Improve instructional programs using principles of curriculum development and modification, and learning theory
ACC2S4	Incorporate essential components into individualized education plans
TS2S1	Identify and facilitate modifications within work and community environments
TS2S2	Arrange and evaluate instructional activities in relation to postschool goals
TS2S3	Identify outcomes and instructional options specific to the community and the individual
TS2S4	Use support systems to facilitate self-advocacy in transition planning

Standard 3: Research and Inquiry

Knowledge	
ACC3K1	Evidence-based practices validated for specific characteristics of learners and settings
TS3K1	Theoretical and applied models of transition
TS3K2	Research on relationships between individual outcomes and transition practices

Skills	
ACC3S1	Identify and use the research literature to resolve issues of professional practice
ACC3S2	Evaluate and modify instructional practices in response to ongoing assessment data
ACC3S3	Use educational research to improve instruction, intervention strategies, and curricular materials
	None in addition to the Advanced Common Core

Standard 4: Individual and Program Evaluation	
Knowledge	
ACC4K1	Evaluation process and determination of eligibility
ACC4K2	Variety of methods for assessing and evaluating individuals with exceptional learning needs' performance
ACC4K3	Strategies for identifying individuals with exceptional learning needs
ACC4K4	Evaluate a student's success in the general education curriculum
TS4K1	Procedures and requirements for referring individuals to community service agencies
TS4K2	Implications of individual characteristics with respect to postschool outcomes and support needs
TS4K3	Formal and informal approaches for identifying individuals with exceptional learning needs' interests and preferences related to educational experiences and postschool goals
Skills	
ACC4S1	Design and use methods for assessing and evaluating programs
ACC4S2	Design and implement research activities to examine the effectiveness of instructional practices
ACC4S3	Advocate for evidence-based practices in assessment
ACC4S4	Report the assessment of individuals with exceptional learning needs' performance and evaluation of instructional programs
TS4S1	Match skills and interests of the individuals to skills and demands required by vocational and postschool settings
TS4S2	Interpret results of career and vocational assessment for individuals, families, and professionals
TS4S3	Use a variety of formal and informal career, transition, and vocational assessment procedures
TS4S4	Evaluate and modify transition goals on an ongoing basis
TS4S5	Assess and develop natural support systems to facilitate transition to postschool environments
Standard 5: Professional Development and Ethical Practice	
Knowledge	
ACC5K1	Legal rights and responsibilities of individuals with exceptional learning needs, staff, and parents/guardians
ACC5K2	Moral and ethical responsibilities of educators
ACC5K3	Human rights of individuals with exceptional learning needs and their families
TS5K1	Scope and role of transition specialist

TS5K2	Scope and role of agency personnel related to transition services
TS5K3	Organizations and publications relevant to the field of transition

Skills	
ACC5S1	Model ethical behavior and promote professional standards
ACC5S2	Implement practices that promote success for individuals with exceptional learning needs
ACC5S3	Use ethical and legal discipline strategies
ACC5S4	Disseminate information on effective school and classroom practices
ACC5S5	Create an environment which supports continuous instructional improvement
ACC5S6	Develop and implement a personalized professional development plan
TS5S1	Show positive regard for the capacity and operating constraints of community organizations involved in transition services
TS5S2	Participate in activities of professional organizations in the field of transition
TS5S3	Ensure the inclusion of transition-related goals in the educational program plan
TS5S4	Develop post-school goals and objectives, using interests and preferences of the individual

Standard 6: Collaboration

Knowledge	
ACC6K1	Methods for communicating goals and plans to stakeholders
ACC6K2	Roles of educators in integrated settings
TS6K1	Methods to increase transition service delivery through interagency agreements and collaborative funding
TS6K2	Transition planning strategies that facilitate input from team members

Skills	
ACC6S1	Collaborate to enhance opportunities for learners with exceptional learning needs
ACC6S2	Apply strategies to resolve conflict and build consensus
TS6S1	Design and use procedures to evaluate and improve transition education and services in collaboration with team members
TS6S2	Provide information to families about transition education, services, support networks, and postschool options
TS6S3	Involve team members in establishing transition policy

TS6S4	Provide transition-focused technical assistance and professional development in collaboration with team members
TS6S5	Collaborate with transition-focused agencies
TS6S6	Develop interagency strategies to collect, share, and use student assessment data
TS6S7	Use strategies for resolving differences in collaborative relationships and interagency agreements
TS6S8	Assist teachers to identify educational program planning team members
TS6S9	Assure individual, family, and agency participation in transition planning and implementation

NOTES:

"Individuals with exceptional learning needs" is used throughout to include individuals with disabilities and individuals with exceptional gifts and talents

"Exceptional Condition" is used throughout to include both single and co-existing conditions These may be two or more disabling conditions or exceptional gifts or talents co-existing with one or more disabling conditions

"Special Curricula" is used throughout to denote curricular areas not routinely emphasized or addressed in general curricula; (e.g., social, communication, motor, independence, self-advocacy)

Special Education Administrators

Standard 1: Leadership and Policy	
Knowledge	
ACC1K1	Needs of different groups in a pluralistic society
ACC1K2	Evidence-based theories of organizational and educational leadership
ACC1K3	Emerging issues and trends that potentially affect the school community and the mission of the school
ACC1K4	National and state education laws and regulations
ACC1K5	Current legal, regulatory, and ethical issues affecting education
ACC1K6	Responsibilities and functions of school committees and boards
SA1K1	Models, theories, and philosophies that provide the foundation for the administration of programs and services for individuals with exceptional learning needs and their families
SA1K2	Historical and social significance of the laws, regulations, and policies as they apply to the administration of programs and the provision of services for individuals with exceptional learning needs and their families
SA1K3	Local, state, and national fiscal policies and funding mechanisms in education, social, and health agencies as they apply to the provision of services for individuals with exceptional learning needs and their families
Skills	
ACC1S1	Promote a free appropriate public education in the least restrictive environment
ACC1S2	Promote high expectations for self, staff, and individuals with exceptional learning needs
ACC1S3	Advocate for educational policy within the context of evidence-based practices
ACC1S4	Mentor teacher candidates, newly certified teachers and other colleagues
SA1S1	Interprets and applies current laws, regulations, and policies as they apply to the administration of services to individuals with exceptional learning needs and their families
SA1S2	Applies leadership, organization, and systems change theory to the provision of services for individuals with exceptional learning needs and their families
SA1S3	Develops a budget in accordance with local, state, and national laws in education, social, and health agencies for the provision of services for individuals with exceptional learning needs and their families
SA1S4	Engages in recruitment, hiring, and retention practices that comply with local, state, and national laws as they apply to personnel serving individuals with exceptional learning needs and their families
SA1S5	Communicates a personal inclusive vision and mission for meeting the needs of individuals with exceptional learning needs and their families

Standard 2: Program Development and Organization

Knowledge

ACC2K1	Effects of the cultural and environmental milieu of the individual and the family on behavior and learning
ACC2K2	Theories and methodologies of teaching and learning, including adaptation and modification of curriculum
ACC2K3	Continuum of program options and services available to individuals with exceptional learning needs with exceptional learning needs
ACC2K4	Prereferral intervention processes and strategies
ACC2K5	Process of developing individualized education plans
ACC2K6	Developmentally appropriate strategies for modifying instructional methods and the learning environment
SA2K1	Programs and services within the general curriculum to achieve positive school outcomes for individuals with exceptional learning needs
SA2K2	Programs and strategies that promote positive school engagement for individuals with exceptional learning needs
SA2K3	Instruction and services needed to support access to the general curriculum for individuals with exceptional learning needs

Skills

ACC2S1	Develop programs including the integration of related services for individuals based on a thorough understanding of individual differences
ACC2S2	Connect educational standards to specialized instructional services
ACC2S3	Improve instructional programs using principles of curriculum development and modification, and learning theory
ACC2S4	Incorporate essential components into individualized education plans
SA2S1	Develops and implements a flexible continuum of services based on effective practices for individuals with exceptional learning needs and their families
SA2S2	Develops and implements programs and services that contribute to the prevention of unnecessary referrals
SA2S3	Develops and implements an administrative plan that supports the use of instructional and assistive technologies

Standard 3: Research and Inquiry

Knowledge

ACC3K1	Evidence-based practices validated for specific characteristics of learners and settings
SA3K1	Research in administrative practices that supports individuals with exceptional learning needs and their families

	Skills
ACC3S1	Identify and use the research literature to resolve issues of professional practice
ACC3S2	Evaluate and modify instructional practices in response to ongoing assessment data
ACC3S3	Use educational research to improve instruction, intervention strategies, and curricular materials
SA3S1	Engages in data-based decision-making for the administration of educational programs and services that supports exceptional individuals with exceptional learning needs and their families
SA3S2	Develops data-based educational expectations and evidence-based programs that account for the impact of diversity on individuals with exceptional learning needs and their families
SA3S3	Joins and participates in professional administrative organizations to guide administrative practices when working with individuals with exceptional learning needs and their families

Standard 4: Individual and Program Evaluation

	Knowledge
ACC4K1	Evaluation process and determination of eligibility
ACC4K2	Variety of methods for assessing and evaluating individuals with exceptional learning needs' performance
ACC4K3	Strategies for identifying individuals with exceptional learning needs
ACC4K4	Evaluate a student's success in the general education curriculum
SA4K1	Models, theories, and practices used to evaluate educational programs and personnel serving individuals with exceptional learning needs and their families

	Skills
ACC4S1	Design and use methods for assessing and evaluating programs
ACC4S2	Design and implement research activities to examine the effectiveness of instructional practices
ACC4S3	Advocate for evidence-based practices in assessment
ACC4S4	Report the assessment of individuals with exceptional learning needs' performance and evaluation of instructional programs
SA4S1	Advocates for and implements procedures for the participation of individuals with exceptional learning needs in accountability systems
SA4S2	Develops and implements ongoing evaluations of education programs and personnel
SA4S3	Provides ongoing supervision of personnel working with individuals with exceptional learning needs and their families
SA4S4	Designs and implements evaluation procedures that improve instructional content and practices

Standard 5: Professional Development and Ethical Practice

Knowledge

ACC5K1	Legal rights and responsibilities of individuals with exceptional learning needs, staff, and parents/guardians
ACC5K2	Moral and ethical responsibilities of educators
ACC5K3	Human rights of individuals with exceptional learning needs and their families
SA5K1	Ethical theories and practices as they apply to the administration of programs and services with individuals with exceptional learning needs and their families
SA5K2	Adult learning theories and models as they apply to professional development programs
SA5K3	Professional development theories and practices that improve instruction and instructional content for individuals with exceptional learning needs with exceptional learning needs
SA5K4	Impact of diversity on educational programming expectations for individuals with exceptional learning needs
SA5K5	Principles of representative governance that support the system of special education administration

Skills

ACC5S1	Model ethical behavior and promote professional standards
ACC5S2	Implement practices that promote success for individuals with exceptional learning needs
ACC5S3	Use ethical and legal discipline strategies
ACC5S4	Disseminate information on effective school and classroom practices
ACC5S5	Create an environment which supports continuous instructional improvement
ACC5S6	Develop and implement a personalized professional development plan
SA5S1	Communicates and demonstrates a high standard of ethical administrative practices when working with staff serving individuals with exceptional learning needs and their families
SA5S2	Develops and implements professional development activities and programs that improve instructional practices and lead to improved outcomes for individuals with exceptional learning needs with exceptional learning needs and their families

Standard 6: Collaboration

Knowledge

ACC6K1	Methods for communicating goals and plans to stakeholders
ACC6K2	Roles of educators in integrated settings
SA6K1	Collaborative theories and practices that support the administration of programs and services for with individuals with exceptional learning needs and their families

SA6K2	Administrative theories and models that facilitate communication among all stakeholders
SA6K3	Importance and relevance of advocacy at the local, state, and national level for individuals with exceptional learning needs and their families

Skills	
ACC6S1	Collaborate to enhance opportunities for learners with exceptional learning needs
ACC6S2	Apply strategies to resolve conflict and build consensus
SA6S1	Utilizes collaborative approaches for involving all stakeholders in educational planning, implementation, and evaluation
SA6S2	Strengthens the role of parent and advocacy organizations as they support individuals with exceptional learning needs and their families
SA6S3	Develops and implements intra- and interagency agreements that create programs with shared responsibility for individuals with exceptional learning needs and their families
SA6S4	Develops seamless transitions of individuals with exceptional learning needs across educational continuum and other programs from birth through adulthood
SA6S5	Implements collaborative administrative procedures and strategies to facilitate communication among all stakeholders
SA6S6	Engages in leadership practices that support shared decision making
SA6S7	Demonstrates the skills necessary to provide ongoing communication, education, and support for families of individuals with exceptional learning needs
SA6S8	Consults and collaborates in administrative and instructional decisions at the school and district levels

NOTES:

"Individuals with exceptional learning needs" is used throughout to include individuals with disabilities and individuals with exceptional gifts and talents

"Exceptional Condition" is used throughout to include both single and co-existing conditions These may be two or more disabling conditions or exceptional gifts or talents co-existing with one or more disabling conditions

"Special Curricula" is used throughout to denote curricular areas not routinely emphasized or addressed in general curricula; (e.g., social, communication, motor, independence, self-advocacy)

Special Education Early Childhood Specialists in Early Childhood Special Education/Early Intervention (Birth to Eight)

Standard 1	Leadership and Policy[12]

Knowledge

ACC1K1	Needs of different groups in a pluralistic society
ACC1K2	Evidence-based theories of organizational and educational leadership
ACC1K3	Emerging issues and trends that potentially affect the school community and the mission of the school
ACC1K4	National and State education laws and regulations
ACC1K5	Current legal, regulatory, and ethical issues affecting education
ACC1K6	Responsibilities and functions of school committees and boards
AEC1K1	Sociocultural, historical, and political forces that influence diverse delivery systems, including mental health
AEC1K2	Policy and emerging trends that affect infants and young children, families, resources, and services
AEC1K3	Community resources on national, state, and local levels that impact program planning and implementation, and the individualized needs of the child and family

Skills

ACC1S1	Promote a free appropriate public education in the least restrictive environment
ACC1S2	Promote high expectations for self, staff, and individuals with exceptional learning needs
ACC1S3	Advocate for educational policy within the context of evidence-based practices
ACC1S4	Mentor teacher candidates, newly certified teachers and other colleagues

[12] Special terminology was developed in the Knowledge and Skills Subcommittee meeting (April 2006) to simplify the wording of the standards for All Beginning Special Educational Professionals in Early Childhood Special Education/Early Intervention (Birth to age 8) These terms adhere to the "editing and smoothing guidelines" of the Knowledge and Skills Subcommittee They are included here for continuity with the advanced ECSE standards.

Infants and Young Children: all children birth to age 8 years

Exceptional Needs: in response to Exceptional Learning Needs (ELN) specified in the CEC standards, "infants and young children with exceptional needs" will be used, and not exceptional learning needs, since infants and young children have developmental needs as well as learning needs.

Infants and Young Children with Exceptional Needs: refers to infants and young children, birth to age 8 years, who have, or are at risk for, developmental delays and disabilities.

Development and Learning: terms to be used, and in that order, to convey the focus of the following knowledge and skills for personnel – to support the developmental and learning needs of infants and young children, and their families.

IFSP/IEP Family or Educational Plan: The language of the standards requires spelling out IFSP and IEP Knowledge and Skills Subcommittee suggests using "family or educational plan" to (a) simplify the expressions and (b) include Canadian terminology in the standards DEC respectfully requests the use of "individualized plan" to simplify the language since the IFSP is an educational plan too.

Developmental Domains: Term to be used to simplify the listing of the five developmental domains specified in federal law – cognitive, communicative, social-emotional, motor, and adaptive development.

AEC1S1	Advocate on behalf of infants and young child with exceptional needs, and their families, at local, state, national levels
AEC1S2	Provide leadership to help others understand policy and research that guide recommended practices
AEC1S3	Provide leadership in the collaborative development of community-based services and resources
AEC1S4	Provide effective supervision and evaluation

Standard 2: Program Development and Organization

Knowledge

ACC2K1	Effects of the cultural and environmental milieu of the individual and the family on behavior and learning
ACC2K2	Theories and methodologies of teaching and learning, including adaptation and modification of curriculum
ACC2K3	Continuum of program options and services available to individuals with exceptional learning needs with exceptional learning needs
ACC2K4	Prereferral intervention processes and strategies
ACC2K5	Process of developing individualized education plans
ACC2K6	Developmentally appropriate strategies for modifying instructional methods and the learning environment
AEC2K1	Range of delivery systems for programs and services available for infants and young children and their families

Skills

ACC2S1	Develop programs including the integration of related services for individuals based on a thorough understanding of individual differences
ACC2S2	Connect educational standards to specialized instructional services
ACC2S3	Improve instructional programs using principles of curriculum development and modification, and learning theory
ACC2S4	Incorporate essential components into individualized education plans
AEC2S1	Apply various curriculum theories and early learning standards, and evaluate their impact
AEC2S2	Design, implement, and evaluate home and community-based programs and services
AEC2S3	Integrate family and social systems theories to develop, implement, and evaluate family and educational plans
AEC2S4	Address medical and mental health issues and concerns when planning, implementing, and evaluating programs and services
AEC2S5	Incorporate and evaluate the use of universal design and assistive technology in programs and services

AEC2S6	Use recommended practices to design, implement, and evaluate transition programs and services
AEC2S7	Design, implement, and evaluate plans to prevent and address challenging behaviors across settings
AEC2S8	Design, implement, and evaluate developmentally responsive learning environments, preventative strategies, program wide behavior supports, and tiered instruction

Standard 3: Research and Inquiry

Knowledge

ACC3K1	Evidence-based practices validated for specific characteristics of learners and settings
	None in addition to the Advanced Common Core

Skills

ACC3S1	Identify and use the research literature to resolve issues of professional practice
ACC3S2	Evaluate and modify instructional practices in response to ongoing assessment data
ACC3S3	Use educational research to improve instruction, intervention strategies, and curricular materials
AEC3S1	Create and/or disseminate new advances and evidence-based practices
AEC3S2	Apply interdisciplinary knowledge from the social sciences and the allied health fields
AEC3S3	Help others understand early development and its impact across the life span
AEC3S4	Interpret and apply research to the provision of quality services and program practices to infants and young children, and their families, in a variety of educational and community settings

Standard 4: Individual and Program Evaluation

Knowledge

ACC4K1	Evaluation process and determination of eligibility
ACC4K2	Variety of methods for assessing and evaluating individuals with exceptional learning needs' performance
ACC4K3	Strategies for identifying individuals with exceptional learning needs
ACC4K4	Evaluate a student's success in the general education curriculum
AEC4K1	Policy and research implications that promote recommended practices in assessment and evaluation
AEC4K2	Systems and theories of child and family assessment

Skills

ACC4S1	Design and use methods for assessing and evaluating programs
ACC4S2	Design and implement research activities to examine the effectiveness of instructional practices

ACC4S3	Advocate for evidence based practices in assessment
ACC4S4	Report the assessment of individuals with exceptional learning needs' performance and evaluation of instructional programs
AEC4S1	Provide leadership in the development and implementation of unbiased assessment and evaluation procedures that include family members as an integral part of the process
AEC4S2	Provide leadership in the development and implementation of unbiased assessment and evaluation procedures for childcare and early education environments and curricula
AEC4S3	Provide leadership when selecting effective formal and informal assessment instruments and strategies

Standard 5: Professional Development and Ethical Practice

Knowledge

ACC5K1	Legal rights and responsibilities of individuals with exceptional learning needs, staff, and parents/guardians
ACC5K2	Moral and ethical responsibilities of educators
ACC5K3	Human rights of individuals with exceptional learning needs and their families
AEC5K1	Specialized knowledge in at least one developmental period or one particular area of disability or delay

Skills

ACC5S1	Model ethical behavior and promote professional standards
ACC5S2	Implement practices that promote success for individuals with exceptional learning needs
ACC5S3	Use ethical and legal discipline strategies
ACC5S4	Disseminate information on effective school and classroom practices
ACC5S5	Create an environment which supports continuous instructional improvement
ACC5S6	Develop and implement a personalized professional development plan
AEC5S1	Engage in reflective inquiry and professional self-assessment
AEC5S2	Participate in professional mentoring and other types of reciprocal professional development activities
AEC5S3	Participate actively in organizations that represent recommended practices of early intervention and early childhood special education on a national, state, and local level

Standard 6: Collaboration

Knowledge

ACC6K1	Methods for communicating goals and plans to stakeholders
ACC6K2	Roles of educators in integrated settings

AEC6K1	Roles and responsibilities of personnel in the development and implementation of team-based early childhood special education and early intervention services
AEC6K2	Theories, models, and research that support collaborative relationships
Skills	
ACC6S1	Collaborate to enhance opportunities for learners with exceptional learning needs
ACC6S2	Apply strategies to resolve conflict and build consensus
AEC6S1	Implement and evaluate leadership and models of collaborative relationships
AEC6S2	Collaborate with stakeholders in developing and implementing positive behavior support plans to prevent and address challenging behavior

NOTES:

Individual with exceptional learning needs is used throughout to include individuals with disabilities and individuals with exceptional gifts and talents

Exceptional Condition is used throughout to include both single and co-existing conditions These may be two or more disabling conditions or exceptional gifts or talents co-existing with one or more disabling conditions

Special Curricula is used throughout to denote curricular areas not routinely emphasized or addressed in general curricula; e.g., social, communication, motor, independence, self-advocacy

Special Education Deaf and Hard-of-Hearing Specialist

Standard 1: Leadership and Policy	
Knowledge	
ACC1K1	Needs of different groups in a pluralistic society
ACC1K2	Evidence-based theories of organizational and educational leadership
ACC1K3	Emerging issues and trends that potentially affect the school community and the mission of the school
ACC1K4	National and state education laws and regulations
ACC1K5	Current legal, regulatory, and ethical issues affecting education
ACC1K6	Responsibilities and functions of school committees and boards
DHH1K1	Socio-cultural, historical, and political forces that influence diverse delivery systems
DHH1K2	Standards for universal newborn hearing screening and early intervention
DHH1K3	Standards for interpreters
DHH1K4	Standards for teachers of individuals who are deaf and hard of hearing who have additional disabilities
Skills	
ACC1S1	Promote a free appropriate public education in the least restrictive environment
ACC1S2	Promote high expectations for self, staff, and individuals with exceptional learning needs
ACC1S3	Advocate for educational policy within the context of evidence-based practices
ACC1S4	Mentor teacher candidates, newly certified teachers and other colleagues
DHH1S1	Provide guidance on policy and recommended practices for individuals who are deaf and hard of hearing
DHH1S2	Advocate for the provision of advanced language and communication skills for teachers, families, and individuals who are deaf and hard of hearing
DHH1S3	Provide leadership for transition among programs and communication options
DHH1S4	Coordinate activities of related service providers including interpreters and paraeducators
Standard 2: Program Development and Organization	
Knowledge	
ACC2K1	Effects of the cultural and environmental milieu of the individual and the family on behavior and learning

ACC2K2	Theories and methodologies of teaching and learning, including adaptation and modification of curriculum
ACC2K3	Continuum of program options and services available to individuals with exceptional learning needs with exceptional learning needs
ACC2K4	Prereferral intervention processes and strategies
ACC2K5	Process of developing individualized education plans
ACC2K6	Developmentally appropriate strategies for modifying instructional methods and the learning environment
DHH2K1	Multiple service options for individuals who are deaf or hard of hearing including mental health services

Skills

ACC2S1	Develop programs including the integration of related services for individuals based on a thorough understanding of individual differences
ACC2S2	Connect educational standards to specialized instructional services
ACC2S3	Improve instructional programs using principles of curriculum development and modification, and learning theory
ACC2S4	Incorporate essential components into individualized education plans
DHH2S1	Address all aspects of the communication environment that lead to inadequate learning
DHH2S2	Structure the learning environment to encourage self-advocacy

Standard 3: Research and Inquiry

Knowledge

ACC3K1	Evidence based practices validated for specific characteristics of learners and settings
	None in addition to the Advanced Common Core

Skills

ACC3S1	Identify and use the research literature to resolve issues of professional practice
ACC3S2	Evaluate and modify instructional practices in response to ongoing assessment data
ACC3S3	Use educational research to improve instruction, intervention strategies, and curricular materials
DHH3S1	Disseminate new research-based advances and evidence-based practices
DHH3S2	Design and implement literacy development programs and transition programs

Standard 4: Individual and Program Evaluation

Knowledge

ACC4K1	Evaluation process and determination of eligibility
ACC4K2	Variety of methods for assessing and evaluating individuals with exceptional learning needs' performance
ACC4K3	Strategies for identifying individuals with exceptional learning needs
ACC4K4	Evaluate a student's success in the general education curriculum
DHH4K1	Policy and research implications that promote recommended practices in assessment and evaluation

Skills

ACC4S1	Design and use methods for assessing and evaluating programs
ACC4S2	Design and implement research activities to examine the effectiveness of instructional practices
ACC4S3	Advocate for evidence-based practices in assessment
ACC4S4	Report the assessment of individuals with exceptional learning needs' performance and evaluation of instructional programs
DHH4S1	Design, implement, and evaluate procedures that enhance individuals with exceptional learning needs effective participation in school, system, and statewide assessments

Standard 5: Professional Development and Ethical Practice

Knowledge

ACC5K1	Legal rights and responsibilities of individuals with exceptional learning needs, staff, and parents/guardians
ACC5K2	Moral and ethical responsibilities of educators
ACC5K3	Human rights of individuals with exceptional learning needs and their families
DHH5K1	Ethical practices that acknowledge diversity among the deaf, hard-of-hearing, and hearing communities

Skills

ACC5S1	Model ethical behavior and promote professional standards
ACC5S2	Implement practices that promote success for individuals with exceptional learning needs
ACC5S3	Use ethical and legal discipline strategies
ACC5S4	Disseminate information on effective school and classroom practices
ACC5S5	Create an environment which supports continuous instructional improvement

ACC5S6	Develop and implement a personalized professional development plan
DHH5S1	Ethically implement current assistive and instructional technologies
DHH5S2	Acquire advanced qualifications and skills

Standard 6: Collaboration

Knowledge

ACC6K1	Methods for communicating goals and plans to stakeholders
ACC6K2	Roles of educators in integrated settings
	None in addition to the Advanced Common Core

Skills

ACC6S1	Collaborate to enhance opportunities for learners with exceptional learning needs
ACC6S2	Apply strategies to resolve conflict and build consensus
DHH6S1	Collaborate with stakeholders in developing and implementing equal access to programs in urban, urban-fringe, or rural settings

NOTES:

"Individuals with exceptional learning needs" is used throughout to include individuals with disabilities and individuals with exceptional gifts and talents

"Exceptional Condition" is used throughout to include both single and co-existing conditions These may be two or more disabling conditions or exceptional gifts or talents co-existing with one or more disabling conditions

"Special Curricula" is used throughout to denote curricular areas not routinely emphasized or addressed in general curricula; (e.g., social, communication, motor, independence, self-advocacy)

Section 6: Paraeducators Serving Individuals With Exceptional Learning Needs

This section provides information about the increasingly critical role of paraeducators in special education service delivery, the CEC standards for paraeducator preparation, and tools paraeducators and paraeducator training programs can use to ensure that they are meeting the standards.

For more than 50 years, paraeducators have helped special educators provide important services to individuals with exceptional learning conditions. Historically, they provided services ranging from clerical tasks to assisting with individualized functional living tasks. Today they have become an essential part of the special education team in delivering individualized services and playing an increasingly prominent role in the instruction of individuals with exceptional learning needs at all ages. According to the Study of Personnel Needs in Special Education (SPENSE, 2003.), today paraeducators in the United States spend at least 10% of their time on the following activities:

- Providing instructional support in small groups
- Providing one-to-one instruction
- Modifying materials
- Implementing behavior plans
- Monitoring hallways, study halls
- Meeting with teachers
- Collecting data on individuals with exceptional learning needs
- Providing personal care assistance

The qualified special education paraeducator performs tasks prescribed and supervised by a fully licensed special education professional. Qualified paraeducators deliver individualized services to individuals with exceptional learning needs in a wide variety of settings, including general education classes, community-based functional learning sites, and just about everywhere that a special education professional can be found. Paraeducators bring a wide variety of backgrounds and experience to their jobs (SPENSE, 2003). In the United States, 29% have high school diplomas, 38% have completed some college, and 32% hold an associate's degree or higher. Paraeducators with college experience have increased confidence in collaborating and communicating with teachers. The majority of paraeducators are supervised by special education teachers and overwhelmingly they feel supported by their special education supervisors.

To ensure that paraeducators have the required skills for their expanded roles, in collaboration with the National Resource Center for Paraeducators, CEC validated the following knowledge and skill set for paraeducators who serve individuals with exceptional learning needs. In addition, CEC has validated a set of corollary knowledge and skills for paraeducators of individuals with deaf-blindness (i.e., paraeducator interveners for individuals with deaf-blindness). CEC expects that agencies will ensure that all paraeducators working with individuals with exceptional learning needs have, at a minimum, mastered the Paraeducator Common Core and appropriate specialization knowledge and skills through ongoing, effective, preservice and continuing education with professional educators and training that is specifically targeted for paraeducators.

Paraeducators should have available ongoing, effective, continuing training with professional educators and training that is specifically targeted for paraeducators.

KNOWLEDGE AND SKILLS FOR PARAEDUCATORS IN SPECIAL EDUCATION

Standard 1: Foundations

Knowledge

SEP1K1	Purposes of programs for individuals with exceptional learning needs
SEP1K2	Basic educational terminology regarding individuals with exceptional learning needs, programs, roles, and instructional activities

Skills

	None

Standard 2: Development and Characteristics of Learners

Knowledge

SEP2K1	Effects an exceptional condition(s) can have on an individual's life

Skills

	None

Standard 3: Individual Learning Differences

Knowledge

SEP3K1	Rights and responsibilities of families and children as they relate to individual learning needs
SEP3K2	Indicators of abuse and neglect

Skills

SEP3S1	Demonstrate sensitivity to the diversity of individuals and families

Standard 4: Instructional Strategies

Knowledge

SEP4K1	Basic instructional and remedial strategies and materials
SEP4K2	Basic technologies appropriate to individuals with exceptional learning needs

Skills

SEP4S1	Use strategies, equipment, materials, and technologies, as directed, to accomplish instructional objectives
SEP4S2	Assist in adapting instructional strategies and materials as directed

SEP4S3	Use strategies as directed to facilitate effective integration into various settings
SEP4S4	Use strategies that promote the learner's independence as directed
SEP4S5	Use strategies as directed to increase the individual's independence and confidence

Standard 5: Learning Environments/Social Interactions

Knowledge

SEP5K1	Demands of various learning environments
SEP5K2	Rules and procedural safeguards regarding the management of behaviors of individuals with exceptional learning needs

Skills

SEP5S1	Establish and maintain rapport with learners
SEP5S2	Use universal precautions and assist in maintaining a safe, healthy learning environment
SEP5S3	Use strategies for managing behavior as directed
SEP5S4	Use strategies as directed, in a variety of settings, to assist in the development of social skills

Standard 6: Language

Knowledge

SEP6K1	Characteristics of appropriate communication with stakeholders

Skills

Standard 7: Instructional Planning

Knowledge

	None

Skills

SEP7S1	Follow written plans, seeking clarification as needed
SEP7S2	Prepare and organize materials to support teaching and learning as directed

Standard 8: Assessment

Knowledge

SEP8K1	Rationale for assessment

Skills	
SEP8S1	Demonstrate basic collection techniques as directed
SEP8S2	Make and document objective observations as directed

Standard 9: Professional and Ethical Practice

Knowledge	
SEP9K1	Ethical practices for confidential communication about individuals with exceptional learning needs
SEP9K2	Personal cultural biases and differences that affect one's ability to work with others

Skills	
SEP9S1	Perform responsibilities as directed in a manner consistent with laws and policies
SEP9S2	Follow instructions of the professional
SEP9S3	Demonstrate problem-solving, flexible thinking, conflict management techniques, and analysis of personal strengths and preferences
SEP9S4	Act as a role model for individuals with exceptional learning needs
SEP9S5	Demonstrate commitment to assisting learners in achieving their highest potential
SEP9S6	Demonstrate the ability to separate personal issues from one's responsibilities as a paraeducator
SEP9S7	Maintain a high level of competence and integrity
SEP9S8	Exercise objective and prudent judgment
SEP9S9	Demonstrate proficiency in academic skills, including oral and written communication
SEP9S10	Engage in activities to increase one's own knowledge and skills
SEP9S11	Engage in self-assessment
SEP9S12	Accept and use constructive feedback
SEP9S13	Demonstrate ethical practices as guided by the CEC Code of Ethics and other standards and policies

Standard 10: Collaboration

Knowledge	
SEP10K1	Common concerns of families of individuals with exceptional learning needs
SEP10K2	Roles of stakeholders in planning an individualized program

Skills	
SEP10S1	Assist in collecting and providing objective, accurate information to professionals
SEP10S2	Collaborate with stakeholders as directed
SEP10S3	Foster respectful and beneficial relationships
SEP10S4	Participate as directed in conferences as members of the educational team
SEP10S5	Function in a manner that demonstrates a positive regard for the distinctions between roles and responsibilities of paraeducators and those of professionals

Standard 1: Foundations

Knowledge

SEP1K1	Purposes of programs for individuals with exceptional learning needs
SEP1K2	Basic educational terminology regarding individuals with exceptional learning needs, programs, roles, and instructional activities
DBI1K1	Definition of deaf-blindness
DBI1K2	Differences between congenital and acquired deaf-blindness
DBI1K3	Implications of the age of onset of vision and hearing loss, the types and degrees of loss, and the presence of additional disabilities on development and learning
DBI1K4	Anatomy and function of the eyes and ears

Skills

	None

Standard 2: Development and Characteristics of Learners

Knowledge

SEP2K1	Effects an exceptional condition(s) can have on an individual's life
DBI2K1	Impact of combined vision and hearing loss on development and learning
DBI2K2	Differences between concept development and skill development, and the impact of deaf-blindness on each
DBI2K3	Process of intervention for individuals with deaf-blindness
DBI2K4	Impact of deaf-blindness on bonding, attachment, and social interaction
DBI2K5	Impact of deaf-blindness on psychological development and on the development of self-identity
DBI2K6	Impact of deaf-blindness related to isolation, stress, and vulnerability
DBI2K7	Impact of deaf-blindness on aspects of sexuality
DBI2K8	Impact of additional disabilities on individuals with deaf-blindness
DBI2K9	Brain development and the neurological implications of combined vision and hearing loss

Skills

	None

Standard 3: Individual Learning Differences

Knowledge

SEP3K1	Rights and responsibilities of families and children as they relate to individual learning needs
SEP3K2	Indicators of abuse and neglect
DBI3K1	Specific causes of the deaf-blindness
DBI3K2	Strengths and needs of the individual
DBI3K3	Likes and dislikes of the individual
DBI3K4	Learning style and communication of the individual
DBI3K5	Audiological and ophthalmological conditions and functioning of the individual
DBI3K6	Additional disabilities of the individual, if present
DBI3K7	Effects of additional disabilities on individual, if present

Skills

SEP3S1	Demonstrate sensitivity to the diversity of individuals and families
DBI3S1	Facilitation of the individual's understanding and development of concepts

Standard 4: Instructional Strategies

Knowledge

SEP4K1	Basic instructional and remedial strategies and materials
SEP4K2	Basic technologies appropriate to individuals with exceptional learning needs
DBI4K1	Strategies that promote visual and auditory development
DBI4K2	The use of calendar systems

Skills

SEP4S1	Use strategies, equipment, materials, and technologies, as directed, to accomplish instructional objectives
SEP4S2	Assist in adapting instructional strategies and materials as directed
SEP4S3	Use strategies as directed to facilitate effective integration into various settings
SEP4S4	Use strategies that promote the learner's independence as directed
SEP4S5	Use strategies as directed to increase the individual's independence and confidence
DBI4S1	Provide one-on-one intervention
DBI4S2	Use routines and functional activities as learning opportunities

DBI4S3	Facilitate direct learning experiences
DBI4S4	Use techniques to increase anticipation, motivation, communication, and confirmation
DBI4S5	Facilitate interdependence for the individual
DBI4S6	Vary the level and intensity of input and the pacing of activities
DBI4S7	Adapt materials and activities to the individual's needs, as directed
DBI4S8	Use strategies that provide opportunities to solve problems and to make decisions and choices
DBI4S9	Implement intervention strategies for the individual's daily care, self-help, transition, and job training
DBI4S10	Use prescribed strategies to respond to the individual's behavior
DBI4S11	Provide the individual with opportunities for self-determination
DBI4S12	Use touch to supplement auditory and visual input and to convey information
DBI4S13	Facilitate individual's use of touch for learning and interaction
DBI4S14	Facilitate individual's use of the other senses to supplement learning modalities
DBI4S15	Utilize strategies that support the development of body awareness, spatial relationships, and related concepts
DBI4S16	Make adaptations for the cognitive and physical needs of the individual
DBI4S17	Important adaptations consistent with the medical needs of the individual as directed
DBI4S18	Utilize strategies to promote sensory integration
DBI4S19	Utilize strategies that promote independent and safe movement and active exploration of the environment
DBI4S20	Implement positioning and handling as directed by the occupational therapist, physical therapist, orientation and mobility specialists
DBI4S21	Promote the use of sighted guide, trailing, and protective techniques as directed by the orientation and mobility specialists
DBI4S22	Implement strategies for travel as directed by an orientation and mobility specialist
DBI4S23	Implement the use of mobility devices as directed by the orientation and mobility specialist

Standard 5: Learning Environments/Social Interactions

Knowledge

SEP5K1	Demands of various learning environments
SEP5K2	Rules and procedural safeguards regarding the management of behaviors of individuals with exceptional learning needs

Skills	
SEP5S1	Establish and maintain rapport with learners
SEP5S2	Use universal precautions and assist in maintaining a safe, healthy learning environment
SEP5S3	Use strategies for managing behavior as directed
SEP5S4	Use strategies as directed, in a variety of settings, to assist in the development of social skills
DBI5S1	Establish a trusting relationship with the individual
DBI5S2	Provide an atmosphere of acceptance, safety, and security that is reliable and consistent for the individual
DBI5S3	Promote positive self-esteem and well-being in the individual
DBI5S4	Promote social interactions and the development of meaningful relationships with an ever expanding number of people
DBI5S5	Use and maintain amplification, cochlear implants, and assistive listening devices as directed
DBI5S6	Use and maintain glasses, low-vision devices, and prostheses as directed
DBI5S7	Maximize the use of residual vision and hearing
DBI5S8	Make adaptations for auditory needs as directed
DBI5S9	Make adaptations for visual needs as directed
DBI5S10	Utilize health and safety practices

Standard 6: Language

Knowledge	
SEP6K1	Characteristics of appropriate communication with stakeholders
DBI6K1	Basic communication development
DBI6K2	Impact of deaf-blindness on communication and interaction
DBI6K3	Modes/forms of communication and devices used by individuals who are deaf-blind

Skills	
DBI6S1	Facilitate language and literacy development
DBI6S2	Observe and identify the communicative behaviors and intents
DBI6S3	Implement methods and strategies for effectively conveying information to the individual
DBI6S4	Respond to the individual's attempts at communication
DBI6S5	Use communication techniques specific to the individual

DBI6S6	Incorporate/embed language and communication into all routines and activities
DBI6S7	Use strategies for eliciting expressive communication
DBI6S8	Use strategies to promote turn-taking
DBI6S9	Use strategies to enhance and expand communication

Standard 7: Instructional Planning

Knowledge

	None

Skills

SEP7S1	Follow written plans, seeking clarification as needed
SEP7S2	Prepare and organize materials to support teaching and learning as directed

Standard 8: Assessment

Knowledge

SEP8K1	Rationale for assessment
DBI8S1	Collect data and monitor progress as directed

Skills

SEP8S1	Demonstrate basic collection techniques as directed
SEP8S2	Make and document objective observations as directed

Standard 9: Professional And Ethical Practice

Knowledge

SEP9K1	Ethical practices for confidential communication about individuals with exceptional learning needs
SEP9K2	Personal cultural biases and differences that affect one's ability to work with others
DBI9K1	The role of the intervener in the process of intervention
DBI9K2	The roles and responsibilities of interveners in various settings
DBI9K3	The difference between interveners, paraeducators, interpreters, aides, caregivers, and special education assistants

Skills

SEP9S1	Perform responsibilities as directed in a manner consistent with laws and policies

SEP9S2	Follow instructions of the professional
SEP9S3	Demonstrate problem-solving, flexible thinking, conflict management techniques, and analysis of personal strengths and preferences
SEP9S4	Act as a role model for individuals with exceptional learning needs
SEP9S5	Demonstrate commitment to assisting learners in achieving their highest potential
SEP9S6	Demonstrate the ability to separate personal issues from one's responsibilities as a paraeducator
SEP9S7	Maintain a high level of competence and integrity
SEP9S8	Exercise objective and prudent judgment
SEP9S9	Demonstrate proficiency in academic skills, including oral and written communication
SEP9S10	Engage in activities to increase one's own knowledge and skills
SEP9S11	Engage in self-assessment
SEP9S12	Accept and use constructive feedback
SEP9S13	Demonstrate ethical practices as guided by the CEC Code of Ethics and other standards and policies
DBI9S1	Adhere to the identified code of ethics including confidentiality
DBI9S2	Pursue ongoing professional development specific to their role and responsibilities

Standard 10: Collaboration

Knowledge

SEP10K1	Common concerns of families of individuals with exceptional learning needs
SEP10K2	Roles of stakeholders in planning an individualized program
DBI10K1	The roles and supervisory responsibilities of team members and consultants

Skills

SEP10S1	Assist in collecting and providing objective, accurate information to professionals
SEP10S2	Collaborate with stakeholders as directed
SEP10S3	Foster respectful and beneficial relationships
SEP10S4	Participate as directed in conferences as members of the educational team
SEP10S5	Function in a manner that demonstrates a positive regard for the distinctions between roles and responsibilities of paraeducators and those of professionals
DBI10S1	Utilize teaming skills in working with team members

DBI10S2	Share observations of individual's communication skills with others
DBI10S3	Communicate and problem-solve with the IFSP/IEP team about the student's needs as appropriate
DBI10S4	Interact with families as directed

SPECIAL EDUCATION PARAEDUCATOR FORMS

The CEC publication *Parability* is a great reference for paraeducator standards and Special Education Paraeducator Forms. These forms are tools paraeducators and paraeducator training programs can use to ensure that they are meeting the CEC Standards for Special Education Paraeducators. Form 1 (see page 202) is a tool paraeducator training programs can use to evaluate whether or not their program sufficiently addresses the CEC Standards for the Preparation of Special Education Paraeducators. Preparation programs can use the chart in several ways. If developing a new program, faculty can use the chart to ensure that the essential knowledge and skills are included in the course curriculum. This can be done by cross-referencing each of the standards to the course content, field experiences. Programs can also use these standards to ensure that their assessments adequately evaluate the knowledge and skills of special education paraeducators. This can be done by cross-referencing required assessments to each of the standards. Form 2 (see page 207) is a self-evaluation instrument designed to be used by candidates in paraeducator training programs to evaluate their progress in learning and applying the paraeducator knowledge and skills. Candidates can use this as a self-assessment tool as they move through the program, checking each knowledge and skill as it is mastered. This could also be used as a summative assessment at the end of the training program.

REFERENCES

Study of Personnel Needs in Special Education, Table 2.91. (2003). Retrieved October 24, 2008, from http://ferdig.coe.ufl. edu/spense/scripts/tables/htdocs/TABLE2_9.htm

FORM 1

Special Education Paraeducator Training Program Evaluation:
Are the Standards Addressed and Assessed?

Standard	What opportunities do candidates have to master this standard?	How does the program assess that candidates have mastered this standard?
Standard 1: Foundations		
Knowledge		
PE1K1	Purposes of programs for individuals with exceptional learning needs		
PE1K2	Basic educational terminology regarding students, programs, roles, and instructional activities		
Standard 2: Development and Characteristics of Learners		
Knowledge		
PE2K1	Effects an exceptional condition(s) can have on an individual's life		
Standard 3: Individual Learning Differences		
Knowledge		
PE3K1	Rights and responsibilities of families and children as they relate to individual learning needs		
PE3K2	Indicators of abuse and neglect		
Skills		
PE3S1	Demonstrate sensitivity to the diversity of individuals and families		
Standard 4: Instructional Strategies		
Knowledge		
PE4K1	Basic instructional and remedial strategies and materials		

Standard		What opportunities do candidates have to master this standard?	How does the program assess that candidates have mastered this standard?
PE4K2	Basic technologies appropriate to individuals with exceptional learning needs		

Skills

PE4S1	Use strategies, equipment, materials, and technologies, as directed, to accomplish instructional objectives		
PE4S2	Assist in adapting instructional strategies and materials as directed		
PE4S3	Use strategies as directed to facilitate effective integration into various settings		
PE4S4	Use strategies that promote the learner's independence as directed		
PE4S5	Use strategies as directed to increase the individual's independence and confidence.		

Standard 5: Learning Environments and Social Interactions

Knowledge

PE5K1	Demands of various learning environments		
PE5K2	Rules and procedural safeguards regarding the management of behaviors of individuals with exceptional learning needs		

Skills

PE5S1	Establish and maintain rapport with learners		
PE5S2	Use universal precautions and assist in maintaining a safe, healthy learning environment		
PE5S3	Use strategies for managing behavior as directed		

Standard	What opportunities do candidates have to master this standard?	How does the program assess that candidates have mastered this standard?
PE5S4	Use strategies as directed, in a variety of settings, to assist in the development of social skills		
Standard 6: Language			
Knowledge			
PE6K1	Characteristics of appropriate communication with stakeholders		
Standard 7: Instructional Planning			
Skills			
PE7S1	Follow written plans, seeking clarification as needed		
PE7S2	Prepare and organize materials to support teaching and learning as directed		
Standard 8: Assessment			
Knowledge			
PE8K1	Rationale for assessment		
Skills			
PE8S1	Demonstrate basic collection techniques as directed		
PE8S2	Make and document objective observations as directed		
Standard 9: Professional and Ethics Practice			
Knowledge			
PE9K1	Ethical practices for confidential communication about individuals with exceptional learning needs		

Standard		What opportunities do candidates have to master this standard?	How does the program assess that candidates have mastered this standard?
PE9K2	Personal cultural biases and differences that affect one's ability to work with others		
Skills			
PE9S1	Perform responsibilities as directed in a manner consistent with laws and policies		
PE9S2	Follow instructions of the professional		
PE9S3	Demonstrate problem-solving, flexible thinking, conflict management techniques, and analysis of personal strengths and preferences		
PE9S4	Act as a role model for individuals with exceptional learning needs		
PE9S5	Demonstrate commitment to assisting learners in achieving their highest potential		
PE9S6	Demonstrate the ability to separate personal issues from one's responsibilities as a paraeducator		
PE9S7	Maintain a high level of competence and integrity		
PE9S8	Exercise objective and prudent judgment		
PE9S9	Demonstrate proficiency in academic skills, including oral and written communication		
PE9S10	Engage in activities to increase one's own knowledge and skills		
PE9S11	Engage in self-assessment		
PE9S12	Accept and use constructive feedback		

Standard		What opportunities do candidates have to master this standard?	How does the program assess that candidates have mastered this standard?
PE9S13	Demonstrate ethical practices as guided by the CEC Code of Ethics and other standards and policies		

Standard 10: Collaboration

Knowledge

PE10K1	Common concerns of families of individuals with exceptional learning needs		
PE10K2	Roles of stakeholders in planning an individualized program		

Skills

PE10S1	Assist in collecting and providing objective, accurate information to professionals.		
PE10S2	Collaborate with stakeholders as directed		
PE10S3	Foster respectful and beneficial relationships		
PE10S4	Participate as directed in conferences as members of the educational team		
PE10S5	Function in a manner that demonstrates a positive regard for the distinctions between roles and responsibilities of paraeducators and those of professionals		

FORM 2
Special Education Paraeducator Self-Evaluation:
Have I Mastered the Standards?

Standard		What is my level of mastery of this standard?	
		Novice	*Proficient*
Standard 1: Foundations			
Knowledge			
PE1K1	Purposes of programs for individuals with exceptional learning needs		
PE1K2	Basic educational terminology regarding students, programs, roles, and instructional activities		
Standard 2: Development and Characteristics of Learners			
Knowledge			
PE2K1	Effects an exceptional condition(s) can have on an individual's life		
Standard 3: Individual Learning Differences			
Knowledge			
PE3K1	Rights and responsibilities of families and children as they relate to individual learning needs		
PE3K2	Indicators of abuse and neglect		
Skills			
PE3S1	Demonstrate sensitivity to the diversity of individuals and families		
Standard 4: Instructional Strategies			
Knowledge			
PE4K1	Basic instructional and remedial strategies and materials		
PE4K2	Basic technologies appropriate to individuals with exceptional learning needs		

Standard		What is my level of mastery of this standard?	
		Novice	Proficient
Skills			
PE4S1	Use strategies, equipment, materials, and technologies, as directed, to accomplish instructional objectives		
PE4S2	Assist in adapting instructional strategies and materials as directed		
PE4S3	Use strategies as directed to facilitate effective integration into various settings		
PE4S4	Use strategies that promote the learner's independence as directed		
PE4S5	Use strategies as directed to increase the individual's independence and confidence.		
Standard 5: Learning Environments and Social Interactions			
Knowledge			
PE5K1	Demands of various learning environments		
PE5K2	Rules and procedural safeguards regarding the management of behaviors of individuals with exceptional learning needs		
Skills			
PE5S1	Establish and maintain rapport with learners		
PE5S2	Use universal precautions and assist in maintaining a safe, healthy learning environment		
PE5S3	Use strategies for managing behavior as directed		
PE5S4	Use strategies as directed, in a variety of settings, to assist in the development of social skills		

Standard	What is my level of mastery of this standard?	
	Novice	Proficient
Standard 6: Language		
Knowledge		
PE6K1 Characteristics of appropriate communication with stakeholders		
Standard 7: Instructional Planning		
Skills		
PE7S1 Follow written plans, seeking clarification as needed		
PE7S2 Prepare and organize materials to support teaching and learning as directed		
Standard 8: Assessment		
Knowledge		
PE8K1 Rationale for assessment		
Skills		
PE8S1 Demonstrate basic collection techniques as directed		
PE8S2 Make and document objective observations as directed		
Standard 9: Professional and Ethics Practice		
Knowledge		
PE9K1 Ethical practices for confidential communication about individuals with exceptional learning needs		
PE9K2 Personal cultural biases and differences that affect one's ability to work with others		
Skills		
PE9S1 Perform responsibilities as directed in a manner consistent with laws and policies		
PE9S2 Follow instructions of the professional		

Standard		What is my level of mastery of this standard?	
		Novice	Proficient
PE9S3	Demonstrate problem-solving, flexible thinking, conflict management techniques, and analysis of personal strengths and preferences		
PE9S4	Act as a role model for individuals with exceptional learning needs.		
PE9S5	Demonstrate commitment to assisting learners in achieving their highest potential.		
PE9S6	Demonstrate the ability to separate personal issues from one's responsibilities as a paraeducator		
PE9S7	Maintain a high level of competence and integrity		
PE9S8	Exercise objective and prudent judgment		
PE9S9	Demonstrate proficiency in academic skills, including oral and written communication		
PE9S10	Engage in activities to increase one's own knowledge and skills		
PE9S11	Engage in self-assessment		
PE9S12	Accept and use constructive feedback		
PE9S13	Demonstrate ethical practices as guided by the CEC Code of Ethics and other standards and policies		

Standard 10: Collaboration

Knowledge

PE10K1	Common concerns of families of individuals with exceptional learning needs		
PE10K2	Roles of stakeholders in planning an individualized program		

Standard		What is my level of mastery of this standard?	
		Novice	Proficient
Skills			
PE10S1	Assist in collecting and providing objective, accurate information to professionals.		
PE10S2	Collaborate with stakeholders as directed		
PE10S3	Foster respectful and beneficial relationships		
PE10S4	Participate as directed in conferences as members of the educational team		
PE10S5	Function in a manner that demonstrates a positive regard for the distinctions between roles and responsibilities of paraeducators and those of professionals		

Appendices

CEC often gets questions regarding the knowledge and skills in several domains of interest. For convenience, the knowledge and skills from the CEC Initial Common Core that are relevant to the following subjects have been excerpted. There are additional knowledge and skills relevant to these topics in the respective Initial and Advanced Knowledge and Skill Sets.

Supervision of Paraeducators

Number	Standard
ICC5S15	Structure, direct, and support the activities of paraeducators, volunteers, and tutors
ICC7K5	Roles and responsibilities of the paraeducators related to instruction, intervention, and direct service
ICC10S11	Observe, evaluate, and provide feedback to Paraeducators

A foundation assumption of the CEC standards is that all special education professionals will use evidence-based research in their decision-making. This is indicated in the standards by the numerous times the standards call for teachers to use "effective" strategies. Two Common Core Standards also deal specifically with this issue.

Evidence-Based Practice and Use Of Research

Number	Standard
ICC1K1	Models, theories, philosophies, and research methods that form the basis for special education practice
ICC4K1	Evidence-based practices validated for specific characteristics of learners and settings
ICC7S13	Make responsive adjustments to instruction based on continual observations
ICC7S15	Evaluate and modify instructional practices in response to ongoing assessment data
ICC9K4	Methods to remain current regarding research-validated practice
ICC9S13	Demonstrate commitment to engage in evidence-based practices

Multicultural Competence

Number	Standard
ICC1K5	Issues in definition and identification of individuals with exceptional learning needs, including those from culturally and linguistically diverse backgrounds
ICC1K8	Historical points of view and contribution of culturally diverse groups
ICC1K9	Impact of the dominant culture on shaping schools and the individuals who study and work in them
ICC1K10	Potential impact of differences in values, languages, and customs that can exist between the home and school
ICC2K3	Characteristics and effects of the cultural and environmental milieu of the individual with exceptional learning needs and the family
ICC3K2	Impact of learners' academic and social abilities, attitudes, interests, and values on instruction and career development
ICC3K3	Variations in beliefs, traditions, and values across and within cultures and their effects on relationships among individuals with exceptional learning needs, family, and schooling
ICC3K4	Cultural perspectives influencing the relationships among families, schools, and communities as related to instruction
ICC3K5	Differing ways of learning of individuals with exceptional learning needs including those from culturally diverse backgrounds and strategies for addressing these differences
ICC5K4	Teacher attitudes and behaviors that influence behavior of individuals with exceptional learning needs
ICC5K7	Strategies for preparing individuals to live harmoniously and productively in a culturally diverse world
ICC5K8	Ways to create learning environments that allow individuals to retain and appreciate their own and each other's respective language and cultural heritage
ICC5K9	Ways specific cultures are negatively stereotyped
ICC5K10	Strategies used by diverse populations to cope with a legacy of former and continuing racism
ICC5S1	Create a safe, equitable, positive, and supportive learning environment in which diversities are valued
ICC5S13	Organize, develop, and sustain learning environments that support positive intracultural and intercultural experiences
ICC5S14	Mediate controversial intercultural issues among students within the learning environment in ways that enhance any culture, group, or person
ICC6K1	Effects of cultural and linguistic differences on growth and development

ICC6K2	Characteristics of one's own culture and use of language and the ways in which these can differ from other cultures and uses of languages
ICC6K3	Ways of behaving and communicating among cultures that can lead to misinterpretation and misunderstanding
ICC6S2	Use communication strategies and resources to facilitate understanding of subject matter for students whose primary language is not the dominant language
ICC7S8	Develop and select instructional content, resources, and strategies that respond to cultural, linguistic, and gender differences
ICC7S14	Prepare individuals to exhibit self-enhancing behavior in response to societal attitudes and actions
ICC8S2	Administer nonbiased formal and informal assessments
ICC8S6	Use assessment information in making eligibility, program, and placement decisions for individuals with exceptional learning needs, including those from culturally and/or linguistically diverse backgrounds
ICC9K1	Personal cultural biases and differences that affect one's teaching
ICC9S6	Demonstrate sensitivity for the culture, language, religion, gender, disability, socio-economic status, and sexual orientation of individuals
ICC10K4	Culturally responsive factors that promote effective communication and collaboration with individuals with exceptional learning needs, families, school personnel, and community members
ICC10S10	Communicate effectively with families of individuals with exceptional learning needs from diverse backgrounds

Student Self-Determination

Number	Standard
ICC4S2	Teach individuals to use self-assessment, problem-solving, and other cognitive strategies to meet their needs
ICC4S5	Use procedures to increase the individual's self-awareness, self-management, self-control, self-reliance, and self-esteem
ICC5S8	Teach self-advocacy
ICC5S9	Create an environment that encourages self-advocacy and increased independence
ICC7S3	Involve the individual and family in setting instructional goals and monitoring progress
ICC7S14	Prepare individuals to exhibit self-enhancing behavior in response to societal attitudes and actions
ICC8S7	Report assessment results to all stakeholders using effective communication skills
ICC10S4	Assist individuals with exceptional learning needs and their families in becoming active participants in the educational team
ICC10S5	Plan and conduct collaborative conferences with individuals with exceptional learning needs and their families

ICC10S7	Use group problem-solving skills to develop, implement, and evaluate collaborative activities

Collaboration and Co-Teaching

Number	Standard
ICC10K1	Models and strategies of consultation and collaboration
ICC10K2	Roles of individuals with exceptional learning needs, families, and school and community personnel in planning of an individualized program
ICC10K3	Concerns of families of individuals with exceptional learning needs and strategies to help address these concerns
ICC10K4	Culturally responsive factors that promote effective communication and collaboration with individuals with exceptional learning needs, families, school personnel, and community members
ICC10S1	Maintain confidential communication about individuals with exceptional learning needs
ICC10S2	Collaborate with families and others in assessment of individuals with exceptional learning needs
ICC10S3	Foster respectful and beneficial relationships between families and professionals
ICC10S4	Assist individuals with exceptional learning needs and their families in becoming active participants in the educational team
ICC10S5	Plan and conduct collaborative conferences with individuals with exceptional learning needs and their families
ICC10S6	Collaborate with school personnel and community members in integrating individuals with exceptional learning needs into various settings
ICC10S7	Use group problem-solving skills to develop, implement, and evaluate collaborative activities
ICC10S8	Model techniques and coach others in the use of instructional methods and accommodations
ICC10S9	Communicate with school personnel about the characteristics and needs of individuals with exceptional learning needs
ICC10S10	Communicate effectively with families of individuals with exceptional learning needs from diverse backgrounds
ICC10S11	Observe, evaluate, and provide feedback to paraeducators

CEC carries out the development of professional standards through the Professional Standards and Practice Standing Committee (PSPSC) and its relevant subcommittees. The CEC Preparation Standards begin with the validation of knowledge and skill sets for the respective specialty areas in special education. These sets delineate the specialized knowledge and skills that practicing professionals should have mastered for safe and effective practice. Each of the knowledge and skills are founded on a literature base that is available at the CEC Professional Standards website.

In turn, CEC distills the knowledge and skill sets into the Initial and Advanced Roles Content Standards. These content standards are rich narratives of the responsibilities special educators in initial and advanced roles respectively. They span across the various specialty areas.

It should be noted in its partnership with NCATE, CEC conducts its reviews of program reports for national recognition at the content standard level. Undergirding each of the narrative content standards are validated knowledge and skill sets for the Common Core and each of the Areas of Specialization. While CEC reviews preparation programs at the Content Standard level, **not** at the knowledge and skill level, CEC expects preparation programs to incorporate the knowledge and skills into their curriculum, and that the program assessments reflect the content, issues, and contexts of the knowledge and skills in the respective areas of specialization.

Any program that prepares candidates for their first special education license will use initial level standards regardless of whether the preparation program is at the graduate or undergraduate level. Programs preparing already licensed special educators for advanced roles will use the advanced standards. Following is a flowchart to help program faculty to identify the appropriate knowledge and skill sets for a program.

Figure A1 Architecture of the CEC Preparation Standards

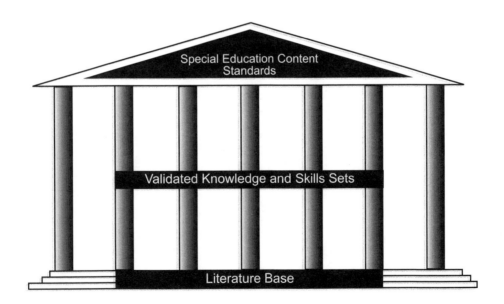

Figure 2.0 NCATE Classification of Initial & Advanced Level Programs

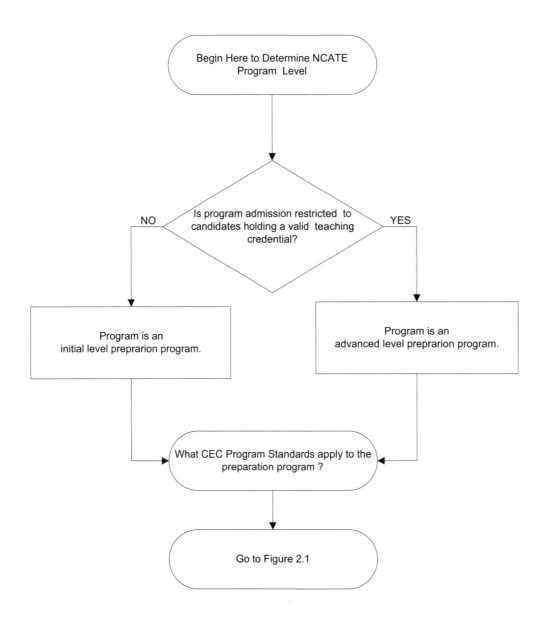

Figure 2.1 CEC Initial Special Education Preparation Standards

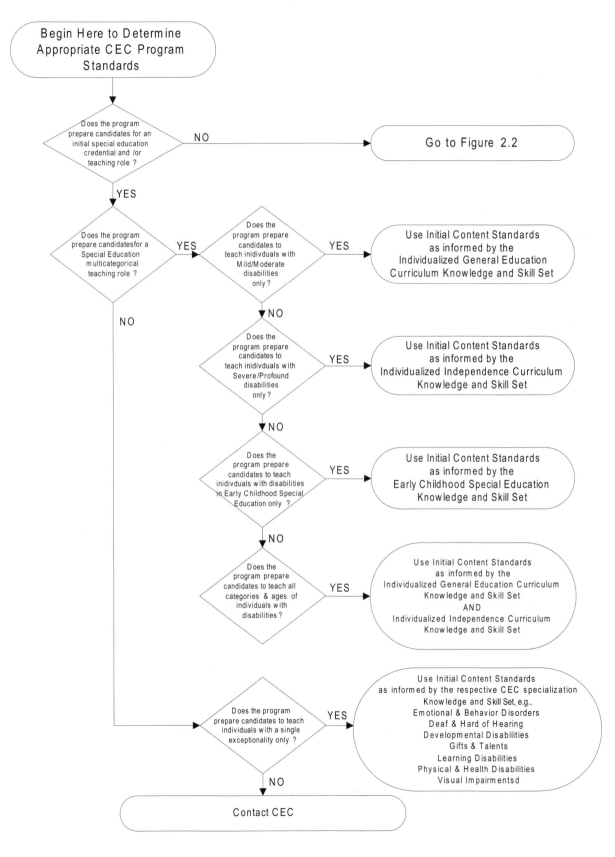

Figure 2.2 CEC Advanced Special Education Preparation Standards

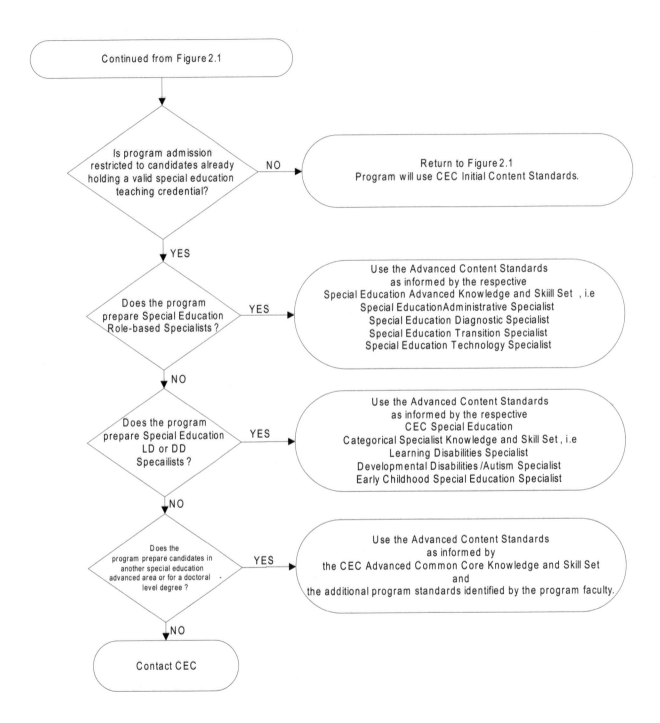

Tenative Schedule

Validation Study	Sponsor	Partner	Status
2004			
Research Standards Addendum to ICC	DR		Approved
2005			
Initial DD	DDD		Approved
Advanced Common Core	K&S		Approved
2006			
Initial ECSE	DEC	NAEYC	Approved
Initial G&T	TAG	NAGC	Approved
2007			
Early Childhood Special Education Specialist	DEC	NAEYC	Approved
Special Education Administrator	CASE		Approved
2008			
Initial Emotional/Behavior Disorders	CCBD		Approved
Transition Specialist	DCDT		Cancelled
Educational Diagnostic Specialist	CEDS		Approved
Initial Deaf and Hard of Hearing	DCDD	CED	Approved
Deaf/Hard of Hearing Specialist	DCDD	CED	Approved
Initial Physical and Health Disabilities	DPHD		Approved
Physical Health and Disabilities Specialist	DPHD		Cancelled for 2008
Initial Visual Impairments	DVI		Complete
2009			
Special Education Technology Specialist	TAM	ISTE	2009
Deaf/Blind Specialist	DVI		Smoothed 09 2008

Validation Study	Sponsor	Partner	Status
Inclusion Specialist	TED		2009
Visual Impairments Specialist	DVI	AER States DB Project	Planning
DD/Autism Specialist	DDD	ASA/O CALI	Smoothed 09 2008
Initial DD/Autism	DDD	ASA/O CALI	Smoothed 09 2008
Emotional/Behavior Disorders Specialist	CCBD		In Study
2010			
Learning Disabilities Specialist	DLD	CLD	In Process
Individualized General Curriculum	K&S		Planning
Individualized Independent Curriculum	K&S		Planning
Special Education Paraeducators	Ad Hoc		Planning
Initial Common Core	K&S		Planning
2011			
Initial Learning Disabilities	DLD	CLD	Cancelled (to be rescheduled in 2010)

Validation Study Procedures

The following process was approved in 2003 for the development, validation, and revalidation of the Knowledge and Skill Standards. The process was amended to ensure that there was an explicit documentation of the research and literature base for the standards. Please note that any member or recognized unit within CEC may recommend additions or amendments to the Knowledge and Skill Standards by submitting the request to the Assistant Executive Director for Professional Standards at CEC Headquarters.

1. The PSPSC determines Knowledge and Skill sets to be developed and/or revalidated. The PSPSC identifies a set group facilitator (SF) to guide the process.

2. The KSS Chair and SF establish a small focused work group.

3. The work group identifies possible items for validation, documents the professional literature that supports each proposed knowledge and skill statement, summarizes the literature base, formats the items, and submits this information to the KSS.

4. The KSS reviews the work of the group to ensure readiness of the standards for survey.

5. The PSPU conducts the survey of CEC members using a targeted stratified random sample and Knowledge and Skill statements and submits its results to the KSS Chair and the SF.

6. A select group of experts, selected by the PSPSC Chair in consultation with the SF, reviews the standards and the survey data.

7. The KSS reviews and approves the revalidated or validated set of Knowledge and Skills.

8. The PSPSC oversees the process, makes a determination regarding the KSS recommendations, and submits its decision to the CEC Board of Directors.

The Knowledge and Skill Standards are designed to address the knowledge and skills that a professional who is entering a new special education position in order to practice safely and effectively. Preparation programs should conduct a systematic analysis of the courses of study to assure that the candidates they prepare have mastery of the appropriate knowledge and skills.

Guidelines for Editing Proposed Knowledge and Skill Statements

❑ Use simple active voice.

❑ Write statements as what a teacher does not what a student learns or does.

❑ Keep statements general but convey the knowledge or skill clearly.

❑ Do not write statements for specific methods or strategies, e.g., the xyz learning strategy or the xyz reading method.

❑ Avoid qualifiers, such as "appropriate." Selective use of "effective" or "effectively" is permitted.

❑ Eliminate statements that are redundant with a statement in the Initial or Advanced Common Core.

❑ Remove long and partial lists unless there are only a few inclusive items.

❑ Remove parenthetical information.

❑ Remove examples when the meaning of the statement is clear without them.

❑ Use terminology consistently:

Individuals with exceptional learning needs (rather than individuals with exceptionalities or student, child…, and so forth)

Families (rather than parents, caregivers, and so forth); "child" may be appropriate in statements that focus on the family

Strategies (rather than methods, techniques, and so forth) [1]

Individuals from diverse backgrounds (rather than "culturally and/or linguistically diverse" backgrounds)

Laws and policies (not regulations, rules, guidelines, and so forth)

Stakeholders

Paraeducators

Nonbiased (rather than unbiased)

❑ Eliminate redundant statements, and combine closely related statements.

❑ Delete knowledge items that are prerequisites for skill items.

❑ Keep specificity level similar across statements.

❑ Do not write statements to influence the content of other disciplines,

❑ Do not duplicate NCATE basic standards.

❑ Equip teachers to be effective teachers.

Working Glossary

General Curriculum: The general curriculum is the curriculum available to and used in teaching all students. The general curriculum is determined by the state, provincial and local definition of what a student should know. Often specified at a given grade level, the general curriculum is based on a set of state or local standards in such areas as English language arts, mathematics, science, health, social studies, fine arts, and physical education.

Special Curriculum: Special curriculum is any modified or expanded curriculum that enables individuals with exceptional learning needs to access the general education curriculum and enables individuals with

---

[1] In the field of learning disabilities, the term strategy only refers to strategies students use in learning. In the field of Learning Disabilities, the term *method* refers to what the teacher uses.

exceptional learning needs to function in society. Special curricula may include but are not limited to:

- Social interaction skills
- Life skills
- Orientation and mobility
- Leisure/recreation
- Augmentative and alternative communication
- Assistive technology
- Self-advocacy
- Compensatory skills
- Learning skills
- Study skills
- Research skills
- Problem solving
- Sexuality

Stakeholders: Stakeholders include individuals and/or agencies having a stake in the outcome of a procedure, program, or setting in which an individual with an exceptional learning need participates. The term may include, but is not limited to, an individual with exceptional learning needs, family, teachers, paraeducators, administrators, community members, and support service providers.

Post School: Education, training, and service options available after a student terminates his/her school (K-12) career as mandated by state/provincial laws and policies, that may include but are not limited to: vocational/professional schools/programs, community colleges, colleges/universities, vocational/rehabilitation, military, supported employment, and sheltered workshops.

Families: Families includes a broad range of relationships across individuals with mutual concerns and intent to care for each other. These relationships include but go beyond biological ties. Family constellations take many forms including but not limited to the nuclear family, blended families, extended families, and a variety of nontraditional families.

Development Validation Studies Procedures

CEC carries out the development of professional standards through the Professional Standards and Practice Standing Committee (PSPSC) and its relevant subcommittees. One of the major responsibilities of the PSPSC has been the development, validation, and updating of the knowledge and skills bases in the various areas of special education.

In 1989, the PSPSC established the first Knowledge and Skills Subcommittee (KSS), co-chaired by Barbara Sirvis, of New York, and Bill Swan, of Georgia, and composed of CEC division representatives and past CEC Teachers of the Year. It set out to accomplish the following two major tasks:

- Identify a common core of knowledge and skills for all beginning special education teachers

- Create specialty sets of knowledge and skills that are necessary to teach in a particular area of exceptionality or age group

The KSS gathered materials from literature; state, provincial, and local governments; institutions of higher education; and elsewhere. The KSS then identified and organized thousands of competencies into major categories, culled them down to 195 statements, and determined the importance of each by surveying a 1,000-person sample of CEC membership. Based on the response (54%), the KSS reduced the number of statements to 107. CEC adopted these validated statements, which became "The CEC Common Core of Knowledge and Skills Essential for All Beginning Special Education Teachers," published in the fall 1992 issue of *TEACHING Exceptional Children.* Alan Koenig, of Texas, assumed the chairmanship of the 1993 KSS and began developing specialty sets of knowledge and skills to supplement the Common Core. The exceptionality and age-specific CEC divisions took the lead, developing sets of knowledge and skills necessary to teach in their areas of specialization. The KSS worked with the divisions to ensure that the specialty sets were formatted properly and that the statements supplemented the Common Core. The KSS also developed a survey, which was sent to a random sample of the division's membership to validate the specialty sets. Each survey was sent to a sample of CEC members, half of whom were teachers and other direct service providers. Modifications were made in consultation with the division. There was concurrence with the work the division produced. In 1996, after initial publication of *What Every Special Educator Must Know,* comments were received from the field regarding the knowledge and skills statements. After review of all of the comments, CEC approved in the spring of 1996 a number of technical and clarifying changes. These were included in the second edition of this publication. In 1996, the KSS began to develop a procedure for developing a set of standards that would be curriculum-referenced rather than disability-category-specific. In 1998, the KSS, now chaired by Rachelle Bruno of Kentucky, completed the development of this Curriculum Referenced Licensing and Program Accreditation Framework. This new framework was approved by the PSPSC in April 1998. The KSS also approved Knowledge and Skill sets for educational diagnosticians and special education administrators.

The special education paraeducator knowledge and skills were approved in 1998 with the close collaboration of the National Resource Center for Paraeducators, the National Education Association, and the American Federation of Teachers. In 2000, the KSS, now chaired by Kathlene Shank of Illinois, successfully completed a revision of the Common Core and a Knowledge and Skill set for Technology Specialist and Transition Specialists. The KSS also began a major effort to refine and update the standards. In order to provide assistance to the more than 30 states that use the 10 Interstate New Teacher and Assessment and Support Consortium (INTASC) principles, the KSS reorganized all of the CEC Knowledge and Skill standards from the 8 domain areas to the 10 domains that coordinate with the INTASC principles. They then edited all of the Knowledge and Skill sets to eliminate redundancy and to increase the precision of the language. In addition, several new items were validated and added to the Common Core in the areas of multicultural competence, access to the general education curriculum, technology, and collaboration. KSS then wrote the CEC Content Standards that are used by teacher preparation programs as the benchmark for a candidate performance assessment system. Instead of lists of knowledge and skill standards, the 2001 Content Standards consisted of 10 narrative standards. These standards were written to reflect the content of the validated common core knowledge and skills in each of the 10 domain areas of the Knowledge and Skill Standards. The Knowledge and Skill Standards inform the Content Standards. The 10 Initial Content Standards are the same for all initial programs.

In 2004, the Subcommittee on Knowledge and Skills strengthened the Initial Common Core specific to research related knowledge and skills. Four new knowledge and skill statements were added to the common core. Also, in 2004 the Subcommittee initiated a process of developing Advanced Standards. In 2005, with Kathlene Shank now serving as Chair of the CEC Professional Standards Committee, Scott Sparks assumed leadership of the Subcommittee on Knowledge and Skills, and the Subcommittee finalized the six Advanced Content Standards and finalized the advanced level common core knowledge and skills.

Under the leadership of Scott Sparks, the Subcommittee on Knowledge and Skills between 2005 and publication of this edition revalidated the initial sets of knowledge and skills for Teachers of Individuals: Early Childhood, Gifted and Talented, Emotional and Behavior Disorders, Deaf and Hard of Hearing, Physical and Health Disabilities, and Visual Impairments. In addition, Transition Specialist knowledge and skills were realigned to the six advanced content standards and the following advanced knowledge and skill sets were validated: Early Childhood, Early Intervention Specialist; Special Education Administrator; Diagnostician; Deaf and Hard of Hearing Specialist; and Physical and Health Disabilities Specialist.

Brief Timeline of CEC Professional Standards Events

1922   CEC declares the establishment of professional standards for the field of special education as a fundamental aim of CEC.

1962   Professional Standards is the theme of the CEC national convention.

1963   CEC purpose statement includes standards for professional personnel.

1965   CEC holds National Conference on Professional Standards.

1966   CEC publishes Professional Standards for Personnel in the Education of Exceptional Children.

1976   CEC publishes Guidelines for Personnel in the Education of Exceptional Children.
        CEC and the National Council for Accreditation of Teacher Education (NCATE) form a partnership for approving training programs.

1980   NCATE adopts CEC standards for recognizing special education preparation programs.

1981   CEC Delegate Assembly charges CEC to develop, promote, and implement preparation and certification standards, and a code of ethics.

1982   CEC mission statement calls CEC to establish and promote appropriate professional standards.

1983   CEC adopts Code of Ethics, Standards for Professional Practice, Standards for the Preparation of Special Education Personnel, and Standards for Entry to Professional Practice, and charges the Professional Standard & Practice Standing Committee with their implementation.

1984   NCATE adopts CEC revised standards. NCATE adopts their "Redesign" where colleges and universities submit their folios to the respective professional organizations.

1985   NCATE adopts Guidelines for Program Approval of both basic and advanced special education preparation programs.

1986   CEC adopts guidelines for folio preparation. CEC begins reviewing folios of programs seeking national accreditation.

1987   CEC publishes Standards and Guidelines for Curriculum Excellence in Personnel Preparation Programs in Special Education.

1989   CEC Delegate Assembly adopts policy framework for CEC Standards for Entry to Professional Practice.

1990   NCATE adopts CEC revised Guidelines for Program Approval of both basic and advanced special education preparation programs.

1992   CEC adopts the Common Core of Knowledge and Skills Essential for All Beginning Special Education Teachers. CEC adopts non-NCATE Guidelines for Program Approval for institutions of higher education (IHE) including institutional, faculty, and program resources.

1993   CEC revises the Standards for Entry to Professional Practice. CEC revises non-NCATE Guidelines for Program Approval for IHEs including institutional, faculty, and program resources.

1995   CEC adopts initial areas of specialization knowledge and skill standards. New standards published and submitted for NCATE adoption. CEC publishes *What Every Special Educator Must Know: The International Standards for the Preparation and Certification of Special Education Teachers (1st Edition)*.

1996   CEC publishes *What Every Special Educator Must Know: The International Standards for the Preparation and Certification of Special Education Teachers (2nd edition)*.

1997   CEC initiates the Professionally Recognized Special Educator, a national special education certification program with certificates for special education teachers, administrators, and diagnosticians. NCATE initiates the NCATE 2000 project that shifts the focus of program accreditation to candidate performance.

1998   CEC adopts Knowledge and Skill Sets for Transition Specialists, Special Education Administrators, Educational Diagnosticians, and Special Education Paraeducators. CEC revises the Standards for Entry to Professional Practice. CEC approves Guidelines for Continuing Education. CEC adopts revisions to the Common Core of Knowledge and Skills Essential for All Beginning Special Education Teachers. CEC adopts the Curriculum-

Referenced Licensing and Program Accreditation Framework. CEC publishes *What Every Special Educator Must Know: Ethics, Standards, and Guidelines (3rd Edition)*.

2000   CEC edits the Knowledge and Skill Standards to improve clarity and reduce redundancy. CEC adds Multicultural knowledge and Skills to the CEC Common Core. CEC publishes *What Every Special Educator Must Know: Ethics, Standards, and Guidelines (4th Edition)*. CEC reorganizes Knowledge and Skill sets into 10 domains that coordinate with the domains of the Interstate New Teacher and Assessment and Support Consortium's (INTASC) Core Principles. CEC revises its procedures for programs developing performance assessment systems.

2001   NCATE approves CEC performance standards and review procedures.

2003   CEC revises procedures for Knowledge and Skill Validation Studies and initiates process by which each knowledge and skill is supported by a documented literature, research, and/or practice base. *What Every Special Educator Must Know: Ethics, Standards, and Guidelines (5th Edition)* is published.

2004   Research additions are made to the initial common core and work is begun on development of advanced standards

2005   Knowledge and Skills for Teachers of Individuals with Developmental Disabilities are up-dated and revalidated.

2006   CEC approves the 6 Advanced

Special Education Content Standards and the advanced common core knowledge and skills. The advanced knowledge and skill sets for Technology Specialist and Transition Specialist are reorganized around the six advanced content standards.

2007   The Professional Standards and Practices Committee submits report on "Promoting Standards" to the CEC Board. CEC implements a pilot of procedures to study and describe the evidence bases of professional practices. CEC approves revalidated initial knowledge and skills sets for Teachers of Individuals with Gifts and Talents and for Teachers of individuals in Early Childhood Special Education and advanced knowledge and skills for Early Childhood and Early Intervention Specialist.

2008   Revalidated initial sets for Teachers of Individuals with Emotional and Behavior Disorders, Deaf and Hard of Hearing, Physical and Health Disabilities, and Visual Impairments are approved. Advanced knowledge and skill sets are validated and approved by CEC for Special Education Administrator; Diagnostician; Deaf and Hard of Hearing Specialist; and Physical and Health Disabilities Specialist. CEC approves beta test of the Evidence-Based Practices Initiative.

2009   CEC publishes *What Every Special Educator Must Know: Ethics, Standards, and Guidelines (6ᵗʰ Edition)*.

The National Board for Professional Teaching Standards has organized the standards for accomplished teachers of students with exceptional needs into the following 14 standards. The standards have been ordered to facilitate understanding, not to assign priorities. They each describe an important facet of accomplished teaching; they often occur concurrently because of the seamless quality of accomplished practice. These standards serve as the basis for National Board Certification in this field.

Preparing for Student Learning

I. Knowledge of Students

Accomplished teachers of students with exceptional needs consistently use their knowledge of human development and learning and their skills as careful observers of students to understand students' knowledge, aptitudes, skills, interests, aspirations, and values.

II. Knowledge of Special Education

Accomplished teachers of students with exceptional needs draw on their knowledge of the philosophical, historical, and legal foundations of special education and their knowledge of effective special education practice to organize and design instruction. In addition, they draw on their specialized knowledge of specific disabilities to set meaningful goals for their students.

III. Communications

Accomplished teachers of students with exceptional needs know the importance of communications in learning. They know how to use communication skills to help students access, comprehend, and apply information; to help them acquire knowledge; and to enable them to develop and maintain interpersonal relationships.

IV. Diversity

Accomplished teachers of students with exceptional needs create an environment in which equal treatment, fairness, and respect for diversity are modeled, taught, and practiced by all, and they take steps to ensure access to quality learning opportunities for all students.

V. Knowledge of Subject Matter

Accomplished teachers of students with exceptional needs command a core body of knowledge in the disciplines and draw on that knowledge to establish curricular goals, design instruction, facilitate student learning, and assess student progress.

Advancing Student Learning

VI. Meaningful Learning

Accomplished teachers of students with exceptional needs work with students to explore in purposeful ways important and challenging concepts, topics, and issues to build competence and confidence.

VII. Multiple Paths to Knowledge

Accomplished teachers of students with exceptional needs use a variety of approaches to help students strengthen understanding and gain command of essential knowledge and skills.

VIII. Social Development

Accomplished teachers of students with exceptional needs cultivate a sense of efficacy and independence in their students as they develop students' character, sense of civic and social responsibility, respect for diverse individuals and groups, and ability to work constructively and collaboratively with others.

Supporting Student Learning

IX. Assessment

Accomplished teachers of students with exceptional needs design and select a variety of assessment strategies to obtain useful and timely information about student learning and development and to help students reflect on their own progress.

X. Learning Environment

Accomplished teachers of students with exceptional needs establish a caring, stimulating, and safe community for learning in which democratic values are fostered and students assume responsibility for learning, show willingness to take intellectual risks, develop self-confidence, and learn to work not only independently but also collaboratively.

XI. *Instructional Resources*

Accomplished teachers of students with exceptional needs select, adapt, create, and use rich and varied resources, both human and material.

XII. *Family Partnerships*

Accomplished teachers of students with exceptional needs work collaboratively with parents, guardians, and other caregivers to understand their children and to achieve common educational goals.

Professional Development and Outreach

XIII. *Reflective Practice*

Accomplished teachers of students with exceptional needs regularly analyze, evaluate, and strengthen the quality of their practice.

XIV. *Contributing to the Profession and to Education*

Accomplished teachers of students with exceptional needs work independently and collaboratively with colleagues and others to improve schools and to advance knowledge, policy, and practice in their field. For more information, see www.nbpts.org .

APPENDIX 6: CEC INITIAL COMMON CORE AND INTASC KNOWLEDGE AND SKILLS INDEX

CEC Professional Entry Level Standards are built on research that informs the field on best practice in the education of children with exceptionalities. From this research, CEC validated Knowledge and Skill Standards that delineate the knowledge and skills that entry-level special educators master in order to serve individuals with specific exceptionalities safely and effectively. Using the Knowledge and Skill Sets as a base, CEC developed 10 Initial Content Standards (indexed to the INTASC Core Principles) that describe in rich narrative what all special education teachers should know and be able to do. Table 6.1 delineates the coordination of CEC Initial Common Core with the INTASC standards for special educators. Programs preparing candidates multicategorically and other areas of specialization are reminded that they must align with these areas of specialization, which lie beyond the INTASC standards.

Special Education Standard 1: Foundations

Knowledge		INTASC
ICC1K1	Models, theories, philosophies, and research methods that form the basis for special education practice	1.01, 2.04
ICC1K2	Laws, policies, and ethical principles regarding behavior management planning and implementation	1.04, 1.13
ICC1K3	Relationship of special education to the organization and function of educational agencies	1.04, 1.13
ICC1K4	Rights and responsibilities of students, parents, teachers, and other professionals, and schools related to exceptional learning needs	1.04, 1.11, 1.13, 8.08, 10.07
ICC1K5	Issues in definition and identification of individuals with exceptional learning needs, including those from culturally and linguistically diverse backgrounds	1.04, 1.13, 3.04, 8.07, 8.09
ICC1K6	Issues, assurances and due process rights related to assessment, eligibility, and placement within a continuum of services)	1.04, 8.07
ICC1K7	Family systems and the role of families in the educational process	1.11, 3.07, 10.10
ICC1K8	Historical points of view and contribution of culturally diverse groups	10.04
ICC1K9	Impact of the dominant culture on shaping schools and the individuals who study and work in them	3.04, 10.04
ICC1K10	Potential impact of differences in values, languages, and customs that can exist between the home and school	3.03, 3.04, 6.03, 10.02, 10.04
Skill		
ICC1S1	Articulate personal philosophy of special education	

Special Education Standard 2: Development and Characteristics of Learners

Knowledge		INTASC
ICC2K1	Typical and atypical human growth and development	1.07, 2.01
ICC2K2	Educational implications of characteristics of various exceptionalities	1.08, 3.05, 2.01, 7.06
ICC2K3	Characteristics and effects of the cultural and environmental milieu of the individual with exceptional learning needs and the family	2.07, 3.03, 3.06, 6.01, 8.09
ICC2K4	Family systems and the role of families in supporting development	2.07, 3.07, 10.03
ICC2K5	Similarities and differences of individuals with and without exceptional learning needs	2.01
ICC2K6	Similarities and differences among individuals with exceptional learning needs	2.05
ICC2K7	Effects of various medications on individuals with exceptional learning needs	

Special Education Standard 3: Individual Learning Differences

Knowledge		INTASC
ICC3K1	Effects an exceptional condition(s) can have on an individual's life	1.08, 2.01, 2.05, 3.02, 3.06, 10.10
ICC3K2	Impact of learners' academic and social abilities, attitudes, interests, and values on instruction and career development	1.07, 2.05, 3.02, 10.10
ICC3K3	Variations in beliefs, traditions, and values across and within cultures and their effects on relationships among individuals with exceptional learning needs, families, and schooling	3.03, 3.09, 8.09, 9.04, 10.02, 10.04, 10.10
ICC3K4	Cultural perspectives influencing the relationships among families, schools and communities as related to instruction	3.03, 3.04, 3.06, 3.07, 3.09, 9.04, 10.02, 10.04
ICC3K5	Differing ways of learning of individuals with exceptional learning needs including those from culturally diverse backgrounds and strategies for addressing these differences	1.08, 2.01, 2.06, 3.04, 3.09, 9.04

Special Education Standard 4: Instructional Strategies

Skills		
ICC4S1	Use strategies to facilitate integration into various settings	1.08, 2.06, 3.05, 4.04, 4.10, 4.13, 6.02, 6.04, 7.02
ICC4S2	Teach individuals to use self-assessment, problem solving, and other cognitive strategies to meet their needs	4.07
ICC4S3	Select, adapt, and use instructional strategies and materials according to characteristics of the individual with exceptional learning needs	1.03, 2.06, 4.01, 4.04, 4.05, 4.10, 4.13

ICC4S4	Use strategies to facilitate maintenance and generalization of skills across learning environments	4.01, 4.03, 4.10, 4.13
ICC4S5	Use procedures to increase the individual's self-awareness, self-management, self-control, self-reliance, and self-esteem	4.01, 4.10
ICC4S6	Use strategies that promote successful transitions for individuals with exceptional learning needs	1.09, 4.01, 4.10, 7.06

Special Education Standard 5: Learning Environments and Social Interactions

Knowledge		*INTASC*
ICC5K1	Demands of learning environments	1.08, 4.13, 5.02, 5.06, 7.07
ICC5K2	Basic classroom management theories and strategies for individuals with exceptional learning needs	5.06
ICC5K3	Effective management of teaching and learning	2.04, 4.02, 5.04, 5.06
ICC5K4	Teacher attitudes and behaviors that influence behavior of individuals with exceptional learning needs	6.05
ICC5K5	Social skills needed for educational and other environments	5.02, 5.03, 7.07
ICC5K6	Strategies for crisis prevention and intervention	5.07
ICC5K7	Strategies for preparing individuals to live harmoniously and productively in a culturally diverse world	5.03
ICC5K8	Ways to create learning environments that allow individuals to retain and appreciate their own and each other's respective language and cultural heritage	5.01
ICC5K9	Ways specific cultures are negatively stereotyped	
ICC5K10	Strategies used by diverse populations to cope with a legacy of former and continuing racism	
Skills		
ICC5S1	Create a safe, equitable, positive, and supportive learning environment in which diversities are valued	2.02, 4.11, 5.01, 5.04, 10.03
ICC5S2	Identify realistic expectations for personal and social behavior in various settings	2.02, 4.11, 7.01, 7.07
ICC5S3	Identify supports needed for integration into various program placements	1.08, 2.06, 4.05, 4.07, 4.11, 6.08, 7.07
ICC5S4	Design learning environments that encourage active participation in individual and group activities	2.03, 4.04, 4.11, 5.01, 5.04, 5.05, 7.04
ICC5S5	Modify the learning environment to manage behaviors.	2.08, 7.04

ICC5S6	Use performance data and information from all stakeholders to make or suggest modifications in learning environments	1.08, 7.01, 7.04, 7.05, 7.08, 8.03, 8.07, 8.08, 9.05
ICC5S7	Establish and maintain rapport with individuals with and without exceptional learning needs	3.01
ICC5S8	Teach self-advocacy	1.07, 5.02, 5.08
ICC5S9	Create an environment that encourages self-advocacy and increased independence	2.08, 4.07, 5.04, 5.08, 7.04
ICC5S10	Use effective and varied behavior management strategies	2.04, 4.02, 5.05, 5.06
ICC5S11	Use the least intensive behavior management strategy consistent with the needs of the individual with exceptional learning needs	5.05
ICC5S12	Design and manage daily routines	5.07
ICC5S13	Organize, develop, and sustain learning environments that support positive intracultural and intercultural experiences	5.01, 5.03, 5.06
ICC5S14	Mediate controversial intercultural issues among students within the learning environment in ways that enhance any culture, group, or person	5.06
ICC5S15	Structure, direct, and support the activities of paraeducators, volunteers, and tutors	5.06, 10.03
ICC5S16	Use universal precautions	

Special Education Standard 6: Communication

Knowledge		*INTASC*
ICC6K1	Effects of cultural and linguistic differences on growth and development	3.08, 6.03
ICC6K2	Characteristics of one's own culture and use of language and the ways in which these can differ from other cultures and uses of languages	3.08, 6.03, 9.02
ICC6K3	Ways of behaving and communicating among cultures that can lead to misinterpretation and misunderstanding	6.03
ICC6K4	Augmentative and assistive communication strategies	4.08, 6.01, 6.04, 6.06, 6.07, 7.09
Skills		
ICC6S1	Use strategies to support and enhance communication skills of individuals with exceptional learning needs	5.08, 6.01, 6.02, 6.04, 6.06, 6.07, 6.08
ICC6S2	Use communication strategies and resources to facilitate understanding of subject matter for students whose primary language is not the dominant language	3.08

Special Education Standard 7: Instructional Planning

Knowledge		INTASC
ICC7K1	Theories and research that form the basis of curriculum development and instructional practice	1.02, 1.06
ICC7K2	Scope and sequences of general and special curricula	1.02, 1.06, 7.02, 7.03, 7.06
ICC7K3	National, state or provincial, and local curricula standards	7.06
ICC7K4	Technology for planning and managing the teaching and learning environment	4.08, 7.06
ICC7K5	Roles and responsibilities of the paraeducator related to instruction, intervention, and direct service	7.06, 10.03
Skills		
ICC7S1	Identify and prioritize areas of the general curriculum and accommodations for individuals with exceptional learning needs	1.03, 1.11, 4.09, 4.11, 6.02, 7.02, 7.01, 7.03, 7.06, 7.09, 8.10
ICC7S2	Develop and implement comprehensive, longitudinal individualized programs in collaboration with team members	1.11, 4.09, 4.11, 6.02, 7.01, 7.03, 7.06, 7.09
ICC7S3	Involve the individual and family in setting instructional goals and monitoring progress	1.11, 3.07, 7.05, 7.08, 8/04
ICC7S4	Use functional assessments to develop intervention plans	7.09, 8.02, 8.07
ICC7S5	Use task analysis	8.02, 8.07
ICC7S6	Sequence, implement, and evaluate individualized learning objectives	1.11, 4.09, 7.01, 7.06
ICC7S7	Integrate affective, social, and life skills with academic curricula	1.03, 1.07, 7.06, 7.09
ICC7S8	Develop and select instructional content, resources, and strategies that respond to cultural, linguistic, and gender differences	4.09, 7.03, 7.06
ICC7S9	Incorporate and implement instructional and assistive technology into the educational program	1.03, 1.10, 4.09, 6.01, 6.07, 6.08
ICC7S10	Prepare lesson plans	4.09
ICC7S11	Prepare and organize materials to implement daily lesson plans	4.09, 7.01
ICC7S12	Use instructional time effectively	4.09, 7.01
ICC7S13	Make responsive adjustments to instruction based on continual observations	4.06, 7.05, 8.10
ICC7S14	Prepare individuals to exhibit self-enhancing behavior in response to societal attitudes and actions	4.07, 7.09

Special Education Standard 8: Assessment

Knowledge		INTASC
ICC8K1	Basic terminology used in assessment	8.01
ICC8K2	Legal provisions and ethical principles regarding assessment of individuals	1.04, 1.13, 8.01, 8.11
ICC8K3	Screening, prereferral, referral, and classification procedures	1.04, 1.05, 2.08, 3.04, 3.06, 8.01, 8.07
ICC8K4	Use and limitations of assessment instruments	8.01
ICC8K5	National, state or provincial, and local accommodations and modifications	1.05, 8.03, 8.05, 8.11

Skills		
ICC8S1	Gather relevant background information	2.08, 8.07, 8.08
ICC8S2	Administer nonbiased formal and informal assessments	8.02, 8.06
ICC8S3	Use technology to conduct assessments	8.03
ICC8S4	Develop or modify individualized assessment strategies	8.02, 8.03, 8.11
ICC8S5	Interpret information from formal and informal assessments	8.06
ICC8S6	Use assessment information in making eligibility, program, and placement decisions for individuals with exceptional learning needs, including those from culturally and/or linguistically diverse backgrounds	2.08, 3.04, 3.06, 8.07
ICC8S7	Report assessment results to all stakeholders using effective communication skills	8.04, 8.06, 8.07
ICC8S8	Evaluate instruction and monitor progress of individuals with exceptional learning needs	4.06
ICC8S9	Create and maintain records	8.10

Special Education Standard 9: Professional and Ethical Practice

Knowledge		INTASC
ICC9K1	Personal cultural biases and differences that affect one's teaching	9.02, 9.07
ICC9K2	Importance of the teacher serving as a model for individuals with exceptional learning needs	
ICC9K3	Continuum of lifelong professional development	9.03, 9.06
ICC9K4	Methods to remain current regarding research-validated practice	9.03, 9.06

Skills			
ICC9S1	Practice within the CEC Code of Ethics and other standards of the profession	9.06
ICC9S2	Uphold high standards of competence and integrity and exercise sound judgment in the practice of the professional	9.07
ICC9S3	Act ethically in advocating for appropriate services	10.06
ICC9S4	Conduct professional activities in compliance with applicable laws and policies	1.13
ICC9S5	Demonstrate commitment to developing the highest education and quality-of-life potential of individuals with exceptional learning needs	9.06, 10.06
ICC9S6	Demonstrate sensitivity for the culture, language, religion, gender, disability, socio-economic status, and sexual orientation of individuals	9.02, 9.07
ICC9S7	Practice within one's skill limit and obtain assistance as needed	9.07, 10.01
ICC9S8	Use verbal, nonverbal, and written language effectively	10.05
ICC9S9	Conduct self-evaluation of instruction	9.01, 9.05
ICC9S10	Access information on exceptionalities	1.10, 4.12, 9.03, 9.06
ICC9S11	Reflect on one's practice to improve instruction and guide professional growth	9.01
ICC9S12	Engage in professional activities that benefit individuals with exceptional learning needs, their families, and one's colleagues	4.12, 9.03, 9.06, 10.06

Special Education Standard 10: Collaboration

Knowledge			INTASC
ICC10K1	Models and strategies of consultation and collaboration	10.05, 10.06
ICC10K2	Roles of individuals with exceptional learning needs, families, and school and community personnel in planning of an individualized program	1.11, 6.02, 7.01, 7.03, 10.01, 10.07
ICC10K3	Concerns of families of individuals with exceptional learning needs and strategies to help address these concerns	3.06, 10.04, 10.08
ICC10K4	Culturally responsive factors that promote effective communication and collaboration with individuals with exceptional learning needs, families, school personnel, and community members	3.06, 10.04
Skill			
ICC10S1	Maintain confidential communication about individuals with exceptional learning needs	8.08, 10.05

ICC10S2	Collaborate with families and others in assessment of individuals with exceptional learning needs	6.02, 8.07, 8.08, 10.07
ICC10S3	Foster respectful and beneficial relationships between families and professionals	2.07, 8.08, 10.01, 10.05, 10.09
ICC10S4	Assist individuals with exceptional learning needs and their families in becoming active participants in the educational team	1.12, 7.07, 7.08, 10.02, 10.04, 10.08
ICC10S5	Plan and conduct collaborative conferences with individuals with exceptional learning needs and their families	5.08, 7.07, 7.08, 10.05, 10.07, 10.08
ICC10S6	Collaborate with school personnel and community members in integrating individuals with exceptional learning needs into various settings	1.12, 4.11, 7.01, 7.02, 7.03, 7.06, 8.08, 10.02, 10.06, 10.07, 10.09
ICC10S7	Use group problem-solving skills to develop, implement and evaluate collaborative activities	10.05, 10.07
ICC10S8	Model techniques and coach others in the use of instructional methods and accommodations	4.09, 4.03, 10.05, 10.07
ICC10S9	Communicate with school personnel about the characteristics and needs of individuals with exceptional learning needs	2.01, 2.05, 7.01, 7.03, 8.08, 10.05, 10.07
ICC10S10	Communicate effectively with families of individuals with exceptional learning needs from diverse backgrounds	2.07, 7.08, 10.04, 10.08
ICC10S11	Observe, evaluate and provide feedback to paraeducators	10.03

The following procedures are designed for preparation programs that seek CEC National Recognition outside of the NCATE CEC partnership. To earn CEC National Recognition special education preparation programs must address the following CEC Standards for the Preparation of Special Education Personnel.

a. Programs preparing individuals for entry level or advanced special education professional roles shall adhere to CEC professional standards, by seeking CEC official recognition through the evidence-based process of program review.

b. Program review includes examination of evidence to document quality practice in:

(1) **Conceptual Framework** Programs have a conceptual framework that establishes the programs vision and its relationship to the programs components and curricula.

(2) Candidate Content, Pedagogical, and Professional Knowledge, Skills, and Dispositions

    i. **Content Standards**. Programs ensure that prospective special educators have mastered the CEC Special Education Content Standards for their respective roles.

    ii. **Liberal Education**. Programs ensure that prospective special educators have a solid grounding in the liberal curricula ensuring proficiency in reading, written and oral communications, calculating, problem solving, and thinking.

    iii. **General Curriculum.**

    (a) Programs ensure that prospective special educators possess a solid base of understanding of the general content area curricula i.e., math, reading, English/language arts, science, social studies, and the arts, sufficient to collaborate with general educators in:

    Teaching or collaborative teaching academic subject matter content of the general curriculum to students with exceptional learning needs across a wide range of performance levels.

Designing appropriate learning and performance accommodations and modifications for students with exceptional learning needs in academic subject matter content of the general curriculum.

(b) Programs preparing special educators for secondary level practice and licensure in which the teachers may assume sole responsibility for teaching academic subject matter classes, ensure that the prospective special educators have a subject matter content knowledge base sufficient to assure that their students can meet state curriculum standards.

(3) **Assessment System and Program Evaluation**. Programs have an assessment system to collect and analyze data on the applicant qualifications, candidates and graduate performance, and program operations sufficient to evaluate and improve the program.

(4) **Field Experiences and Clinical Practice.** Programs with their school partners have designed, implemented, and evaluated field experiences and clinical practica sufficient for prospective special educators to develop and apply knowledge, skills, and dispositions essential to the roles for which they are being prepared.

(5) **Diversity**. Programs with their school partners have designed, implemented, and evaluated curriculum and experiences sufficient for prospective special educators to develop and apply their knowledge, skills, and dispositions necessary to help all students learn. The curricula and experiences include working with diverse faculty, candidates, and P-12 exceptional students.

(6) **Faculty Qualification, Performance, and Development**. The program faculty is qualified and model best professional practice in their scholarship, service, and teaching.

(7) **Program Governance and Resources**. The program has appropriate leadership, authority, budget, facilities, and resources to address professional, institutional, and state standards.

CEC Policy
October 2004

Special Education Mentoring Program Implementation Checklist

Components of Special Education Mentoring Program	Status	Notes
Collaboration: Clear Mentoring Program objectives are developed collaboratively		
Information: Information on roles, expectations, policies, provisions and desired outcomes is shared and understood by all stakeholders.		
Resources: Resources are adequately planned and funded		
Participation: All first year special education teachers participate.		
Special Education Coordination: Mentoring activities are coordinated with general education mentoring programs but specifically addresses special education concerns.		
Mentor & Teacher Relationship: Mentor and new teacher relationship is for support and guidance, not for evaluation or supervision.		
Program Responsibility: An Administrator is assigned specific responsibility to coordinate and oversee mentoring program.		
Compensation: Mentors receive appropriate compensation based on choices.		
Program Evaluation: Formative and summative information is used, including feedback from mentoring team.		
Beginning Teacher Roles and Responsibilities	*Status*	*Notes*
Attends all training sessions		
Requests assistance proactively		

*Check ( ) and date all components that meet criteria on the date of review. Notes. Space is provided for notes on items to improve, resources to consider, etc.

	Status	Notes
Schedules and attends sessions with mentor teacher		
Remains open and responsive to feedback/suggestions		
Observes other teachers		
Conducts self-assessment and uses reflective skills		
Participates in evaluation of program		
Mentor Teacher Roles and Responsibilities	**Status**	**Notes**
Attends all training sessions		
Provides support and guidance		
Acclimates beginning teacher to school and community culture		
Observes beginning teacher regularly		
Provides post-observation feedback in timely manner		
Models appropriate classroom and professional behaviors		
Maintains professional and confidential relationship		
Participates in evaluation of program		
Mentor Program Coordinator Roles and Responsibilities	**Status**	**Notes**
Manages the mentoring program		
Ensures building administrators are informed and supportive		
Develops district policy guidelines for mentoring		

*Check ( ) and date all components that meet criteria on the date of review. Notes. Space is provided for notes on items to improve, resources to consider, etc.

	Status	Notes
Guides development and adoption of resource materials and conducts inservice training for new teachers and mentors		
Arranges and conducts regular meetings with new teachers and mentors		
Ensures implementation, evaluation, and improvement of mentoring program		
Helps provide more intensive support for individual teachers as needed		
Qualities of Mentors	**Status**	**Notes**
Must be special education teachers preferably in same school		
Must be special education teachers teaching same population at same grade level		
Must be special education teachers who volunteer		
Must be special education teachers with 3-5 years special education experience in current district		
Must be special education teachers nominated as master teachers		
Orientation and Training	**Status**	**Notes**
Beginning teachers hired **prior** to school opening Mentors participate in inservice before school Beginning teachers hired **after** opening are paired with mentors and provided orientation to program as soon as possible		
Mentor teacher training provided prior to school year with additional sessions throughout year		
Mentor teachers have opportunity to meet regularly with other mentors to share materials, strategies, and successes and concerns		
Mentor Teacher Training Includes	**Status**	**Notes**
Role and expectations of the mentor		

*Check ( ) and date all components that meet criteria on the date of review. Notes. Space is provided for notes on items to improve, resources to consider, etc.

Needs of new teachers and their role and responsibilities in the mentoring process		
Effective communication skill Development incorporating adult principles		
Consultation strategies - how to give constructive feedback and social support		
Time management and organizational strategies		
Classroom observation skills		
Updates on IEP development and implementation changes		
Updates on special education laws and paperwork requirements		
Advising and coaching skills		
Behavior management strategies across grade levels and disabilities		
Collaboration and problem-solving skills		
Curriculum and instructional strategies		

*Check ( ) and date all components that meet criteria on the date of review. Notes. Space is provided for notes on items to improve, resources to consider, etc.

Section Three - Part 1

Basic Commitments and Responsibilities to Exceptional Children

CHAPTER 01

RESPONSIBILITIES OF THE COUNCIL FOR EXCEPTIONAL CHILDREN

Paragraph 1- Purpose

The Council for Exceptional Children is an association of professional and other persons whose principal purpose is to obtain opti¬mal educational opportunity for all children and youth with exceptionalities. These children's needs differ sufficiently from other children's so that they require special educational and related services in addition to those presently available through regular education programs and other human service delivery systems. While the legal criteria that define children and youth with exceptionalities vary greatly from one governmental jurisdiction to another, The Council for Exceptional Children is primarily concerned about children and youth having sensory deficits, physical handicaps, mental retardation, behavioral disorders, communication disorders, special learning disabilities, multiple handicaps, gifts and talents, and children who are developmentally delayed or abused and neglected. Children and youth with exceptionalities are found in all communities regardless of socioeconomic or cultural factors.

Paragraph 2 - Governmental Relations

Public policy legislation, litigation, appropriation, regulation, and negotiated agreements are the means by which children and youth with exceptionalities have been guaranteed the educational opportunities of our society. The Council is deeply committed to the effective implementation of existing public policy in the interest of children and youth with exceptionalities. In addition, The Council seeks extension and creation of public policy in a manner which will encourage and augment quality service programs at all governmental levels. To provide the scope and kind of services needed, The Council endorses public policies that strengthen and enhance instructional programs for all children and youth. While such general provisions should benefit the exceptional child, The Council believes that specific policy provisions are necessary to

offer those children and youth with exceptional needs the opportunity to develop to their fullest potential. In carrying out its governmental activities, The Council will be guided by the policies adopted by its members and by the directives of its governance.

Paragraph 3 - Advocacy by Members

The Council believes that all persons concerned about the education of children and youth with exceptionalities must initiate and maintain efforts to ensure that appropriate public policy is adopted, fully implemented, and enforced.

The Council recognizes that the provision of public services to children and youth with exceptionalities is a function of the governmental process. For this reason, The Council urges and supports the active involvement of its members in activities which will build greater awareness on the part of parents, communities, and governmental officials regarding the needs of children and youth with exceptionalities and will extend appropriate information to such bodies in their efforts to carry out the objectives of this policy statement.

The Council believes that it is the responsibility of all persons concerned about the needs of children and youth with exceptionalities to continually seek to improve government provisions for their education. In this regard, The Council pledges its assistance in providing needed information and in helping to develop the necessary strategies to attain improvement of educational services for children and youth with exceptionalities.

In our democratic societies, we have created systems of law to protect the individual from the abuses of society, particularly from abuses of the agencies established by society to serve its needs. In the attempt to provide what appear to be needed services, the rights of the individual may be overlooked. For this reason, The Council urges constant vigilance on the part of all persons engaged in the education of children and youth with exceptionalities to assure that the rights of these individuals and their families are understood and observed. The Council further suggests that all public programs and private programs utilizing public funds be open to review and that flexibility be provided to allow for judicial consideration of such matters.

Paragraph 4 - Accessibility

The Council for Exceptional Children provides a physical and emotional environment which is sensitive to the needs, feelings, and opinions of persons with varying mobility and communication needs. CEC makes special efforts to encourage the participation of members with exceptionalities in its activities and the utilization of its services. The Council for Exceptional Children:

a. Identifies CEC members and other professionals with exceptionalities who would make use of communication, accessibility, and mobility resources.

b. Facilitates communication between professionals with exceptionalities and CEC Headquarters staff.

c. Orients CEC members and headquarters staff to the needs of professionals with exceptionalities.

d. Informs professionals with exceptionalities about the resources available through CEC to enable their equitable participation in all CEC activities.

e. Guarantees that all CEC sponsored activities are conducted in accessible and usable facilities and communication modes to ensure full and equitable participation of professionals with exceptionalities.

CHAPTER 02

EDUCATIONAL RIGHTS AND RESPONSIBILITIES

Paragraph 1 - Education is the Right of All Children

The principle of education for all is based on democracy's philosophical premise that every person is valuable in his or her own right and should be afforded equal opportunities to develop his or her full potential. Thus, no democratic society should deny educational opportunities to any child, regardless of the child's potential for making a contribution to society. Since the passage of the first public school laws in the mid-nineteenth century, this principle has received general endorsement and qualified execution. While lip service has been paid to the intent of the principle, various interpretations of the terms "education" and "all children" have deprived many children of their rights.

The ordinary educational opportunities provided by the schools have tended to neglect or exclude children with unusual learning needs: the gifted and talented; those having sensory deficits, physical handicaps, mental retardation, behavioral disorders, communication disorders, specific learning disabilities, or multiple handicaps; and children who are developmentally delayed or abused and neglected. These children need special education and, in order to be able to benefit fully from this education, they need the opportunity to view themselves as acceptable to society. They need stable and supportive home lives, wholesome community interactions, and the opportunity to view themselves and others in a healthy manner.

Because of their exceptionality, many children need to begin their school experiences at an earlier age than is customary; many need formal educational services well into adulthood; and many require health and social services that are closely coordinated with school programs. Meeting these needs is essential to the total development of children with exceptionalities as individuals and as members of society.

For some decades now, educators and schools have been responding to the challenges of educating children with exceptionalities. Still, not all children are being provided for fully; the intellectually gifted child, for example, and many other children who need highly specialized services, are not receiving them. The community should extend its demand that school personnel learn to understand and serve the individual needs of these children as well as those more easily accommodated in the educational system. The surge of interest among educators in individualizing instruction hopefully will mean more sensitivity to the educational needs of all children, and particularly those with special needs.

Programs for children and youth with exceptionalities should be varied in nature and conducted in a variety of settings, depending on the individual needs of the child, the child's family, and the community. It is The Council's belief that society should have the legal responsibility to extend the opportunity for every individual to be educated to the full extent of his or her capacities, whatever they may be or however they may be attenuated by special circumstances. There is no dividing line which excludes some children and includes others in educational programs. Clearly, every exceptional child has the right to a free appropriate public education which may not in any instance be compromised because of inadequacies in the educational system or existing public policies.

Paragraph 2 - Government Responsibilities for Special Education in Intermediate and Local School Districts

Intermediate and local school districts carry major responsibility for the quality of educational services to children and youth with exceptionalities and for leadership and coordination with other agencies to achieve comprehensive child centered services. Intermediate and local school districts should provide continuing leadership for all educational services in the community, including participation in the financing of every education program in the district and of any program outside the district which serves children and youth with exceptionalities at the district's request.

The Council believes that school districts should be responsible for an annual review of children and youth with exceptionalities who are legal residents of the district to assure that their education is proceeding adequately, even though they may be receiving their educational services outside their district of residence.

Paragraph 3 - State or Provincial Governments

The basic responsibility for guaranteeing an education to all children rests with state or provincial governments through their state or provincial education agencies; however, the fulfillment of this responsibility is effected in cooperation with federal and local education authorities. The Council believes that it is the responsibility of the state/province to guarantee each child comprehensive educational opportunities without cost to the child or the child's family. Special financial support should be offered to the intermediate and local districts or combinations of these units so that no excess local cost is involved in providing specialized quality programs, services, and facilities. While the cost of services for children and youth with exceptionalities varies greatly, such considerations should not affect the goal of optimal programming for every child. The Council believes that no financial incentive should be provided to encourage the adoption of a less than optimal education program. A particular responsibility of state/province governments is to provide progressive leadership and direction to coordinated state/provincial programs of special education and to provide coordination among the several departments of government other than education which may be called upon to serve children and youth with exceptionalities and their families.

Paragraph 4 - Federal Governments of the United States and Canada

The Council believes the federal government should give major attention to guaranteeing educational opportunities to children and youth whose education has been neglected. The federal government has a responsibility for assuring that the rights of children with exceptionalities are not violated. Because education of children and youth with exceptionalities has, in general, been a neglected area, special categories of support should be directed to meeting their needs. Federal financial aid should be directed to state or provincial governments for the education of children with exceptionalities.

The federal government should provide for support of professional leadership in the field of special education with emphasis on assessment of needs, planning of needed programs, preparation of personnel, and research.

The federal government should provide financial support to colleges, universities, and other appropriate agencies to assist in operating programs to prepare all needed personnel to conduct comprehensive special education programs and services.

The federal government should provide financial support to school districts and combinations of school districts that wish to provide innovative or exemplary programs for children and youth with exceptionalities or that, for any reason, enroll an unusually high proportion of children and youth with special needs.

The federal government should provide major support to programs in the field of special education that serve regional or national needs such as the education of migrant children.

In instances where the federal government assumes primary responsibility for the education of a group of children (i.e., American Indian and Alaska Native children in Bureau of Indian Affairs operated and contracted schools and the education of dependents in Department of Defense schools and programs), it must also provide appropriate special education to these groups. As one means of accomplishing this goal, the Department of Interior, Bureau of Indian Affairs, should maintain a specific budget line item for special education and related services for children with exceptionalities.

Paragraph 5 - Intergovernmental Planning

The success of the functions of federal, state/provincial, and local government requires close cooperative planning of a short- and long-term nature. Such planning requires excellence in communicative skills and facilities. Such plans for the education of children and youth with exceptionalities should form the basis for new and improved legislative and government policies at all levels of government.

Paragraph 6 - Compulsory Services and Attendance

The provision for universal education of children in a democratic society has been translated as a commitment to providing educational opportunities for every child, whatever may be his or her socioeconomic status; cultural or racial origins; physical, intellectual, or emotional status; potential contribution to society; and educational needs. This commitment to every child thus includes a commitment to children with unusual learning needs and to those with outstanding abilities and talents. Although providing education for these children may require a variety of specialized services and instructional programs, some costly and some requiring radical innovations in traditional educational structures, there is no basis for including some children and excluding others where the principle of universal education is concerned.

Some of the specialized services that may be essential if children with exceptionalities are to attend school include the provision of specialized transportation, functional architectural environments, personalized equipment and aids, individualized instructional programs, and special education and support personnel. Certainly the fiscal requirements for such programs may be great; if they are not instituted and maintained, however, the cost of neglect is infinitely greater and must be borne mainly by the children as well as by their families, communities, and society as a whole.

The commitment to education for all encompasses the responsibility for providing special forms of education to children and youth with exceptional characteristics and needs. This responsibility extends to all types of exceptionalities, regardless of the degree to which a child may eventually be able to contribute to society. To this end, The Council supports efforts to eliminate exclusionary clauses in compulsory school attendance laws and other such laws and administrative practices which deny children and youth with exceptionalities the educational opportunity they require.

Paragraph 7 - Maintenance of Educational Opportunity

The requirement to provide a free, appropriate, public education is constitutionally based and cannot be abrogated for any child or group of children, regardless of any characteristics, disabilities, or traits of such children. Many children, including children with exceptionalities have been excluded from schools on the unacceptable grounds that they are disruptive, are perceived to be uneducable, or have undesirable characteristics.

Schools today face a growing challenge in educating students who are dangerously violent or destructive. In order for educational environments to be acceptably conducive to learning, behavior which impedes the ability of children to learn and teachers to teach must be minimized or eliminated. Schools have the responsibility to immediately consider changing the educational setting for any students who behave in a dangerously violent or destructive manner. If such an alternative educational placement is determined to be appropriate, such students must be placed in educational settings designed to meet their learning, safety, and behavioral management needs.

Few students receiving appropriate special education services become a danger to self and/or others. Rather, students with disabilities are more likely to be victimized than their nondisabled peers and would benefit directly from safer schools.

Policy: The exemption, exclusion, or expulsion of any child from receiving a free, appropriate, public education creates a greater problem for society and therefore should not be permitted. At the same time violent and destructive behavior is unacceptable in our schools. Acknowledging that such behavior occurs, CEC believes that schools have the responsibility to quickly and unilaterally move students who exhibit dangerously violent or destructive behavior to an alternative educational setting in which ongoing safety/behavioral goals and educational goals are addressed by appropriately trained or qualified personnel. This setting must meet the school's dual responsibilities of providing an appropriate, public education and a safe learning/working environment in an age and culturally appropriate manner.

Alternative placements and programs should meet standards of quality that promote learning environments that benefit students in positive and productive ways. Less than desirable alternative placements that serve to merely contain students without meaningful learner benefits should not be used. If the student has a disability, this setting must be selected by the student's individualized education program committee. If the student does not have a disability, another appropriate education committee should make this decision. If the alternative setting is contested, the current alternative setting will continue until the resolution of applicable due process procedures for a student with or without disabilities.

During the time a student is in an alternative educational setting, the local education agency must conduct a committee meeting (in the case of a student with a disability, an individualized education program committee meeting) as soon as possible. During this meeting, the following must be considered:

a. Whether the student's violent behavior was an isolated incident and is not likely to happen again;

b. Whether the environment in which the violent behavior occurred was appropriate given the student's age, cultural background, disability, related needs, and characteristics;

c. Whether or not there are new characteristics within the student or environment necessitating further evaluation or, in the case of a student with a disability, a revision of the individualized education program;

d. Whether the student's return to the previous educational setting with appropriate supports and related services would provide safety for self and others; and

e. Whether the placement was the least restrictive environment for the student.

In determining an appropriate temporary placement for a student or when developing a new program if one is necessary, educators, parents, and other appropriate professionals should consider a variety of possibilities, such as:

a. Maintaining the current placement with additional support services.

b. Providing educational alternatives to suspension that afford students quality learning experiences.

c. Utilizing documented effective behavioral interventions, curricular modifications, and

accommodation strategies appropriate to the student's culture and designed to assist the student in controlling behavior.

Schools should ensure that all general and special educators involved in implementing the student's education program have opportunities for staff development to acquire the knowledge and skills necessary for effective implementation of the student's program. Providing systematic education about appropriate behavior to all students in the educational environment is also necessary. CEC also stresses the importance of the involvement and commitment of families and communities. CEC recommends that school districts, in collaboration with state/provincial agencies, community agencies, and juvenile justice systems, create appropriate alternative settings. The creation and maintenance of appropriate educational settings provide positive opportunities for all to work and learn and thus reduce the likelihood of future inappropriate behavior.

Paragraph 8 - Responsibility of the Schools for Early Childhood Education

Schools have traditionally assumed educational responsibility for children beginning at about age 5 or 6 and ending with late adolescence. Increasingly, it is apparent that formal educational experiences at earlier ages would pay rich dividends in the full development of the capabilities of many children with exceptionalities. Special educators have useful knowledge and many techniques for working with very young children with exceptionalities. What is needed is the identification of children who could benefit from early education and the actual implementation of programs.

Communities should make their schools responsible for conducting search and census operations through which children who may need specialized education at very early ages can be identified. The voluntary enrollment of such children by their parents is inadequate because many parents may not be aware of the child's special needs or of available forms of assistance. Procedures for child study that encourage adaptations to the particular needs of very young children with exceptionalities are an important part of early education programs.

Schools should provide educational services for individuals according to their needs and regardless of age.

Schools should actively seek out children who may have specialized educational needs in the first years of their lives. A particular commitment should be made to initiate home care training programs for parents of infants with special needs, to establish specialized early childhood and kindergarten programs, and to utilize specialized components of regular early education programs to serve children with exceptionalities.

Paragraph 9 - Services to Children with Exceptionalities Ages Birth Through Five

The provision of services to children with exceptionalities from birth through 5 years of age must be made a priority. It is the premise of The Council that lack of such services currently represents the most serious impediment to the development of children with exceptionalities. There is mounting evidence of the effectiveness of programs for very young children with exceptionalities and their families.

Services to young children with exceptionalities are presently provided by a variety of systems at national, state, provincial, and local levels. There is little systematic coordination between agencies, and major service gaps remain unfilled. A national initiative is needed to establish plans for systematic coordination among the social, educational, and health agencies currently serving children with exceptionalities from birth through 5 years so as to ensure maximum benefits for these children and their families, and to plan for the future provision of additional programs to fill major gaps in service to this population.

Wide variations in service arrangements are necessary to meet the individual needs of children. The Council strongly supports the principle that services for young children with exceptionalities, whenever appropriate, be provided in a context which includes children without exceptionalities. Effective integrated experiences can further the development of children with exceptionalities and also can form the roots of respect for diversity in all children. Since the success of integrated programs relies heavily on the provision of specialized teacher training and supportive resources, the importance of such supports should be reflected in legislative and funding directives.

In expanding services for children with exceptionalities from birth through 5 years, it is essential that the central role of the parent in the young child's development be recognized. Programs must be designed to incorporate parental participation and to provide support for families in their role as the child's primary care provider. The training of teachers of young children with exceptionalities should be expanded to include skills in working with parents in mutually helpful ways so that parental and agency efforts in helping the child are strengthened.

Paragraph 10 - Responsibilities for Providing Continuing Education Services to Exceptional Youth

The Council believes that education is a lifelong process and that, instead of age, competency and maximal development should be the terminating factor with regard to formal schooling. It also believes that individuals with learning problems, particularly exceptional youth, frequently need education and periodic reeducation beyond the traditional school attendance ages to encourage their continuing development. These options might include postsecondary education, vocational education, job training, employment counseling, community living skills, and placement services in order to maximize their ability to contribute to society.

Paragraph 11 - Migrant Exceptional Students

Exceptional students who are mobile, due to their parents' migrant employment, experience reduced opportunities for an appropriate education and a reduced likelihood of completing their education. Child-find and identification policies and practices, designed for a stationary population, are inadequate for children who move frequently. Incomplete, delayed, or inadequate transfer of records seriously impedes educational continuity. Interstate/provincial differences in special education eligibility requirements, programs and resources, minimum competency testing, and graduation requirements result in repetition of processing formalities, gaps in instruction, delays in the resumption of services, an inability to accumulate credits for graduation, and other serious inequities. In addition to the disruption of learning, mobility disrupts health care, training, teacher-student rapport, and personal relationships.

The Council believes that educational policies and practices should be developed at federal, state/provincial, and local levels to improve access to education for migrant children and youth with exceptionalities. These policies should include:

a. A national system for the maintenance and transferal of special education records for migrant students with exceptionalities.

b. Intrastate/provincial and interstate/provincial cooperation in the transfer of records and of credits.

c. Flexibility in high school credit accumulation for migrant students with exceptionalities.

d. Joint planning, coordination, and shared responsibility among special education, migrant education, bilingual education, and related programs.

e. Funding patterns that adjust for variations in enrollment.

f. Flexible scheduling and other programming options that adjust for student mobility.

g. Routine monitoring of activities undertaken to identify the migrant exceptional student and to ensure educational continuity.

h. Ongoing research efforts to promote, improve, support, and evaluate the education of migrant students with exceptionalities.

i. Personnel training.

j. Parent and family information programs to facilitate record transfer.

Paragraph 12 - Children with Exceptionalities in Charter Schools

CEC vigorously supports educational reforms within the public schools which promote rigorous learning standards, strong educational outcomes, shared decision making, diverse educational offerings, and the removal of unnecessary administrative requirements. Charter schools, a form of public schools, are one approach many believe can be effective in achieving these objectives. However, such schools must reflect this country's commitment to free and universal public education, with equality of educational opportunity for all including students with disabilities.

Regardless of who takes responsibility for the delivery of educational services for children with disabilities who attend a charter school, the chartering agency – and, ultimately, state or provincial authorities -- must ensure that the rights of children with exceptionalities are upheld. It is the position of CEC that the following criteria with respect to children with disabilities be adhered to when parents, professionals, and school district authorities consider the development of charter school policy, the content of contracts or agreements establishing individual charter schools, and the actual operation of charter schools.

Student Access. Charter schools must be required to abide by the same federal or provincial nondiscrimination and equal education opportunity laws that apply to other public schools. Charter schools must not discriminate in their admissions policies, nor should they charge tuition or other mandatory fees. Disability status cannot be used as a criterion for excluding a child with a disability from attending a charter school, and policies governing admissions and students' participation in the school program should not inadvertently exclude children with disabilities.

Provision of Free, Appropriate Public Education. As public schools, charter schools must be required to provide a free, appropriate, public education to students with disabilities, and to ensure all of the other basic fundamental procedural rights in accordance with applicable federal and provincial laws, such as the Individuals with Disabilities Education Act and Section 504 of the Rehabilitation Act in the United States, including children's physical access to the education program offered. Enrollment in a charter school cannot be used to deny to a student with disabilities the free, appropriate education to which they have a right.

Financing the Education of Children with Disabilities. Educational and other services required by children with disabilities, including special education and related services, can be provided directly by the charter school, or through alternative arrangements with other public schools, with local school districts, or with state or provincial education agencies. State, provincial and local policies for charter schools and, when appropriate, charter agreements themselves should explicitly identify responsibility for providing and paying for any special services associated with educating children with disabilities in charter schools, including the cost of building renovations and the provision of education and related services.

Accountability. Charter schools must be held accountable by state or provincial education agencies and, when appropriate local school districts, for providing special education and related services to children with disabilities, consistent with applicable federal, provincial and state laws, just as other public schools are. The standards that apply to educating children with disabilities in charter schools must be the same as those that apply to other public schools, and enforcement of these standards must be conducted in a manner that is consistent with enforcement activities and penalties that apply in determining compliance of other public schools.

Paragraph 13 – Safe and Positive School Climate

CEC recognizes the important impact a safe and positive school climate has on the personal development and academic achievement of all students. Research has shown that schools implementing supportive and positive school climate strategies are more successful in creating environments conducive to learning. Recent incidents of school violence, including harassment directed at students with disabilities and/or gifts and talents, have drawn attention to the unacceptable cost of not assuring a safe and positive climate in our schools for all students. Furthermore, students with disabilities may be more at risk because they do not necessarily have the ability to understand and report what is happening to them.

Such incidents, as well as surveys of students and faculty regarding safety, document continuing and pervasive harassment and bullying experienced by students and reveal that these actions are more likely to be perpetrated on the basis of appearance and actual or perceived differences in ethnicity, race, language, abilities, gender, sexual orientation, gender expression, or religion.

As student enrollment becomes increasingly diverse, schools are challenged to assure that all students feel valued and supported. Available research confirms that students feel safer and learn better when schools have clear policies prohibiting harassment and discrimination and when all members of the school community (students, parents, educators, administrators, and other school personnel) actively uphold the right of every student to a safe learning environment. Harassment can take many forms, including cyber bullying and other technological/electronic methods. In addition, although overt acts easily come to the attention of schools, it is essential that covert acts are recognized and addressed. CEC believes that all members of the school community have a critical role to play in assuring that students have access to a safe and supportive school environment.

In light of legal mandates and professional standards that promote the use of evidence-based practices to increase positive academic and social-emotional behaviors among students, CEC believes that special educators must acquire and use a knowledge base of effective practices for promoting supportive school climates in ways that support human and civil rights and promote social justice for the diverse student populations in today's schools.

Discrimination or harassment directed at students or adults on the basis of ethnic and racial backgrounds, language, age, abilities, family status, gender, sexual orientation, socioeconomic status, religious and spiritual values, and geographic location violates the human and/or civil rights of individuals who are the targets of such behavior.

To ensure the creation of sage learning environments that contribute to all students' cognitive, academic, social-emotional, and ethical development, it is the policy of the Council for Exceptional Children that:

All schools should have clear policies that prohibit harassment and discriminatory behaviors of any kind, including those related to ethnic background, language, age, abilities, family status, gender, sexual orientation, socioeconomic status, religious and spiritual values, and geographic location. Students and staff should be clearly informed of such policies and procedures, including data collection, reporting, sanctions, and indemnity to those reporting incidents. Educational efforts at the federal, provincial, state, and local levels should promote policies, guidelines, and universal interventions designed to reduce or prevent discrimination or harassment as well as to create a school climate that is conducive to respect and dignity for all individuals.

Because bullying and harassment create emotional wounds that amplify the hardships of exceptionality as well as jeopardize the emotional and mental well-being of students, teachers, administrators, and other school support personnel with knowledge of harassment or bullying carry the responsibility to report these behaviors to relevant authorities and school personnel similar to the professional obligation to report child abuse.

In recognition that students' families, professionals, and staff may also be at risk of experiencing discrimination on the basis of factors including ethnic and racial backgrounds, language, age, abilities, family status, gender, sexual orientation, socioeconomic status, religious and spiritual values, and geographic location, school policies, activities, and interventions related to a positive school climate should address the needs and safety of adults as well as students.

School-based implementation of anti-discrimination policies must equally support and provide open access for the participation of students in activities and student-led groups designed to enhance a respectful, safe, and positive school climate and to promote respect for diversity in general or with respect to one or more diversity elements.

To support antidiscriminatory policies, schools should provide students, staff, and administrators with access to a range of resources, including designated professionals with expertise in intercultural and diversity-related counseling and human-relations.

School policies should promote practices and curricula that build a sense of community and understanding for and among all students in recognition of the positive relationship between school climate, learning environments, and educational outcomes for all individuals.

Professional development for educators and educational administrators should build schools' capacity to implement a diversity-rich curriculum as well as to respond effectively to instances of harassment, bullying, or intimidation. To this end, such activities should enhance educators' skills and strategies for effectively delivering culturally-sensitive educational experiences within the context of current standards-based curricula. Similarly, professional development for administrators should develop their leadership skills and strategies for developing and implementing anti-discrimination policies and for ensuring positive learning environments for all students. Schools should provide opportunities for parent education to complement professional development for educators.

Teacher and educational leadership preparation programs should prepare educators, administrators, and related services personnel to create safe learning environments and to intervene effectively in the event that harassment or discriminatory behaviors occur. This includes understanding about the range of ways that schools can evaluate school climate comprehensively using evidence-based practices as well as how school climate findings can be used to build authentic learning communities that support positive youth development and academic achievement.

CHAPTER 03

SPECIAL EDUCATION WITHIN THE SCHOOLS

Paragraph 1 - The Relationship Between Special and Regular School Programs

Special education is an integral part of the total educational enterprise, not a separate order. In any school system, special education is a means of enlarging the capacity of the system to serve the educational needs of all children.

The particular function of special education within the schools (and the education departments of other institutions) is to identify children with unusual needs and to aid in the effective fulfillment of those needs. Both regular and special school programs play a role in meeting the educational needs of children with exceptionalities. A primary goal of educators should be to help build accommodative learning opportunities for children with exceptionalities in regular educational programs. In the implementation of this goal, special education can serve as a support system, and special educators can assist regular school personnel in managing the education of children with exceptionalities.

When the special placement of a child is required, the aim of the placement should be to maximize the development and freedom of the child rather than to accommodate the regular classroom.

Special education should function within and as a part of the regular, public school framework. Within this framework, the function of special education should be to participate in the creation and maintenance of a total educational environment suitable for all children.

From their base in the regular school system, special educators can foster the development of specialized resources by coordinating their specialized contributions with the contributions of the regular school system. One of the primary goals of special educators should be the enhancement of regular school programs as a resource for all children.

Paragraph 2 - Administrative Organization

The system of organization and administration developed for special education should be linked with regular education (a) to increase the capability of the total system to make more flexible responses to changes in the behavior of individual pupils and to changing conditions in schools and society, and (b) to permit all elements of the system to influence the policies and programs of the others.

Special education must provide an administrative organization to facilitate achievement for children with exceptionalities of the same educational goals as those pursued by other children. This purpose can be achieved through structures that are sufficiently compatible with those employed by regular education to ensure easy, unbroken passage of children across regular-special education administrative lines for whatever periods of time may be necessary, as well as by structures that are sufficiently flexible to adjust quickly to changing task demands and child growth needs.

The major purpose of the special education administrative organization is to provide and maintain those environmental conditions in schools that are most conducive to the growth and learning of children with special needs.

Under suitable conditions, education within the regular school environment can provide the optimal opportunity for most children with exceptionalities. Consequently, the system for the delivery of special education must enable the incorporation of special help and opportunities in regular educational settings. Children should spend only as much time outside regular class settings as is necessary to control learning variables that are critical to the achievement of specified learning goals.

Paragraph 3 - Scope of Program

Education for children and youth with exceptionalities requires the well planned and purposeful coordination of many disciplines. Special education is a cross-disciplinary, problem-oriented field of services which is directed toward mobilizing and improving a variety of resources to meet the educational needs of children and youth with exceptionalities.

Paragraph 4 - The Goal and Commitment of Special Education

The fundamental purposes of special education are the same as those of regular education: the optimal development of the student as a skillful, free, and purposeful person, able to plan and manage his or her own life and to reach his or her highest potential as an individual and as a member of society. Indeed, special education developed as a highly specialized area of education in order to provide children with exceptionalities with the same opportunities as other children for a meaningful, purposeful, and fulfilling life.

Perhaps the most important concept that has been developed in special education as the result of experiences with children with exceptionalities is that of the fundamental individualism of every child. The aspiration of special educators is to see every child as a unique composite of potentials, abilities, and learning needs for whom an educational program must be designed to meet his or her particular needs. From its beginnings, special education had championed the cause of children with learning problems. It is as the advocates of such children and of the concept of individualization that special education can come to play a major creative role in the mainstream of education.

The special competencies of special educators are more than a collection of techniques and skills. They comprise a body of knowledge, methods, and philosophical tenets that are the hallmark of the profession. As professionals, special educators are dedicated to the optimal education of children with exceptionalities and they reject the misconception of schooling that is nothing but custodial care.

The focus of all education should be the unique learning needs of the individual child as a total functioning organism. All educators should recognize and accept that special and regular education share the same fundamental goals.

Special education expands the capacity of schools to respond to the educational needs of all students.

As advocates of the right of all children to an appropriate education, special educators affirm their professionalism.

Paragraph 5 - Educational Environments for Exceptional Students

Special education takes many forms and can be provided with a broad spectrum of administrative arrangements. Children with special educational needs should be served in regular classes and neighborhood schools insofar as these arrangements are conducive to good educational progress. The Council believes that the goal of educating children with exceptionalities together with children without exceptionalities is desirable if the individual program is such that it will enhance the child's (with exceptionalities) educational, social, emotional, and vocational development.

It is sometimes necessary, however, to provide special supplementary services for children with exceptionalities or to remove them from parts or all of the regular educational program. It may even be necessary to remove some children from their homes and communities in order for them to receive education and related services in residential schools, hospitals, or training centers. The Council believes that careful study and compelling reasons are necessary to justify such removal.

The Council charges each public agency to ensure that a continuum of alternative placements, ranging from regular class programs to residential settings, is available to meet the needs of children with exceptionalities.

Children with exceptionalities enrolled in special school programs should be given every appropriate opportunity to participate in educational, nonacademic, and extracurricular programs and services with children who are not disabled or whose disabilities are less severe.

While special schools for children with exceptionalities and other separate educational facilities may function as part of an effective special educational delivery system, it is indefensible to confine groups of exceptional pupils inappropriately in such settings as a result of the failure to develop a full continuum of less restrictive programs. The Council condemns as educationally and morally indefensible the practice of categorical isolation by exceptionality without full consideration of the unique needs of each student, and the rejection of children who are difficult to teach from regular school situations. When insufficient program options exist and when decisions are poorly made, children with exceptionalities are denied their fundamental rights to free public education. In so acting, education authorities violate the basic tenets of our democratic societies.

Like all children, children with exceptionalities need environmental stability, emotional nurturance, and social acceptance. Decisions about the delivery of special education to children with exceptionalities should be made after careful consideration of their home, school, and community relationships, their personal preferences, and effects on self-concept, in addition to other sound educational considerations.

Paragraph 6 - Inclusive Schools and Community Settings

The Council for Exceptional Children believes all children, youth, and young adults with disabilities are entitled to a free and appropriate education and/or services that lead to an adult life characterized by satisfying relations with others, independent living, productive engagement in the community, and participation in society at large. To achieve such outcomes, there must exist for all children, youth, and young adults a rich variety of early intervention, educational, and vocational program options and experiences. Access to these programs and experiences should be based on individual educational need and desired outcomes. Furthermore, students and their families or guardians, as members of the planning team, may recommend the placement, curriculum option, and the exit document to be pursued.

CEC believes that a continuum of services must be available for all children, youth, and young adults. CEC also believes that the concept of inclusion is a meaningful goal to be pursued in our schools and communities. In addition, CEC believes children, youth, and young adults with disabilities should be served whenever possible in general education classrooms in inclusive neighborhood schools and community settings. Such settings should be strengthened and supported by an infusion of specially trained personnel and other appropriate supportive practices according to the individual needs of the child.

Policy Implications

Schools. In inclusive schools, the building administrator and staff with assistance from the special education administration should be primarily responsible for the education of children, youth, and young adults with disabilities. The administrator(s) and other school personnel must have available to them appropriate support and technical assistance to enable them to fulfill their responsibilities. Leaders in state/provincial and local governments must redefine rules and regulations as necessary, and grant school personnel greater authority to make decisions regarding curriculum, materials, instructional practice, and staffing patterns. In return for greater autonomy, the school administrator and staff should establish high standards for each child, youth, and young adult, and should be held accountable for his or her progress toward outcomes.

Communities. Inclusive schools must be located in inclusive communities; therefore, CEC invites all educators, other professionals, and family members to work together to create early intervention, educational, and vocational programs and experiences that are collegial, inclusive, and responsive to the diversity of children, youth, and young adults. Policy makers at the highest levels of state/provincial and local government, as well as school administration, also must support inclusion in the educational reforms they espouse. Further, the policy makers should fund programs in nutrition, early intervention, health care, parent education, and other social support programs that prepare all children, youth, and young adults to do well in school. There can be no meaningful school reform, nor inclusive schools, without funding of these key prerequisites. As important, there must be interagency agreements and collaboration with local governments and business to help prepare students to assume a constructive role in an inclusive community.

Professional Development. And finally, state/provincial departments of education, local educational districts, and colleges and universities must provide high-quality preservice and continuing professional development experiences that prepare all general educators to work effectively with children, youth, and young adults representing a wide range of abilities and disabilities, experiences, cultural and linguistic backgrounds, attitudes, and expectations. Moreover, special educators should be trained with an emphasis on their roles in inclusive schools and community settings. They also must learn the importance of establishing ambitious goals for their students and of using appropriate means of monitoring the progress of children, youth, and young adults.

Paragraph 7 - Staff Preparation for Placement

Essential to the appropriate placement of the child with an exceptionality is the preparation of the environment for that child through preservice and/or inservice training of staff and any other necessary accommodations.

Teacher training institutions are challenged to instruct all teacher candidates about current trends in the education of exceptional children.

State and provincial departments of education are charged with the responsibility to promote inservice activities that will update all professional educators and provide ongoing, meaningful staff development programs.

Administrators can have a significant positive influence upon the professional lives of teaching staff and, therefore, upon the educational lives of children. Administrative personnel of school districts are, therefore, charged with the responsibility to promote inservice education and interprofessional exchanges which openly confront contemporary issues in the education of all children.

Paragraph 8 - Individualized Education Programs

The creation and operation of a series of alternative settings for exceptional persons to live their lives and to develop to the greatest degree possible requires that service providers continuously strive to deliver the highest quality services possible. The Council believes that the central element for the delivery of all the services required by a person with an exceptionality must be an individually designed program. Such a program must contain the objectives to be attained, resources to be allocated, evaluation procedures and time schedule to be employed, and a termination date for ending the program and procedure for developing a new one. The process for developing an individualized program must adhere to all the procedural safeguards of due process of law and must involve the individual person and his or her family, surrogate, advocate, or legal representative.

Paragraph 9 - Due Process Protections (Procedural Safeguards)

As a final component of quality control, The Council believes that no decisions can be made on behalf of any individual without strict adherence to due process of law. Most significant is our position that all individuals are entitled to adequate representation when such decisions are being made. We support the increasing efforts on the part of governments to officially require the assignment of a surrogate when a family member is not available for purposes of adequately representing the interests of the person with an exceptionality. Ultimately, however, whenever possible, a member of the individual's family provides the most desirable representation. It is also our position that the individual consumer must be given every opportunity to make his or her own decisions, that this is a right provided to all citizens, and that any abridgement of that individual right can only occur upon the proper exercise of law.

Paragraph 10 - Confidentiality

The Council for Exceptional Children urges members to adhere to ethical principles and act in compliance with laws and regulations which protect children and their family's right to privacy and which control the use of confidential information regarding children.

Paragraph 11 - Program Evaluation

Programs designed for the purpose of providing educational opportunities for children and youth with exceptionalities must not be viewed as static, for the end product must always be the exceptional child and his or her personal improvement. For this reason, all programs should contain plans to evaluate their effectiveness, and the results of such evaluations should be presented for public review.

The Council believes that all legislation to fund existing programs or create new programs should contain mechanisms for effective evaluation and that governmental advisory bodies should review the findings of evaluations on a regular basis. External as well as internal systems of evaluation should be developed to aid in the evaluation of programs for children and youth with exceptionalities.

Paragraph 12 - Labeling and Categorizing of Children

The field of special education is concerned with children who have unique needs and with school programs that employ specialized techniques. As the result of early attitudes and programs that stressed assistance for children with severe disabilities, the field developed a vocabulary and practices based on the labeling and categorizing of children. In recent decades, labeling and categorizing were extended to children with milder degrees of exceptionality. Unfortunately, the continued use of labels tends to rigidify the thinking of all educators concerning the significance and purpose of special education and thus to be dysfunctional and even harmful for children.

Words such as "defective," "disabled," "retarded," "impaired," "disturbed," and "disordered," when attached to children with special needs, are stigmatic labels that produce unfortunate results in both the children and in the community's attitudes toward the children. These problems are magnified when the field organizes and regulates its programs on the basis of classification systems that define categories of children according to such terms. Many of these classifications are oriented to etiology, prognosis, or necessary medical treatment rather than to educational classifications. They are thus of little value to the schools. Simple psychometric thresholds, which have sometimes been allowed to become pivotal considerations in educational decision making, present another set of labeling problems.

Special education's most valuable contribution to education is its specialized knowledge, competencies, values, and procedures for individualizing educational programs for individual children, whatever their special needs. Indeed, special educators at their most creative are the advocates of children who are not well served by schools except through special arrangements. To further the understanding of and programming for such children, special educators as well as other educational personnel should eliminate the use of simplistic categorizing.

No one can deny the importance of some of the variables of traditional significance in special education such as intelligence, hearing, and vision. However, these variables in all their complex forms and degrees must be assessed in terms of educational relevance for a particular child. Turning them into typologies that may contribute to excesses in labeling and categorizing children is indefensible and should be eliminated.

In the past, many legislative and regulatory systems have specified criteria for including children in an approved category as the starting point for specialized programming and funding. This practice places high incentives on the labeling of children and undoubtedly results in the erroneous placement of many children.

It is desirable that financial aids be tied to educational programs rather than to children and that systems for allocating children to specialized programs be much more open than in the past.

Special educators should enhance the accommodative capacity of schools and other educational agencies to serve children with special needs more effectively. In identifying such children, special educators should be concerned with the identification of their educational needs, not with generalized labeling or categorizing of children.

Decisions about the education of children should be made in terms of carefully individualized procedures that are explicitly oriented to children's developmental needs.

To further discourage the labeling and categorizing of children, programs should be created on the basis of educational functions served rather than on the basis of categories of children served.

Regulatory systems that enforce the rigid categorization of pupils as a way of allocating them to specialized programs are indefensible. Financial aid for special education should be tied to specialized programs rather than to finding and placing children in those categories and programs.

Paragraph 13 - Group Intelligence Testing

a. Psychological tests of many kinds saturate our society and their use can result in the irreversible deprivation of opportunity to many children, especially those already burdened by poverty and prejudice.

b. Most group intelligence tests are multileveled and standardized on grade samples, thus necessitating the use of interpolated and extrapolated norms and scores.

c. Most group intelligence tests, standardized on LEAs rather than individual students, are not standardized on representative populations.

d. In spite of the use of nonrepresentative group standardization procedures, the norms are expressed in individual scores.

e. Most group intelligence tests, standardized on districts which volunteer, may have a bias in the standardization.

f. Many of the more severely handicapped and those expelled or suspended have no opportunity to influence the norms.

g. Group intelligence tests are heavily weighted with language and will often yield spurious estimates of the intelligence of non-English speaking or language different children.

h. A group intelligence test score, although spurious, may still be a good predictor of school performance for some children.

i. School achievement predicts future school performance as well as group intelligence tests, thus leaving little justification for relying on group intelligence tests.

j. One of the most frequent abuses of group intelligence tests is the use of such tests with populations for which they are inappropriate.

The Council goes on record in full support of the recommendations of the "Classification Project" (Hobbs, The Futures of Children, 1975, pp. 237-239) pertaining to group intelligence testing as follows:

a. "... That there be established a National Bureau of standards for Psychological Tests and Testing."

b. That there be established "minimum guidelines with respect to the utilization of psychological tests for the classification of children."

c. "That organizations that make extensive use of educational and psychological tests...should establish review boards to monitor their testing programs."

Until these three recommendations are accomplished, The Council encourages a moratorium on the use of group intelligence tests by individual school districts for the purpose of identifying children with exceptionalities.

Paragraph 14 - Exit Exams for Students with Exceptionalities

To ensure that exit exams are appropriately carried out regarding students with exceptionalities, it is the position of the Council for Exceptional Children that:

a. No single test score should be used to make critical educational decisions for students with exceptionalities. Multiple measures that document student learning and skills development should be used with accommodations when appropriate, in the decision-making process.

b. All students with exceptionalities must be given the opportunity to learn the material that is covered on exit exams. This includes the provision of individualized instructional services and supports that address the general education curriculum that is aligned with standards, test content, and the student's IEP. An alternate assessment should be an option for a student as recommended by the IEP team.

c. Advance notice should be given to all students with exceptionalities and their parents on the consequences of exit exams. This should include (1) a description of the steps to be taken to prepare students and teachers for the tests themselves; (2) any additional resources/supports that are available to ensure adequate performance on the tests; and (3) a clear statement for parents and students that explains what decisions may be made on the basis of the test results.

d. On-going research should be conducted on the impact of exit exams for students with exceptionalities that address issues, such as, grade-level retention/promotion, referral rates for special education, and any limits on future employment and educational experiences resulting from alternative high school diplomas.

Paragraph 15 - Assessment and Accountability

To ensure that students with disabilities are appropriately assessed under educational assessment and accountability systems, it is the position of the Council for Exceptional Children that:

a. All students with exceptional learning needs shall be included in all assessment and accountability systems, and shall have available the opportunity to participate in general assessments, assessments with accommodations including off-grade level testing or alternate assessments that reflect valid and reliable performance for them, rather than cultural diversity, linguistic diversity, disability, or other exceptionality.

b. All students with exceptional needs in all settings shall be included in the assessment and accountability systems. This includes students in traditional public school placements and students who change schools or placements, as well as all students receiving publicly-funded educational services in settings such as home schools, private schools, charter schools, state-operated programs and in the juvenile justice system.

c. Only assessment processes and instruments that have been developed and validated on student samples that included students who have exceptionalities and that validly demonstrate their performance shall be used. Test designers shall be required to develop universally designed assessments.

d. State and provincial determinations of adequate yearly progress must address the progress made on grade promotions and graduation rates for exceptional students, as well as addressing other appropriate achievement indicators for students with exceptionalities, and toward making well-grounded appraisals of the particular schools.

e. The IEP team will determine student participation in assessments as part of the review of the overall individualized education program and be based on individual student needs.

f. All students with exceptionalities shall be included when assessment scores are publicly reported, whether they participate with or without accommodations or participate through an alternate assessment - subject to personal confidentiality protections. If standards-based reform is to succeed all students must be held to higher standards, and every student must therefore be counted. However, assessment data focused on school system accountability shall never be the sole basis for making individual student educational decisions.

g. To ensure equal access and opportunity for all students and to ensure inclusive accountability in all local and state/provincial accountability indices, the performance on assessments of students with exceptionalities must have the same impact on the final accountability index as the performance of other students, whether or not these students participated with accommodations or in an alternate assessment.

h. Policy makers and all other stakeholders must be committed to the continuing development of a unified system of assessment and accountability for all students.

i. There must be a firm commitment to the continuing improvement of the assessment and accountability system in the challenging years ahead, through the processes of structured monitoring, intensive ongoing evaluation, and systemic professional training based on emerging research and best practice.

j. The successful implementation of an appropriate assessment and accountability system, including its application to students with exceptional needs, requires the cooperative efforts of all teachers, related service personnel, paraprofessionals, administrators, parents, and students in its planning, application, and evaluation.

k. The support of legislators, other policy makers, and state/provincial educational service personnel is essential to guarantee that each student is afforded the opportunity to be assessed with a measure for her/his abilities.

Paragraph 16 - Surgical and Chemical Interventions to Control the Behavior of Human Beings

The Council condemns the inappropriate use of surgical and chemical interventions to control the behavior of human beings. Although these procedures often simplify care and maintenance, the integrity of the individual must transcend any institution's desire for administrative convenience. The Council recognizes that in certain circumstances such interventions may be appropriate; however, they should never be used without the approval of the individual to be treated, or the individual's parents or guardians, or, in circumstances where the individual is a ward of the state, the approval of an appropriate review body before which the individual or his or her representatives are guaranteed all legal due-process rights.

Paragraph 17 - Physical Intervention

The Council recognizes the right to the most effective educational strategies to be the basic educational right of each special education child. Furthermore, The Council believes that the least restrictive positive educational strategies should be used, as it relates to physical intervention, to respect the child's dignity and personal privacy. Additionally, The Council believes that such interventions shall assure the child's physical freedom, social interaction and individual choice. The intervention must not include procedures which cause pain or trauma. Intervention techniques must focus not only on eliminating a certain undesirable behavior, but also upon a determination of the purpose of that behavior, and the provision/instruction of a more appropriate behavior. Lastly, behavior intervention plans must be specifically described in the child's written educational plan with agreement from the education staff, the parents and, when appropriate, the child.

The Council recommends that physical intervention be used only if all the following requirements are met:

a. The child's behavior is dangerous to herself/ himself or others, or the behavior is extremely detrimental to or interferes with the education or development of the child.

b. Various positive reinforcement techniques have been implemented appropriately and the child has repeatedly failed to respond as documented in the child's records.

c. It is evident that withholding physical intervention would significantly impede the child's educational progress as explicitly defined in his/her written educational plan.

d. The physical intervention plan specifically will describe the intervention to be implemented, the staff to be responsible for the implementation, the process for documentation, the required training of staff and supervision of staff as it relates to the intervention and when the intervention will be replaced.

e. The physical intervention plan will become a part of the written educational plan.

f. The physical intervention plan shall encompass the following provisions:

1. A comprehensive analysis of the child's environment including variables contributing to the inappropriate behavior.

2. The plan to be developed by a team including professionals and parents/guardians, as designated by state/provisional and federal law.

3. The personnel implementing the plan shall receive specific training congruent with the contents of the plan and receive ongoing supervision from individuals who ware trained and skilled in the techniques identified in the plan.

4. The health and medical records of the child must be reviewed to ensure that there are no physical conditions present that would contraindicate the use of the physical intervention proposed.

5. The impact of the plan on the child's behavior must be consistently evaluated, the results documented, and the plan modified when indicated.

The Council supports the following prohibitions:

a. Any intervention that is designed to, or likely to, cause physical pain.

b. Releasing noxious, toxic or otherwise unpleasant sprays, mists, or substances in proximity to the child's face.

c. Any intervention which denies adequate sleep, food, water, shelter, bedding, physical comfort, or access to bathroom facilities.

d. Any intervention which is designed to subject, used to subject, or likely to subject the individual to verbal abuse, ridicule or humiliation, or which can be expected to cause excessive emotional trauma.

e. Restrictive interventions which employ a device or material or objects that simultaneously immobilize all four extremities, including the procedure known as prone containment, except that prone containment may be used by trained personnel as a limited emergency intervention.

f. Locked seclusion, unless under constant surveillance and observation.

g. Any intervention that precludes adequate supervision of the child.

h. Any intervention which deprives the individual of one or more of his or her senses.

The Council recognizes that emergency physical intervention may be implemented if the child's behavior poses an imminent and significant threat to his/her physical well-being or to the safety of others. The intervention must be documented and parents/guardians must be notified of the incident.

However, emergency physical intervention shall not be used as a substitute for systematic behavioral intervention plans that are designed to change, replace, modify, or eliminate a targeted behavior.

Furthermore, The Council expects school districts and other educational agencies to establish policies and comply with state/provincial and federal law and regulations to ensure the protection of the rights of the child, the parent/guardian, the education staff, and the school and local educational agency when physical intervention is applied.

Paragraph 18 - Corporal Punishment

The Council for Exceptional Children supports the prohibition of the use of corporal punishment in special education. Corporal punishment is here defined as a situation in which all of the following elements are present: an authority accuses a child of violating a rule and seeks from the child an explanation, whereupon a judgment of guilt is made, followed by physical contact and pain inflicted on the child. The Council finds no conditions under which corporal punishment so defined would be the treatment of choice in special education.

Paragraph 19 - Child Abuse and Neglect

The Council recognizes abused and neglected children as children with exceptionalities. As professionals concerned with the physical, emotional, and mental well-being of children, educators must take an ac-

tive role in the protection of children from abuse and neglect. The Council reminds its members and citizens in general, of the availability of assault and battery statutes and calls upon its members to utilize such statutes when applicable in cases of child abuse. When child abuse occurs, swift action must be taken to report the incident and protect the child. Delays caused by not knowing what to do or failure to take action, contribute to the child's injury. Educators and related personnel are urged to learn how to recognize and report child abuse and neglect and to know the community resources for treating suspected cases.

Paragraph 20 - Managing Communicable and Contagious Diseases

Controlling the spread of communicable and contagious diseases within the schools has always been a problem faced by educators, the medical profession, and the public. Effective policies and procedures for managing such diseases in the schools have historically been developed by health agencies and implemented by the schools. These policies and procedures were primarily designed to manage acute, temporary conditions rather than chronic conditions which require continuous monitoring and remove children from interaction with other children while the condition is contagious or communicable.

Recent public awareness of chronic infectious diseases such as those with hepatitis B-virus, cytomegalovirus, herpes simplex virus, and HIV have raised concerns necessitating the reassessment or at least clarification of school policies and procedures. The Council believes that having a chronic infection does not in itself result in a need for special education. Further, The Council believes that schools and public health agencies should assure that any such infectious and communicable disease policies and procedures:

a. Do not exclude the affected child from the receipt of an appropriate education even when circumstances require the temporary removal of the child from contact with other children.

b. Provide that determination of a nontemporary alteration of a child's educational placement should be done on an individual basis, utilizing an interdisciplinary/interagency approach including the child's physician, public health personnel, the child's parents, and appropriate educational personnel.

c. Provide that decisions involving exceptional children's nontemporary alterations of educational placements or services constitute a change in the child's Individualized Education Program and should thus follow the procedures and protections required.

d. Recognize that children vary in the degree and manner in which they come into contact with other children and school staff.

e. Provide education staff with the necessary information, training, and hygienic resources to provide for a safe environment for students and educational staff.

f. Provide students with appropriate education about infectious diseases and hygienic measures to prevent the spread of such diseases.

g. Provide, where appropriate, infected children with education about the additional control measures that they can practice to prevent the transmission of the disease agent.

h. Enable educational personnel who are medically at high risk to work in environments which minimize such risk.

i. Provide educational personnel with adequate protections for such personnel and their families if they are exposed to such diseases through their employment.

The Council believes that special education personnel preparation programs should:

a. Educate students about infectious diseases and appropriate methods for their management.

b. Counsel students as to how to determine their level of medical risk in relation to certain diseases and the implications of such risk to career choice.

The Council believes that the manner in which policies for managing infectious diseases are developed and disseminated is important to their effective implementation. Therefore the following must be considered integral to any such process:

a. That they be developed through the collaborative efforts of health and education agencies at both the state, provincial and local levels, reflecting state, provincial and local educational, health and legal requirements.

b. That provision is made for frequent review and revision to reflect the ever-increasing knowledge being produced through research, case reports, and experience.

c. That policies developed be based on reliable identified sources of information and scientific principles endorsed by the medical and educational professions.

d. That such policies be understandable to students, professionals, and the public.

e. That policy development and dissemination be a continual process and disassociated from pressures associated with precipitating events.

Paragraph 21 - Career Education

Career education is the totality of experience through which one learns to live a meaningful, satisfying work life. Within the career education framework, work is conceptualized as conscious effort aimed at producing benefits for oneself and/or others. Career education provides the opportunity for children to learn, in the least restrictive environment possible, the academic, daily living, personal-social and occupational knowledge, and specific vocational skills necessary for attaining their highest levels of economic, personal, and social fulfillment.

The individual can obtain this fulfillment though work (both paid and unpaid) and in a variety of other social roles and personal lifestyles, including his or her pursuits as a student, citizen, volunteer, family member, and participant in meaningful leisure time activities.

Children with exceptionalities (i.e., those whose characteristics range from profoundly and severely disabled to those who are richly endowed with talents and/or intellectual giftedness) include individuals whose career potentials range from sheltered to competitive work and living arrangements. Children with exceptionalities require career education experiences which will develop to the fullest extent possible their wide range of abilities, needs, and interests.

It is the position of The Council that individualized appropriate education for children with exceptionalities must include the opportunity for every student to attain his or her highest level of career potential through career education experiences. Provision for these educational experiences must be reflected in an individualized education program for each exceptional child, which must include the following:

a. Nondiscriminatory, ongoing assessment of career interests, needs, and potentials which assures recognition of the strengths of the individual which can lead to a meaningful, satisfying career in a work oriented society. Assessment materials and procedures must not be discriminatory on the basis of race, sex, national origin, or exceptionality.

b. Career awareness, exploration, preparation, and placement experiences in the least restrictive school, living, and community environments that focus on the needs of the exceptional individual from early childhood through adulthood.

c. Specification and utilization of community and other services related to the career development of exceptional individuals (e.g., rehabilitation, transportation, industrial and business, psychological).

d. Involvement of parents or guardians and the exceptional student in career education planning.

Career education must not be viewed separately from the total curriculum. Rather, career education permeates the entire school program and even extends beyond it. It should be an infusion throughout the curriculum by knowledgeable teachers who modify the curriculum to integrate career development goals with current subject matter, goals, and content. It should prepare individuals for the several life roles that make up an individual's career. These life roles may include an economic role, a community role, a home role, an avocational role, a religious or moral role, and an aesthetic role. Thus, career education is concerned with the total person and his or her adjustment for community working and living.

Paragraph 22 - Treatment of Exceptional Persons in Textbooks

The Council proposes the following points as guidelines for early childhood, elementary, secondary, and higher education instructional materials so they more accurately and adequately reflect persons with exceptionalities as full and contributing members of society.

a. In print and non-print educational materials, 10% of the contents should include or represent children or adults with an exceptionality.

b. Representation of persons with exceptionalities should be included in materials at all levels (early childhood through adult) and in all areas of study.

c. The representation of persons with exceptionalities should be accurate and free from stereotypes.

d. Persons with exceptionalities should be shown in the least restrictive environment. They should be shown participating in activities in a manner that will include them as part of society.

e. In describing persons with exceptionalities, the language used should be nondiscriminatory and free from value judgments.

f. Persons with exceptionalities and persons without exceptionalities should be shown interacting in ways that are mutually beneficial

g. Materials should provide a variety of appropriate role models of persons with exceptionalities.

h. Emphasis should be on uniqueness and worth of all persons, rather than on the differences between persons with and without exceptionalities.

i. Tokenism should be avoided in the representation of persons with exceptionalities.

Paragraph 23 - Technology

The Council for Exceptional Children recognizes that the appropriate application and modification of present and future technologies can improve the education of exceptional persons. CEC believes in equal access to technology and supports equal educational opportunities for technology utilization by all individuals. Present technologies include electronic tools, devices, media, and techniques such as (a) computers and microprocessors; (b) radio, television, and videodisc systems; (c) information and communication systems; (d) robotics; and (e) assistive and prosthetic equipment and techniques. The Council believes in exploring and stimulating the utilization of these technologies in school, at home, at work, and in the community.

CEC encourages the development of product standards and consumer education that will lead to the appropriate and efficient matching of technological applications to individual and local conditions. CEC recognizes the need to communicate market needs and market expectations to decision makers in business, industry, and government.

CEC supports the continuous education of professionals who serve exceptional individuals, through (a) collection and dissemination of state-of-the-art information, (b) professional development, and (c) professional preparation of personnel to perform educational and other services for the benefit of exceptional individuals.

Paragraph 24 - Students with Special Health Care Needs

The Council for Exceptional Children believes that having a medical diagnosis that qualifies a student as one with a special health care need does not in itself result in a need for special education. Students with specialized health care needs are those who require specialized technological health care procedures for life support and/or health support during the school day. The Council believes the policies and procedures developed by schools and health care agencies that serve students with special health care needs should: (1) not exclude a student from receipt of appropriate special education and related services; (2) not exclude a student from receipt of appropriate educational services in the least restrictive environment; (3) not require educational agencies to assume financial responsibility for noneducationally related medical services; (4) define clearly the type, nature, and extent of appropriate related services to be provided and the nature of the appropriate provider; (5) assure that placement and service decisions involve interdisciplinary teams of personnel knowledgeable about the student, the meaning of evaluation data, and placement options; (6) promote a safe learning environment, including reasonable standards for a clean environment in which health risks can be minimized for all involved; (7) provide assurance that health care services are delivered by appropriate and adequately trained personnel; (8) provide appropriate medical and legal information about the special health care needs of students for all staff; (9) provide appropriate support mechanisms for students, families, and personnel involved with students with special health care needs; and (10) provide appropriate and safe transportation.

The Council for Exceptional Children believes that special education personnel preparation and continuing education programs should provide knowledge and skills related to: (1) the nature and management of students with special health care needs; (2) exemplary approaches and models for the delivery of services to students with special health care needs; and (3) the importance and necessity for establishing support systems for students, parents/families, and personnel.

Recognizing that this population of students is unique and relatively small, The Council for Exceptional Children still believes that the manner in which policies are developed and disseminated related to students with special health care needs is critically important to effective implementation. In development of policy and procedure for this low-incidence population, the following must be considered integral to any such process: (1) that it be developed through collaborative efforts of health and education agencies at state, provincial, and local levels; (2) that it reflects federal, state, provincial, and local educational, health, and legal requirements; (3) that it provides for frequent review and revision of intervention techniques and programs as a result of new knowledge identified through research, program evaluation and monitoring, and other review mechanisms; (4) that policies are supported by data obtained from medical and educational professions; (5) that policy development is easily understandable by students, professionals, and the public at large; and (6) that policy development and dissemination should be a continual process and disassociated from pressures associated with precipitating events.

Paragraph 25 - Use of Interpreters or Transliterators for Individuals Who are Deaf/Hard of Hearing

CEC recognizes that an increasing number of students who are deaf/hard of hearing are being educated in the public schools. CEC impresses upon the education field the importance of using appropriately trained and qualified persons to interpret and transliterate for students who are deaf/hard of hearing. CEC opposes the practice of using non-related or non-certified individuals to interpret or transliterate in classrooms. Additionally, CEC opposes the notion that "one size fits all" when communication modes and languages are involved. Therefore, CEC supports the following statements.

1. The practice of spontaneously pulling non-professional persons from their regularly assigned duties to fulfill the role of interpreter/transliterator when appropriate training has not been provided should be avoided altogether.

2. School districts, agencies, private schools or other employers/users should exhaust all means of obtaining professional personnel who are competent in the mode of communication used by the students before seeking the assistance of interpreters/transliterators.

3. Individuals certified to assess the communication needs of students who are deaf/hard of hearing should be consulted to determine the appropriate mode or language needed by an individual child. Providing interpretation or transliteration in a mode or language not used by the child is equally as problematic as providing no interpretation/transliteration at all, and the average signer or oral interpreter is often not qualified to make this judgment.

4. Interpreters (from natural sign languages such as ASL or Auslan to the spoken form of the country in which that language is used and vice versa) and transliterators (from English-based sign system, Cued Speech, oral interpreters, and those who use any sign system designed to pattern the grammar of that country's spoken language) should be trained and credentialed in their mode and language of communication along with training in special education procedures and guidelines, normal child development, and the roles and responsibilities of educational interpreters. Professionals using interpreters and transliterators also should receive training in the appropriate use of these individuals to maximize effective communication among professionals, students, and parents.

5. Competencies of interpreters and transliterators must be determined before using their services. Evaluations should be conducted by certified individuals, agencies or organizations from the community familiar with the mode, language, and needs of children and youth. Competencies should include, but are not limited to, high proficiency levels in the spoken language of the country and the target language (eg, spoken English or Czech to ASL or CSL, spoken language such as Spanish to Cued Speech or oral transliteration), knowledge of the culture and linguistic nuances, including Deaf Culture and other cultures of other spoken languages; and knowledge of cross-cultural, gender, and generational differences and expectations.

6. Upon mastery of these competencies, a certification, approval, or rating system should be required to ensure that interpreters and transliterators possess the skills necessary for providing effective services.

CHAPTER 04

ADMINISTRATIVE AND FISCAL IDENTITY

Paragraph 1 - Responsibility Defined

Responsibility for administering special education programs should be clearly defined so that accountability for service effectiveness can be maintained.

In the administration of the special education system, it must be clarified (a) who is to be responsible for various functions and decisions and (b) what procedures can be developed to provide adequate protection of the individual child's rights. When services essential to the improvement of a child's condition are rendered under several administrative auspices, as is so often the case with children and youth with exceptionalities, which agent or agency is to be responsible for providing which aspects of treatment needs to be clearly defined at every level to produce the most effective outcomes for the child.

The major functions commonly assigned to administrators of special education programs include the following:

a. Establishing and maintaining effective ways of identifying children with special education needs.

b. Assessing the special needs of children to determine what kinds of special programs and services should be provided for them.

c. Planning and organizing an appropriate variety of interventions or program alternatives for children with exceptionalities.

d. Marshaling the resources needed to conduct a comprehensive program of special education.

e. Using direction, coordination, and consultation as required to guide the efforts of all those who are engaged in the special education enterprise.

f. Conducting evaluation and research activities to reflect new emphases and to incorporate new knowledge and constantly improve special instruction and the quality of special services.

g. Involving community representatives in planning programs to ensure their understanding and support.

h. Conducting programs for staff development, such as inservice or continuing education.

Paragraph 2 - Leadership

The Council urges state/provincial and local education agencies to develop administrative structures on a policy-making level and to staff such programs with professionally qualified personnel who can provide dynamic leadership. Creative leadership at all levels of government is imperative for the development and improvement of programs for children and youth with exceptionalities. For this reason, The Council supports efforts to improve the quality of leadership and administrative operations in all phases of educational endeavor.

Paragraph 3 - Administrative Hierarchy

Every school system should contain a visible central administrative unit for special education programs and services which is at the same administrative hierarchical level as other major instructional program units.

The parameters of regular and special education should be articulated so that children may be afforded equal educational opportunity through the resources of either or both instructional programs.

Such articulation should be achieved through sensitive negotiations between the responsible agents of both regular and special education who meet in full parity. To protect the rights of all children to equal educational opportunity, the policy-making bodies of school systems should include administrators of both regular and special education.

Programs to meet the needs of children with exceptionalities are no less important than those designed to meet the needs of other children. The importance of programs to meet human needs should not be judged on the basis of the number of clients the programs are expected to serve.

Paragraph 4 - Special Education and School Budgets

Success of all education programs is dependent on the provision of adequate funding. This is essentially true of programs for children and youth with exceptionalities. Often funding for such programs becomes buried in general budgeting procedures. In such cases, children and youth with exceptionalities do not have the opportunity to have their needs directly considered by the decision-making bodies of government. Therefore, The Council urges that efforts be undertaken to assure that budgetary provisions for children and youth with exceptionalities be clearly identified. The Council opposes general funding procedures that would circumvent direct aid to programs for children and youth with exceptionalities.

Since children with exceptionalities have the same rights to education as other children, the educational needs of children with exceptionalities cannot be delayed until the needs and service demands of the majority of children have been satisfied. Educational resources are always likely to be finite. The application of the principle of "the greatest good for the greatest number" to determine which children's needs shall be met first directly contradicts our democratic society's declared commitment to equal educational opportunity for all children. History confirms that the social injustices and ill effects that flow from the application of the majority-first principle to educational budgeting are too serious for this principle to be used in educational financing.

Children with exceptionalities constitute a minority of the school population. The programs serving them represent a comparatively high financial investment in relation to the numbers of children served. In some school systems, money allocated to special education is regarded as an alternative to the improvement of regular school programs. The climate of competitive interests thus produced can jeopardize the stability of special education services.

The interests of the community are ill served if competition for funds is conducted on the basis of special interests. What is needed, rather, is the cooperation of both regular and special educators to educate the public in the desirability of meeting the needs of all children without discrimination or favoritism.

There is every reason to believe that the public interest is best protected when the responsibility for the deployment of public resources is placed in the hands of persons who are qualified by training and experience to make the necessary judgments. Thus, special education should play an active role in determining how resources are to be allocated. However, the community has the ultimate responsibility to determine goals and to evaluate performance.

Resources should be allocated to special education on the basis of programs to be provided, not on the basis of traditional categorical incidence estimates.

The mandate to provide all children with equal educational opportunities requires that all educators, whether regular or special, be equally concerned with the funding of both regular and special education programs. No school system can fulfill the mandate if rivalries for dollars are permitted to supersede the needs of children.

CHAPTER 05

SPECIAL EDUCATION AND THE COMMUNITY OUTSIDE THE EDUCATION SYSTEM

Paragraph 1 - Liaison with Other Agencies and Organizations

Children and youth with exceptionalities and their families require the services of many agencies which deal with their various needs. In most cases, individual agency efforts can be made more effective through a cooperative interagency and interdisciplinary approach whereby special education has a primary function for liaison with other agencies and organizations. This approach will not only encourage a consistent effort on the part of all concerned with the child's education and development, but will provide for joint establishment of the priorities and respective responsibilities for meeting the child's needs. Public policy should be encouraged at the state, provincial, and federal levels for a coordinated approach to multifunded projects under one application procedure to ensure comprehensive services to the child. Such policies should support and facilitate intergovernmental cooperation as well as interagency linkage. The Council encourages policies which promote a coordinated approach to planning for the needs of children and youth with exceptionalities and which strengthen the relationships of special education to public and private agencies providing services. The Council at all levels should consistently support a coordinated effort.

Paragraph 2 - Public Participation

Administrative units at all levels of government responsible for providing leadership must have responsibility for developing policy regarding the education of children and youth with exceptionalities. However, such policy must reflect the thinking of all persons involved in the education of children and youth with exceptionalities. The Council believes that advisory committees can help government agencies assess problems, plan and set priorities, and develop and oversee policies regarding the education of children and youth with exceptionalities. The Council further believes that all policies involving education of children and youth with exceptionalities should be brought before recurring public and legislative scrutiny.

Paragraph 3 - The School and the Family

Parents must have access to all available necessary information in order to be able to make optimal decisions about the child's education and to fulfill the family's obligations to the child.

As a means of strengthening special education programs, the parents of children with exceptionalities and organized community groups should be given a responsible voice in educational policy formation and planning activities.

The primary consumers of educational services, the children, should not be ignored as a valuable resource in the evaluation of the organization and delivery of services.

As a means of strengthening the family in fulfilling its obligations to children with exceptional needs, the schools should provide educationally related counsel-ing and family services. In cases of clear educational neglect, the schools, through qualified professional personnel, should make extraordinary arrangements for educational services.

Access includes making information available at convenient times and locations and providing information in the parent's native language or mode of communication whenever necessary.

Paragraph 4 - Private Sector

The private sector (nonprofit) has long played a significant role in the field of special education. The elements of the private sector (nonprofit) are varied and encompass the full gamut of levels of educational programs and services from preschool education through higher education, research, demonstration projects, personnel training, technology, and the development and production of media and materials. Increasingly, a working relationship has developed between the public and private sectors (nonprofit) regarding children and youth with exceptionalities.

The Council believes that private enterprise (nonprofit) can make major contributions to the development of adequate special education services. The Council urges cooperation between government and private enterprise (nonprofit) to meet the needs of children and youth with exceptionalities. The Council urges that legislation be flexible enough to allow administrative agencies to involve the private sector (nonprofit) in all aspects of program development.

The Council believes that the opportunity for all children to receive an education is a public responsibility, but that program operation of such services may be conducted in varied settings and through a variety of public and private (nonprofit) agencies. For this reason, The Council supports the development and provision of special services in both the public and private sectors (nonprofit) and the support for such services through public funds, under public control and supervision.

The Council believes that when children with exceptionalities receive their education in the private sector (nonprofit) as a matter of public policy, then the appropriate state public agency shall approve the education program and personnel in such facilities, certify that the program is appropriate to the child's educational needs and is provided at no expense to the child or his family, certify that the facility meets appropriate health and safety standards, and guarantee that all rights of children with exceptionalities and their families are maintained.

CHAPTER 06

COMMUNITY-BASED SERVICES

Paragraph 1 - Prerequisites

Significant nationwide trends, both to reduce the populations of institutions and to improve the services provided for those who are institutionalized, necessitate comprehensive public policies on community-based services. Numerous exceptional children and adults reside in institutions. The quantity and quality of educational and other service programs provided in these facilities vary greatly. Considerable evidence, however, has been collected demonstrating that many institutions for exceptional citizens have failed to meet the needs of their residents. Institutionalization, in many instances, has violated basic individual rights and fostered inhumane deprivation. Rights violated include the opportunity to live in a humane environment and be provided with individual programs of treatment designed to allow each person to develop to the greatest degree possible.

Despite public and professional awareness of deplorable institutional conditions, persons with exceptionalities who could not live in natural homes were routinely placed in institutions. Alternative service arrangements were usually not available and an implicit assumption was made that some persons with disabilities were incapable of growth. The lack of quality services and the stigma of negative attitudes must be changed.

The Council, recognizing the necessity for community-based services, maintains that the human services system must adhere to the principle of normalization to avoid destructive individual and societal consequences and adhere to the following prerequisites:

a. Central to a person's growth and dignity is a right to live within the community, with access to high quality and appropriate services.

b. A legal mandate with fixed responsibility must exist providing community services for all persons, including those now institutionalized.

c. The goal of community services is to assure the greatest developmental gains on the part of the individual through maximum flexibility in all services.

d. The ongoing process of normalizing the service system requires developing a continuum of community-based living environments and the selective use of the full range of services available to the entire community.

e. Multiple and diverse methods of safeguarding program quality are essential at every level of responsibility.

f. All programs provided to exceptional persons must include written standards governing service delivery.

g. When a state restricts an individual's fundamental liberty, it must adhere to the principle of least restrictive environment and, further, absolutely guarantee due process.

Paragraph 2 - Characteristics

A comprehensive community-based service system for exceptional persons should reflect the following characteristics:

a. Services must meet the needs of persons of all ages, must accommodate the problems of individuals possessing all degrees of disabilities, and be available when needed and where needed by the individual.

b. Services must be appropriately located in populous neighborhoods and should be compatible with the surrounding community.

c. Services must be based upon a systematic plan for continuity which interrelates with other established services.

d. Services must have a legally vested authority which enables the fixing of responsibility and accountability with implementation power.

e. Services must be designed to permit the placement of exceptional persons in high quality programs in the least restrictive environment.

f. Services must be economically sound in meeting human development needs.

Paragraph 3 - The Need for Flexibility and Development

Because of rapid changes and developments in the environmental factors that influence the characteristics of children and the conditions of their lives, special education should maintain a flexibility that permits it to adapt to changing requirements.

Some of the events and changes that have had major impact on special education in recent years are the following: a rubella epidemic, discovery of preventatives for retrolental fibroplasia, increasing numbers of premature births, increasing awareness of the deleterious effects of poverty and malnutrition, new techniques in surgical intervention, invention of individual electronic hearing aids, and adaptation of low-vision aids. Changes and developments in public health, medicine, technology, and social programs may have only a small total effect on school systems, but they frequently have major impacts on special education programs. Changes in one aspect of special education quickly are reflected in other aspects of the field as, for example, the rapid development of day school programs for children with exceptionalities which has been reflected in a more severely disabled population in residential schools.

Special educators must seek to be highly flexible in the provision of services and the use of technology and techniques to meet the changing needs of children with exceptionalities.

School administrators and special educators have particular responsibility for sustaining their professional awareness and development as a basis for changing programs to meet changing needs.

Paragraph 4 - Prevention of Handicapping Conditions

Increasing knowledge of the biological and social causes of many handicapping conditions now makes some conditions preventable. The Council believes that appropriate prenatal counseling and care and intervention services could prevent or reduce the severity of many handicapping conditions. Therefore, The Council believes that there should be substantial governmental attention and resources devoted to prevention and the amelioration of the impact of handicapping conditions including:

a. Research and development

b. Public awareness

c. Prenatal services

d. Child- and family-centered early intervention services

e. Family and parenting education and support programs for teenagers and other high-risk populations

f. Reduction of social and environmental factors that cause handicapping conditions.

CHAPTER 07

EDUCATION OF THE GIFTED AND TALENTED

Paragraph 1 - Gifted and Talented Children as Exceptional Children

Special education for the gifted is not a question of advantage to the individual versus advantage to society. It is a matter of advantage to both. Society has an urgent and accelerated need to develop the abilities and talents of those who promise high contribution. To ignore this obligation and this resource is not only shortsighted but does violence to the basic concept of full educational opportunity for all.

Special educators should vigorously support programs for the gifted and talented as consistent with their concept of the need for special assistance for all children with exceptionalities. Such programs should reflect both the cognitive and non-cognitive needs of the gifted and talented.

Paragraph 2 - Identification

Gifted and talented children are those who are capable of high performance as identified by professionally qualified personnel. These children require different educational programs and/or services beyond those normally provided by the regular school program in order to realize their full potential in contribution to self and society.

Broad search and an early identification system for the identification of gifted and talented children within all sectors of the population should be the hallmark of an adequate educational system. Identification procedures should also reflect individual means of identifying children with general intellectual ability, specific academic abilities, leadership abilities, and abilities in the fine and performing arts.

Paragraph 3 - Delivery of Services

No single administrative plan or educational provision is totally appropriate for the gifted and talented. Certain administrative and instructional arrangements may provide settings in which the gifted and talented are likely to perform more adequately. In the final analysis, however, the task is one of accommodation to the needs of the individual.

New arrangements and new provisions must be utilized, including freedom to pursue interests which might not fit the prescribed curriculum, opportunities for open blocks of time, opportunities for consultation with persons and use of resources external to the classroom, and opportunities to bypass those portions of the curriculum which have been previously achieved by the individual. These kinds of arrangements must present options across all educational settings and procedures within all programs for the gifted and talented, whether in the regular classroom or in highly specialized situations.

Special education for the gifted and talented demands individualization within special programs in terms of student needs, as well as differentiation between programs for the gifted and talented and programs for other children and adults.

A program of special education for the gifted and talented should provide continuing and appropriate educational experiences from preschool into adult years.

Paragraph 4 - Preparation of School and Leadership Personnel

Special preparation is required for those educators who have either specific or general responsibilities for educating the gifted and talented. Teachers and other professional educators who work with the gifted and talented need special training in both program content and process skills. Such training should be recognized by appropriate certification in the case of teachers and should receive the general support of local, state, provincial, federal, and private interests.

Paragraph 5 - Demonstration Programs

The preparation of school personnel in the education of the gifted and talented should be carried out in settings which permit opportunities to examine relevant research and to observe innovative administrative provisions and exemplary instruction. This requires extensive library services, ongoing research or access to such research, and most importantly, centers in which teachers may observe and try out new styles of teaching appropriate to the education of the gifted and talented.

Special model or demonstration programs should be established to illustrate to educators and others the kind and range of innovative program efforts that are possible and effective in the education of gifted and talented students.

Paragraph 6 - Research and Development

Research and development resources should be focused on the needs of the gifted and talented in order to develop new methodologies and curricula and to allow educators and others to evaluate current and proposed methods.

Paragraph 7 - Parents and the Public

One responsibility of the special educator is to educate the parents of gifted and talented children concerning their children's needs and rights.

The educational needs of the gifted and talented also warrant planned programs of public information, particularly at the local community level. Special educators should accept these responsibilities as an important part of their professional involvement.

Para. 8 - Financial Support

Although programs for the gifted and talented can sometimes be initiated at relatively modest cost, it is important that funds for this purpose be earmarked at local, state or provincial, and national levels.

Principal expenditures should be directed toward the employment of leadership personnel, the development of methods and programs, and of particular importance at the local level, the preparation of persons for the support and implementation of such methods and programs in the schools.

The importance of optimal educational services for the gifted and talented merits the expenditure of funds in appropriate amounts toward this end by all levels of government as well as by other sources.

CHAPTER 08

ETHNIC AND MULTICULTURAL GROUPS

Paragraph 1 - Preamble

The Council believes that all policy statements previously adopted by CEC related to children with and without exceptionalities, as well as children with gifts and talents, are relevant and applicable to both minority and nonminority individuals. In order to highlight concerns of special interest to members of ethnic and multicultural groups, the following policy statements have been developed:

Paragraph 2 - Ethnicity and Exceptionality

The Council recognizes the special and unique needs of members of ethnic and multicultural groups and pledges its full support toward promoting all efforts which will help to bring them into full and equitable participation and membership in the total society.

Paragraph 3 - Identification, Testing, and Placement

The Council supports the following statements related to the identification, testing, and placement of children from ethnic and multicultural groups who are also exceptional.

a. Child-find procedures should identify children by ethnicity as well as type and severity of exceptionality or degree of giftedness.

b. Program service reporting procedures should identify children by ethnicity as well as exceptionality or degree of giftedness.

c. All testing and evaluation materials and methods used for the classification and placement of children from ethnic and multicultural groups should be selected and administered so as not to be racially or culturally discriminatory.

d. Children with exceptionalities who are members of ethnic and multicultural groups should be tested in their dominant language by examiners who are fluent in that language and familiar with the cultural heritage of the children being tested.

e. Communication of test results with parents of children from ethnic and multicultural groups should be done in the dominant language of those parents and conducted by persons involved in the testing or familiar with the particular exceptionality, fluent in that language, and familiar with the cultural heritage of those parents.

All levels of government should establish procedures to ensure that testing and evaluation materials and methods used for the purpose of classification and placement of children are selected and administered so as not to be linguistically, racially, or culturally discriminatory.

Paragraph 4 - Programming and Curriculum Adaptation

The Council supports the following statements related to programming and curriculum adaptation for children from ethnic and multicultural groups:

a. Long-term placement should be avoided unless students are reevaluated at prescribed intervals by individuals qualified in assessing such students with the most appropriate culture-free assessment instruments available.

b. All school districts should take necessary steps to ensure that both students and their parents fully comprehend the implications of and the reasons for proposed programming decisions, including the mature and length of placement. Parents should be fully involved in the decision-making process.

c. Culturally appropriate individualized education programs should be designed which include the child's present level of educational performance, annual goals, short-term objectives, and specific educational services to be provided.

d. It is of utmost importance to identify children's relative language proficiency so that language-appropriate special education programs may be provided (e.g., bilingual special education and special education programs incorporating English-as-a-Second-Language instruction).

e. Children with exceptionalities who are members of ethnic and multicultural groups should have access to special cultural and language programs provided to nonexceptional group members, with the necessary program adaptations to make the program beneficial to the exceptional child or youth.

f. Culturally appropriate educational materials should be readily available in ample quantity so that all students, including those from ethnic and multicultural groups, may benefit from their content.

g. Curriculum should be adapted or developed to meet the unique needs of children from all cultural groups. Curriculum should include a multicultural perspective which recognizes the value of diverse cultural traditions to society as well as the contributions of all cultural groups of American and Canadian society.

h. It is critical for teachers to recognize individual language and cultural differences as assets rather than deficits. Furthermore, those assets should be utilized to enhance education for all children, including those from ethnic and multicultural groups.

Paragraph 5 - Technical Assistance and Training

Special and unique concerns of Council members from ethnic and multicultural groups which are related to technical assistance, training, and services will receive the attention and support of the Special Assistant to the Executive Director for Ethnic and Multicultural Concerns.

Paragraph 6 - Special Projects

a. The Council will continue its interests in projects that meet the needs and concerns of all its membership. Furthermore, The Council will actively search for projects that include special concerns of members from ethnic and multicultural groups.

b. Projects that include special and unique concerns of members from ethnic and multicultural groups to be considered for development and implementation will receive the combined attention and support of various Council staff and the Special Assistant to the Executive Director for Ethnic and Multicultural Concerns.

c. All projects of The Council will include opportunities for perspective and participation by ethnic and multicultural groups in formulation, implementation, and evaluation phases.

Paragraph 7 - Cooperation with Organizations, Disciplines, and Individuals

a. The Council will support efforts to explore with other organizations mutual concerns and issues related to ethnic and multicultural children and their families. In the process, The Council will take care not to intervene in the internal affairs of any of the other organizations.

b. The Council will support efforts to work cooperatively with other organizations in activities and services related to children with exceptionalities from ethnic and multicultural groups and their families.

Paragraph 8 - Use of Interpreters/Translators for Culturally and Linguistically Diverse Individuals (Other than Hard of Hearing)

a. The practice of spontaneously pulling non-professional bilingual persons from their regularly assigned duties to fulfill the role of interpreter/translator when appropriate training has not been provided should be avoided altogether.

b. School districts, agencies, private schools or other employers/users should exhaust all means of obtaining professional personnel who are bilingual before seeking the assistance of interpreters/translators.

c. If the use of interpreters/translators is the only alternative, training should be provided in the briefing, interaction and debriefing processes on interpreting/translating, and in special education procedures and guidelines.

d. Professionals in organizations using interpreters/translators should also be trained in the appropriate use of these personnel to maximize effective communication among professionals, students and parents.

e. Competencies of interpreters/translators must be determined before using their services. Competencies should include, but are not limited to, high proficiency levels in English and the target language; knowledge of cultural and linguistic nuances; knowledge of cross-cultural, gender, and generational differences and expectations.

f. Upon mastery of the competencies, certification or rating through an approved system should be required to ensure that interpreters/translators possess the skills necessary for providing effective services.

CHAPTER 09

SPECIAL EDUCATION'S RESPONSIBILITIES TO ADULTS WITH DISABILITIES

Paragraph 1 - Preamble

The Council believes that most students can learn to become contributing citizens, family members, employees, learners, and active participants in meaningful vocational, recreational, and leisure pursuits. We believe, therefore, that it is an important purpose of education to assist students in the attainment of such outcomes. Further, we believe that education from early childhood through adult education should focus on assuring that students with exceptionalities attain such outcomes.

Paragraph 2 - Collaborative Responsibilities

In order to assist students with exceptionalities to become productive workers and independent adults, special education should work in collaboration with adult service agencies to influence the provision of needed services from such agencies. Collaboration should include:

a. Working with postsecondary vocational/technical institutions, adult education, rehabilitation, and independent living centers that assess, train, and place persons with exceptionalities in meaningful work situations.

b. Interaction and collaboration to provide relevant information to agencies and organizations that will assist them to conduct job site assessments, training follow-up, and continuing training or education for persons with exceptionalities.

c. Assisting appropriate special educators to become knowledgeable about their community's labor market needs and build close working relationships and partnerships with the business and industrial sector so that receptivity toward potential employees with exceptionalities is increased.

d. Promotion of adult and continuing education and literacy service opportunities for adults with exceptionalities.

e. Conducting systematic follow-up studies on former students so that curriculum and instruction can be appropriately modified to be responsive to employment and independent living needs.

f. Advocating the elimination of attitudinal and physical barriers which reduce the ability of these individuals to fully participate in society and increase vocational, recreational, and leisure opportunities.

g. Supporting the participation of special educators on advisory committees and in staff development and inservice training programs of agencies, organizations, and the business and industrial sector that address the needs of adults with exceptionalities and how they can be met.

h. Promoting an early close working relationship with adult service agency personnel, so secondary students can be provided more successful transition from school to adult life, and advocating for the provision of needed adult services by these agencies.

Section Three - Part 2
Professional Standards and Practice

CHAPTER 01

PREPARATION AND UTILIZATION OF PERSONNEL

Paragraph 1 - Right to Quality Instruction

The quality of educational services for children and youth with exceptionalities resides in the abilities, qualifications, and competencies of the personnel who provide the services. There is a serious deficit in the present availability of fully qualified personnel able to extend such services. This lack of competent personnel seriously hampers efforts to extend educational services to all children and youth with exceptionalities. There is a need to investigate new modes for evaluation of professional competence in the desire to accelerate the process of training effective professionals and paraprofessionals in significant numbers to meet the needs of the field. The Council affirms the principle that, through public policy, each student with an exceptionality is entitled to instruction and services by professionally trained and competent personnel. In addition, there is a need for new and appropriate training patterns which allow for broadening the role of special educators in a variety of settings to work in teams with other educators and children and youth with exceptionalities and for training the necessary supportive and ancillary personnel.

Paragraph 2 - Continuing Professional Development

As standards, practice, policy, and service delivery systems change, employing education agencies have a responsibility to assure that all professionals and others involved in the education of individuals with exceptionalities have the requisite knowledge and skills. Accordingly, CEC believes that both general and special education teachers and administrators, and other ancillary staff must have access to state-of-the-art knowledge and documented effective practices designed for students with exceptionalities. Therefore, access to the evolving knowledge base of effective practice is essential to maintaining programs that can respond to the needs of all students with exceptionalities. To this end, CEC calls upon the federal government and professional associations, states/provinces, local school districts, institutions of higher education, and other relevant entities to commit the necessary resources to professional development programs that are grounded in adult learning principles and reflect professional standards for continuing education.

Because effective special education is dependent on the continuous improvement of what special educators know and are able to do, CEC believes that all special education professionals must be committed to and engage in ongoing professional development that advances their practice. We further believe that professionals must have the opportunity to acquire knowledge and skills through a broad array of venues, including, but not limited to, institutions of higher education, professional associations, state/provincial education agencies, and local school districts. We further encourage collaboration among all of these entities in designing and implementing high quality professional development. Employing agencies must provide resources, including release time, to enable each special educator to engage in continuing professional development throughout her/his career. We further believe that employers and professional organizations should recognize and reward special education professionals for improving their knowledge and skills.

Paragraph 3 - Federal Role in Personnel Preparation

Through legislation, the federal government has played a dominant role in supporting initial efforts to prepare personnel for educating children and youth with exceptionalities. The Council believes that the federal government should continue and expand its efforts to train high level leadership personnel, assist through leadership and financial support the development of agencies to prepare personnel, and conduct research in new systems of preparing and utilizing personnel and meeting personnel needs. Definitive data are needed concerning personnel utilization and retention and other factors of personnel usage.

Paragraph 4 - State, Provincial, and Local Role in Personnel Preparation

In recent years, state, provincial, and local governments, in order to improve professional competencies, have made greater efforts to support formal training programs in colleges and universities and facilitate inservice and workshop efforts. The Council believes that such activities should be increased and that greater state, provincial, and local financial support should be given to their development and operation. The Council advocates extension of state, provincial, and federal funding to new and emerging special education services.

Paragraph 5 - National Recruitment

Further efforts need to be undertaken to develop a national program to attract more qualified and motivated individuals into the field of special education. Such a program should include efforts to recruit more members from ethnic and multicultural groups into the field and to provide employment opportunities for those persons trained. The Council believes that such a program must be conducted through national leadership with full involvement and participation of all levels of government and professional organizations. It is only through such a well coordinated effort in recruitment that the field's needs for qualified and motivated personnel can ever be met.

Paragraph 6 - Responsibility of Higher Education

Colleges and universities have an obligation to develop and coordinate their resources in support of programs for exceptional children. The obligation comprises a number of factors:

a. To provide through scholarly inquiry an expanded knowledge base for special education programs.

b. To provide training for various professional and paraprofessional personnel needed to conduct programs for students with exceptionalities.

c. To cooperate in the development and field testing of innovative programs.

d. To provide for the coordinated development of programs across disciplines and professions so that training and service models are congruent with emerging models for comprehensive community services.

e. To provide all students, whether or not they are in programs relating specifically to children with exceptionalities, a basis for understanding and appreciating human differences.

f. To exemplify in their own programs of training,

research, and community service and even in their architecture a concern for accommodating and upgrading the welfare of handicapped and gifted persons.

g. To cooperate with schools, agencies, and community groups in the creation and maintenance of needed special education programs.

Paragraph 7 - Government Role in Research

The Council recommends additional federal funding to bring about effective coordination of services and research efforts in order to provide a national information service encompassing curriculum methods and education technology. Funds from all levels of government should be made available for the development of more effective information and dissemination services. To facilitate more effective dissemination, an interchangeable coding and retrieval system compatible with educational enterprises and disciplines should be established across organization, agency, and government lines. Considering the exceptional child, through the teacher, as the ultimate recipient of services, The Council believes that information and dissemination systems should be coordinated so that a concerted and unified thrust is possible. Such systems should not be unique to geographic areas but national in scope.

Paragraph 8 - Dissemination of Research

The Council sees research and its dissemination as inextricably interrelated. No longer can these two functions be considered as separate entities if children and youth with exceptionalities are to benefit from such enterprises. The Council recommends that all government funded research projects include a means for dissemination that will contribute toward upgrading the instruction of children and youth with exceptionalities.

The Council strongly recommends that government approved dissemination activities be provided for separately in the federal education budget and not subsumed under some other priority. Further, it is recommended that dissemination not only include information delivery, but also include the identification and implementation of better educational practices and a process to train school personnel in the implementation of the improved practices and procedures.

A coordinating process for such a system is mandatory in order to identify, redirect, and deliver information among the various parts of the system. The goal is to constantly survey the information needs of multiple audiences; inform appropriate agencies who can develop materials, methods, programs, and strategies to meet those needs; inform users of worthwhile and proven resources; and encourage their implementation.

Paragraph 9 - Focus of Research

The Council believes that greater emphasis needs to be given to improving educational methods and curriculum for children and youth with exceptionalities. It is suggested that government agencies give particular attention to applied educational research which would provide for the empirical evaluation of educational materials, analysis of teacher pupil interaction, efficacy of media and technology as they relate to the instructional process, and development and evaluation of innovative instructional methods for children and youth with exceptionalities.

Equally important, as has been learned from the developing fields associated with the education of exceptional children, is the belief that research must be conducted regarding how the human service delivery system can be made available to formerly institutionalized persons with exceptionalities. The Council believes that such research should be highly programmatic in nature and should clearly focus on the development of new policies and approaches for the delivery and evaluation of needed and provided services. At a minimum, such research must focus upon the implementation and continuous evaluation of the utilization of the individualized educational program.

Paragraph 10 - Preparation of Personnel for Exceptional Children from Ethnic and Multicultural Groups

The Council supports the following personnel preparation policy recommendations to assist teachers and other professional personnel to improve their skills in meeting the needs of children from ethnic and multicultural groups:

a. Teachers and college faculty members and others who provide training should include information about the diversity of cultural and linguistic differences in their preservice and inservice training programs.

b. Professional personnel should be required to receive training in adapting instruction to accommodate children with different learning styles who are members of ethnic and multicultural groups.

c. College and university preservice training programs should include clinical, practicum, or other field experiences with specific focus on learning about exceptional children from ethnic and multicultural groups.

Paragraph 11 - High Stakes Assessment of Professional Knowledge, Skill, and Dispositions

It is the Council for Exceptional Children's (CEC) policy that, in determining an individual's professional competence, multiple measures rather than a single test score shall be used in the decision making process to enhance the validity and reliability of decisions related to content and pedagogical competence. As a minimum assurance of fairness, when a test is used as part of the decision making process, the individual should be provided multiple opportunities to pass the test. If there is credible evidence that a test score may not accurately reflect the individual's level of performance, the agency shall provide an alternative means by which the individual may demonstrate performance relative to professional standards.

Background: The CEC recognizes the important role that standardized assessments play in documenting teacher competence to ensure that all children are provided with effective teachers. Developments in national, state and provincial policy are moving toward more rigorous assessment and accountability systems for teachers, most notably through provisions such as NCLB. CEC endorses various countries' efforts to ensure that students with exceptional needs are guaranteed well-prepared teachers.

However, CEC is concerned by the growing reliance of policy makers on use of a single high stakes test to make critical decisions about educators' professional competence. Several states in the United States have already adopted policies that permit individuals with a bachelor's degree, but no training in special education, to be fully licensed in special education if they achieve a passing score on a single test. NCLB includes a provision that defines a "highly qualified teacher" as one who passes a single test. Teaching is a complex activity. None of the currently available tests adequately assesses prospective special education teachers in both content and pedagogy. The use of a single test also raises serious validity issues and could have a negative impact on otherwise qualified persons. There is consensus in the teaching community that high stakes decisions should never rest on a single test score.

CHAPTER 02

PROFESSIONAL STANDARDS, RIGHTS, AND RESPONSIBILITIES

Paragraph 1 - Preamble

As public awareness increases and public policies expand, new sets of conditions are created under which professionals in special education must function. While such awareness and policies may be powerful forces for improvement in the field, they do not of themselves deliver appropriate education to persons with exceptionalities. Effective education for persons with exceptionalities is also dependent upon qualified professionals who work under appropriate standards and conditions and are able to ensure their own professional rights and responsibilities.

Professionals must be adequately prepared and have a supportive environment which enables them to meet new demands. As advocates for persons with exceptionalities they must have the right to be responsive to and responsible for the vulnerable persons whom they serve. Finally, professionals must continually advance the knowledge, skills, behaviors, and values that make up the collective basis for practice and decision making for those working in the field. The combined energies of the profession and The Council for Exceptional Children are needed to accomplish these goals.

Therefore, The Council believes that professionals practicing in the field should be able to do so according to recognized standards of practice and a professional code of ethics; and that only persons qualified to provide special educational services should be eligible for employment in instructional, administrative, and support roles in programs serving persons with exceptionalities.

For these reasons, The Council is committed to the development, promotion, and implementation of standards of preparation and practice, code of ethics, and appropriate certification and/or licensure in order to continue its leadership role in supporting professionals who serve persons with exceptionalities.

Paragraph 2 - Code of Ethics

We declare the following principles to be the Code of Ethics for educators of persons with exceptionalities. Members of the special education profession are responsible for upholding and advancing these principles. Members of The Council for Exceptional Children agree to judge and be judged by them in accordance with the spirit and provisions of this Code.

a. Special education professionals are committed to developing the highest educational and quality of life potential of individuals with exceptionalities.

b. Special education professionals promote and maintain a high level of competence and integrity in practicing their profession.

c. Special education professionals engage in professional activities which benefit exceptional individuals, their families, other colleagues, students, or research subjects.

d. Special education professionals exercise objective professional judgment in the practice of their profession.

e. Special education professionals strive to advance their knowledge and skills regarding the education of individuals with exceptionalities.

f. Special education professionals work within the standards and policies of their profession.

g. Special education professionals seek to uphold and improve where necessary the laws, regulations, and policies governing the delivery of special education and related services and the practice of their profession.

h. Special education professionals do not condone or participate in unethical or illegal acts, nor violate professional standards adopted by the Delegate Assembly of CEC.

Paragraph 3: Standards for Professional Practice

3.1 Professionals In Relation To Persons With Exceptionalities And Their Families

a. Instructional Responsibilities

Special education personnel are committed to the application of professional expertise to ensure the provision of quality education for all individuals with exceptionalities. Professionals strive to:

(1) Identify and use instructional methods and curricula that are appropriate to their area of

professional practice and effective in meeting persons' with exceptionalities needs.

(2) Participate in the selection and use of appropriate instructional materials, equipment, supplies, and other resources needed in the effective practice of their profession.

(3) Create safe and effective learning environments which contribute to fulfillment of needs, stimulation of learning, and self-concept.

(4) Maintain class size and case loads which are conducive to meeting the individual instructional needs of individuals with exceptionalities.

(5) Use assessment instruments and procedures that do not discriminate against persons with exceptionalities on the basis of race, color, creed, sex, national origin, age, political practices, family or social background, sexual orientation, or exceptionality.

(6) Base grading, promotion, graduation, and/ or movement out of the program on the individual goals and objectives for individuals with exceptionalities.

(7) Provide accurate program data to administrators, colleagues and parents, based on efficient and objective record keeping practices, for the purpose of decision making.

(8) Maintain confidentiality of information except when information is released under specific conditions of written consent and statutory confidentiality requirements.

b. Management of Behavior

Special education professionals participate with other professionals and with parents in an interdisciplinary effort in the management of behavior. Professionals:

(1) Apply only those disciplinary methods and behavioral procedures which they have been instructed to use and which do not undermine the dignity of the individual or the basic human rights of persons with exceptionalities, such as corporal punishment.

(2) Clearly specify the goals and objectives for behavior management practices in the person's with exceptionalities Individualized Education Program.

(3) Conform to policies, statutes, and rules established by state/ provincial and local agencies relating to judicious application of disciplinary methods and behavioral procedures.

(4) Take adequate measures to discourage, prevent, and intervene when a colleague's behavior is perceived as being detrimental to exceptional students.

(5) Refrain from aversive techniques unless repeated trials of other methods have failed and only after consultation with parents and appropriate agency officials.

c. Support Procedures

(1) Adequate instruction and supervision shall be provided to professionals before they are required to perform support services for which they have not been prepared previously.

(2) Professionals may administer medication, where state/provincial policies do not preclude such action, if qualified to do so or if written instructions are on file which state the purpose of the medication, the conditions under which it may be administered, possible side effects, the physician's name and phone number, and the professional liability if a mistake is made. The professional will not be required to administer medication.

(3) Professionals note and report to those concerned whenever changes in behavior occur in conjunction with the administration of medication or at any other time.

d. Parent Relationships

Professionals seek to develop relationships with parents based on mutual respect for their roles in achieving benefits for the exceptional person. Special education professionals:

(1) Develop effective communication with parents, avoiding technical terminology, using the primary language of the home, and other modes of communication when appropriate.

(2) Seek and use parents' knowledge and expertise in planning, conducting, and evaluating special education and related services for persons with exceptionalities.

(3) Maintain communications between parents and professionals with appropriate respect for privacy and confidentiality.

(4) Extend opportunities for parent education utilizing accurate information and professional methods.

(5) Inform parents of the educational rights of their children and of any proposed or actual practices which violate those rights.

(6) Recognize and respect cultural diversities which exist in some families with persons with exceptionalities.

(7) Recognize that relationship of home and community environmental conditions affects the behavior and outlook of the exceptional person.

e. Advocacy

Special education professionals serve as advocates for exceptional students by speaking, writing, and acting in a variety of situations on their behalf. They:

(1) Continually seek to improve government provisions for the education of persons with exceptionalities while ensuring that public statements by professionals as individuals are not construed to represent official policy statements of the agency that employs them.

(2) Work cooperatively with and encourage other professionals to improve the provision of special education and related services to persons with exceptionalities.

(3) Document and objectively report to one's supervisors or administrators inadequacies in resources and promote appropriate corrective action.

(4) Monitor for inappropriate placements in special education and intervene at appropriate levels to correct the condition when such inappropriate placements exist.

(5) Follow local, state/provincial and federal laws and regulations which mandate a free appropriate public education to exceptional students and the protection of the rights of persons with exceptionalities to equal opportunities in our society.

3.2 *Professional Employment*

a. Certification and Qualification

Professionals ensure that only persons deemed qualified by having met state/provincial minimum standards are employed as teachers, administrators, and related service providers for individuals with exceptionalities.

b. Employment

(1) Professionals do not discriminate in hiring on the basis of race, color, creed, sex, national origin, age, political practices, family or social background, sexual orientation, or exceptionality.

(2) Professionals represent themselves in an ethical and legal manner in regard to their training and experience when seeking new employment.

(3) Professionals give notice consistent with local education agency policies when intending to leave employment.

(4) Professionals adhere to the conditions of a contract or terms of an appointment in the setting where they practice.

(5) Professionals released from employment are entitled to a written explanation of the reasons for termination and to fair and impartial due process procedures.

(6) Special education professionals share equitably the opportunities and benefits (salary, working conditions, facilities, and other resources) of other professionals in the school system.

(7) Professionals seek assistance, including the services of other professionals, in instances where personal problems threaten to interfere with their job performance.

(8) Professionals respond objectively when requested to evaluate applicants seeking employment.

(9) Professionals have the right and responsibility to resolve professional problems by utilizing established procedures, including grievance procedures, when appropriate.

c. Assignment and Role

(1) Professionals should receive clear written communication of all duties and responsibilities, including those which are prescribed as conditions of their employment.

(2) Professionals promote educational quality, and intra- and inter-professional cooperation through active participation in the planning, policy development, management and evaluation of the special education program and the education program at large so that programs remain responsive to the changing needs of persons with exceptionalities.

(3) Professionals practice only in areas of exceptionality, at age levels, and in program models for which they are prepared by their training and/or experience.

(4) Adequate supervision of and support for special education professionals is provided by other professionals qualified by their training and experience in the area of concern.

(5) The administration and supervision of special education professionals provides for clear lines of accountability.

(6) The unavailability of substitute teachers or support personnel, including aides, does not result in the denial of special education services to a greater degree than to that of other educational programs.

d. Professional Development

(1) Special education professionals systematically advance their knowledge and skills in order to maintain a high level of competence and response to the changing needs of persons with exceptionalities by pursuing a program of continuing education including but not limited to participation in such activities as inservice training, professional conferences/workshops, professional meetings, continuing education courses, and the reading of professional literature.

(2) Professionals participate in the objective and systematic evaluation of themselves, colleagues, services, and programs for the purpose of continuous improvement of professional performance.

(3) Professionals in administrative positions support and facilitate professional development.

3.3 *Professionals In Relation To The Profession And To Other Professionals*

a. To the Profession

(1) Special education professionals assume responsibility for participating in professional organizations and adherence to the standards and codes of ethics of those organizations.

(2) Special education professionals have a responsibility to provide varied and exemplary supervised field experiences for persons in undergraduate and graduate preparation programs.

(3) Special education professionals refrain from using professional relationships with students and parents for personal advantage.

(4) Special education professionals take an active position in the regulation of the profession through use of appropriate procedures for bringing about changes.

(5) Special education professionals initiate, support and/or participate in research related to the education of persons with exceptionalities with the aim of improving the quality of educational services, increasing the accountability of programs, and generally benefiting persons with exceptionalities. They:

(a) Adopt procedures that protect the rights and welfare of subjects participating in the research.

(b) Interpret and publish research results with accuracy and a high quality of scholarship.

(c) Support a cessation of the use of any research procedure which may result in undesirable consequences for the participant.

(d) Exercise all possible precautions to prevent misapplication or misuse of a research effort, by self or others.

b. To Other Professionals

Special education professionals function as members of interdisciplinary teams and the reputation of the profession resides with them. They:

(1) Recognize and acknowledge the competencies and expertise of members representing other disciplines as well as those of members in their own disciplines.

(2) Strive to develop positive attitudes among other professionals toward persons with exceptionalities, representing them with an objective regard for their possibilities and their limitations as persons in a democratic society.

(3) Cooperate with other agencies involved in serving persons with exceptionalities through such activities as the planning and coordination of information exchanges, service delivery, evaluation and training, so that no duplication or loss in quality of services may occur.

(4) Provide consultation and assistance, where appropriate, to both regular and special education as well as other school personnel serving persons with exceptionalities.

(5) Provide consultation and assistance, where appropriate, to professionals in non-school settings serving persons with exceptionalities.

(6) Maintain effective interpersonal relations with colleagues and other professionals, helping them to develop and maintain positive and accurate perceptions about the special education profession.

Paragraph 4: Standards for the Preparation of Special Education Personnel

4.1 *Program Recognition*

a. Programs preparing individuals for entry level or advanced special education professional roles shall adhere to CEC's professional standards, by seeking CEC's official recognition through the evidence-based process of program review.

b. Program review includes examination of evidence to document quality practice in:

(1) Conceptual Framework. Programs have a conceptual framework that establishes the programs vision and its relationship to the programs components and curricula.

(2) Candidate Content, Pedagogical, And Professional Knowledge, Skills, And Dispositions

    i. Content Standards. Programs ensure that prospective special educators have mastered the CEC Special Education Content Standards for their respective roles.

    ii. Liberal Education. Programs ensure that prospective special educators have a solid grounding in the liberal curricula ensuring proficiency in reading, written and oral communications, calculating, problem solving, and thinking.

iii. General Curriculum.

    (a) Programs ensure that prospective special educators possess a solid base of understanding of the general content area curricula[1] i.e., math, reading, English/language arts, science, social studies, and the arts, sufficient to collaborate with general educators in:

Teaching or collaborative teaching academic subject matter content of the general curriculum to students with exceptional learning needs across a wide range of performance levels.

Designing appropriate learning and performance accommodations and modifications for students with exceptional learning needs in academic subject matter content of the general curriculum.

    (b) Programs preparing special educators for secondary level practice and licensure in which the teachers may assume sole responsibility for teaching academic subject matter classes, ensure that the prospective special educators have a subject matter content knowledge base sufficient to assure that their students can meet state curriculum standards.

(3) Assessment System and Program Evaluation. Programs have an assessment system to collect and analyze data on the applicant qualifications, candidates and graduate performance, and program operations sufficient to evaluate and improve the program.

(4) Field Experiences and Clinical Practice. Programs with their school partners have designed, implemented, and evaluated field experiences and clinical practica sufficient for prospective special educators to develop and apply knowledge, skills, and dispositions essential to the roles for which they are being prepared.

(5) Diversity. Program with their school partners have designed, implemented, and evaluated curriculum and experiences sufficient for prospective special educators to develop and apply their knowledge, skills, and dispositions necessary to help all students learn. The curricula and experiences include working with diverse faculty, candidates, and P-12 exceptional students.

(6) Faculty Qualification, Performance, and Development. The program faculty is qualified and model best professional practice in their scholarship, service, and teaching.

(7) Program Governance and Resources. The program has appropriate leadership, authority, budget, facilities, and resources to address professional, institutional, and state standards.

Paragraph 5: Standards for Entry Into Professional Practice

a. Requirements for professional practice should be sufficiently flexible to provide for the newly emerging and changing roles of special education professionals and to encourage experimentation and innovation in their preparation.

b. CEC and its divisions should be the lead organizations in establishing minimum standards for entry into the profession of special education. CEC should develop and promote a model that requires no less than a bachelor's degree which encompasses the knowledge and skills consistent with entry level into special education teaching.

c. Each new professional in special education should

---

[1] As used the phrase, "academic subject matter content of the general curriculum", means the content of the general curriculum including math, reading, English/language arts, science, social studies, and the arts. It does not per se include the additional specialized knowledge and skill that special educators must possess in areas such as reading, writing, and math.

receive a minimum of a one-year mentorship, during the first year of his/her professional special education practice in a new role. The mentor should be an experienced professional in the same or a similar role, who can provide expertise and support on a continuing basis.

d. State and provincial education agencies should adopt common knowledge and skills as a basis for providing reciprocity for approval of professional practice across state and provincial lines.

e. Approval of individuals for professional practice in the field of special education should be for a limited period of time with periodic renewal.

f. There should be a continuum of professional development for special educators. The continuum for special education teachers should include at a minimum:

(1) Knowledge and skills required to practice as a teacher in a particular area of exceptionality/age grouping (infancy through secondary).

(2) Knowledge and skills required to excel in the instruction of a particular area of exceptionality/age group (infancy through secondary).

g. Each professional in the field of educating individuals with exceptionalities shall participate an average of 36 contact hours (or an average of 3.6 CEUs) each year of planned, organized, and recognized professional development activities related to the professional's field of practice. Such activities may include a combination of professional development units, continuing education units, college/university coursework, professional organization service (e.g., CEC state and provincial units, chapters, divisions, subdivisions, and caucuses), professional workshops, special projects, or structured discussions of readings from the professional literature. Employing agencies should provide resources to enable each professional's continuing development.

Joni L. Baldwin
University of Dayton

Carol A. Long
Winona State University

The special education preparation program performance assessment system is designed to document that teacher candidates have mastered the knowledge, skills, and dispositions necessary for teaching students safely and effectively with exceptional learning needs. While challenging, it can also be a highly rewarding and a powerful incentive for program improvement. This article describes the basics for developing and implementing the program-wide performance assessment process with an eye on NCATE unit review.

Elements of a Successful Performance-Based Assessment System

Understand the 6 to 8 Assessment Rule

Several years ago, NCATE joined in a collaborative effort with its specialty professional association partners (SPAs) to develop a process by which all teacher education programs could document candidate learning for program recognition with not more than 6 to 8 program-wide assessments. Under the new procedures, six program-wide assessments are required by all programs, with specific types of assessments specified for the first five.

Licensure assessment or other content assessment: most frequently this will be the state mandated Praxis II. It may also be a state developed assessment, or use of a commercial tool such as an NES assessment. The assessment must be aligned with CEC standards to document that the content of the test does address CEC standards (Required).

Content assessment: The content assessment is an assessment that documents candidates have the content knowledge necessary to teach students with exceptional learning needs. This can be any type of assessment, such as a research report, child study, or an essay (Required).

Assessment of planning: This assessment needs to demonstrate that the teacher candidate documenting pedagogical and professional knowledge, skills, and dispositions can plan, taking into consideration all variables of the students and content to be taught (Required).

Student teaching/internship assessment: aligned with CEC standards (Required).

Assessment of candidate impact on student learning: This assessment must document that the students learned what the candidate was teaching. This could be the assessment plan and results from the unit planned in Assessment 3 (if it actually is a different assignment and/or grading template), a behavior change project, or a case study.

Final Required Assessment: The last required assessment is of the faculty's choosing to document missing standards or to clarify specific program standards.

Once the six assessments are determined, the faculty may choose up to two additional assessments to document a missing standards area (Optional).

To be considered program-wide, the assessment must be required of all teacher candidates in the program. For example, if a behavior change project, based in a course only some of your candidates take, it is not a program-wide assessment and cannot be used as such. Typically, the six-to-eight program-wide assessments each cover several CEC standards. However, faculty should decide which standards are an assessment's primary focuses. While it is possible an assessment to touch on each CEC Standard, the faculty should review the assessments carefully to determine which standard(s) are best represented.

Program Standards

The common core and applicable specialized program standards must be addressed for all initial licensure teacher candidates. For example, for categorical programs, such as an Early Childhood Special Education licensure program, the Early Childhood specialty standards must be addressed as well as the Initial Common Core. The same is true for any other categorical preparation programs (i.e., Learning Disabilities, Deaf and Hard of Hearing, Physical and Health Disability). The specific standards for each category must be addressed. For multi-categorical, or non-categorical programs, the Individualized General Education standards (for mild/moderate programs), or Individualized Independence standards (for moderate/severe) should be included. The CEC Standards Flowchart (Appendix 3) can be of assistance in determining the appropriate knowledge and skill sets.

Address the Entire Content Standard

Most of the CEC standards are complex with multiple components. All of these components for each of the Standards should be included in the assessment plan. For example, CEC Standard 8: Assessment requires the teacher candidate to understand assessment (legalities, theory, and practice), conduct both formal and informal assessments, and monitor progress of students as part of the standard. Thus, the assessment system developed by your program needs to document mastery of the multiple components within the CEC Standard. CEC made this relatively easy for you by bolding key words in the descriptions of the standards.

Align Assessments with CEC Content Standards

Providing an alignment matrix for the components of the assessment and the CEC standards will allow the reviewer to assess the relationship between the assessment and the standards more easily. This alignment can then be transferred to the scoring guide for documentation of mastery of the standards.

Develop scoring guides for each assessment

Scoring guides must be sufficiently complete to allow the reviewer to understand what standards are being met by what component of an assessment. Aligning the CEC standards to your scoring guide again provides the reader with a quick analysis of the standards, criteria for mastery, and candidate performance. Many programs use rubrics for the majority of their scoring guides to facilitate consistency across grading and expectations of candidate performance.

Develop a Common Rubric Format

If the faculty chooses to use rubrics, the rubric formats should be consistent across assessments with the rating scale, the format, and wording. Choose a rating scale and descriptors that all graders/raters are willing to use. Do you want a three-, four-, or five-point scale? What are rating descriptors, e.g., unacceptable, acceptable, target or not met, met, exceeds? The key is to use a consistent format, including the direction of your number scale (left to right or right to left), for all rubrics to ease comparison and program review.

Strategies for the Program Review Report

Be consistent in your presentation of the assessments, scoring guides, and data. For each assessment, the report should provide the description of the assessment, alignment of CEC standards with the assessment, and findings/analysis of the data. Attachments for each assessment will be the directions to the candidate (actual assignment), scoring guide/rubric, and data. Following the same format and sequence for each assessment will allow for an accurate and efficient review.

Presenting Data

The report must provide data to document that program candidates are meeting the standards, and/or that changes have been made to the program based upon performance data from the candidates. It is important to provide the data in aggregated format, for each semester or year that the class is taught, for different locations if applicable and for different program groups if possible. The "N" should be provided (number of candidates included), with the number and percentage of candidates per rubric title, or categories (unacceptable, acceptable, target). You could also report this as the number of candidates who earned the rating. The assessment items should be clearly documented, along with the semester and year the data was collected.

Findings

As the faculty collects the data, they should analyze the data to identify areas for improvement in the program. The faculty also documents when no improvements are identified based on the data. This continuous improvement analysis must be described in Section V (Use of Assessment Results to Improve the Program) of the program report.

Connecting CEC Program Review and NCATE Unit Review

NCATE Unit Standards and Accreditation

NCATE accreditation is based on the unit conceptual framework and six standards. The unit's conceptual framework describes the shared vision that guides efforts to prepare candidates to work in P-12 schools. It is the compass for making unit level decisions and the description of the unit's philosophy of education and teacher preparation. The conceptual framework articulates how the unit's graduates can be distinguished from other preparation programs in other institutions. The unit's conceptual framework must be reflected in the unit's responses to the six unit standards.

Standard 1: Candidate Knowledge, Skills, and Dispositions

It is through NCATE Unit Standard 1 that the various program level assessments demonstrate that candidates have mastered the content, pedagogical, and professional knowledge, skills, and dispositions to help all students learn. CEC Content Standards directly coordinate with NCATE Standard 1. In other words, program-wide assessments are designed to align with CEC Content Standards. It is through this relationship that the data from the program-wide assessments are linked to and used in NCATE Unit Standard 1.

Standard 2: Assessment System and Unit Evaluation

The second standard deals with the systematic collection of data for the unit. Data must be collected on applicant qualifications, candidate and graduate performance, and unit operations. Once collected, the data must be analyzed and the findings used to make improvements.

Standard 3: Field Experiences and Clinical Practice

During field-experiences and clinical practice, candidates must demonstrate the knowledge, skills, and dispositions needed to help all students learn.

Standard 4: Diversity

The diversity standard applies to providing experiences with diverse students in P-12 settings and working with diverse higher education and school faculty and diverse fellow candidates.

Standard 5: Faculty Qualifications, Performance, and Development

Faculty must be qualified for their assignments with doctorates or exceptional expertise. Standard 5 also specifies that they model best practice in scholarship, service, and teaching and they must collaborate with colleagues in their disciplines and in schools.

Standard 6: Unit Governance and Resources

The final standard ensures that the unit has the leadership and resources needed to prepare candidates. The review team will look at the budget, support personnel, facilities, and technology resources.

Unit and Program Assessments

Unit accreditation and program recognition are two different processes based on different sets of standards. While program standards are program specific, unit standards, i.e., NCATE standards apply across programs that prepare educators and school personnel. This could mean employing two sets of assessments, one for the program and another set to be aggregated with the rest of the unit. The program assessment data feeds into common unit frameworks for documenting NCATE Standard 1.

In the past, some programs attempted to use assessments designed at the unit level for program assessments. The assessment designed at the unit level by definition will not be program specific, as they must be sufficiently general to cover candidates across programs. For example, Assessment 4 the Student teaching/internship assessment is probably also a Unit assessment. This would be true for all programs in the Unit, but while a single instrument was used to allow for consistent data collection at the Unit level, for the program reports the assessment must be aligned with the SPA standards. Therefore, a single student teaching/internship assessment must be adjusted or amended to align specifically to CEC or other SPA standards.

Your NCATE Coordinator and Program Assessment Coordinator can help you design assessments that collect the data needed for program recognition and they can see that you are also collecting the data the unit requires. Often the two sets of assessments can dovetail or complement each other.

Transition Points

The unit will specify decision or transition points that all candidates must pass. Often the points include admission to Teacher Education or the program, pre-student teaching, exit from student teaching, and a post-graduation follow-up. Transition points are also good times to collect program specific data. This data can be used to learn about new candidates. Follow-up information can be extremely useful. Assessments can be especially useful if administered at key transition points and used to determine candidate status or to target areas for remediation.

Data collection

Faculty will need to collect data using the unit's assessments so your candidates can be counted in the total aggregate but you can add to the unit's assessments or create program specific assessments, too. For example, your unit should have designated dispositions that all candidates should demonstrate. You might review the unit assessment and add to it items that address the CEC Code of Ethics.

Be systematic about collecting data. Set up regular meetings to review findings, refine assessments, and make decisions based on data. Attitude is extremely important. View this as not one more thing to do but as an opportunity to improve your program.